The Way of Awen

Journey of a Bard

First published by O Books, 2010
O Books is an imprint of John Hunt Publishing Ltd., The Bothy, Deershot Lodge, Park Lane, Ropley,
Hants, SO24 0BE, UK
office1@o-books.net
www.o-books.net

Distribution in:	South Africa
	Stephan Phillips (pty) Ltd
UK and Europe	Email: orders@stephanphillips.com
Orca Book Services Ltd	Tel: 27 21 4489839 Telefax: 27 21 4479879
tradeorders@orcabookservices.co.uk	
directorders@orcabookservices.co.uk	Text copyright Kevan Manwaring 2009
Tel: 01235 465521 Fax: 01235 465555	
Int. code (44)	Design: Tom Davies
USA and Canada	ISBN: 978 1 84694 311 9
NBN	
custserv@nbnbooks.com	All rights reserved. Except for brief quotations
Tel: 1 800 462 6420 Fax: 1 800 338 4550	in critical articles or reviews, no part of this
	book may be reproduced in any manner without
Australia and New Zealand	prior written permission from the publishers.
Brumby Books	
sales@brumbybooks.com.au	The rights of Kevan Manwaring as author have
Tel: 61 3 9761 5535 Fax: 61 3 9761 7095	been asserted in accordance with the
	Copyright, Designs and Patents Act 1988.
Far East (offices in Singapore, Thailand,	
Hong Kong, Taiwan)	
Pansing Distribution Pte Ltd	
kemal@pansing.com	A CIP catalogue record for this book is available
Tel: 65 6319 9939 Fax: 65 6462 5761	from the British Library.

Printed by Digital Book Print

O Books operates a distinctive and ethical publishing philosophy in
all areas of its business, from its global network of authors to
production and worldwide distribution.

The Way of Awen

Journey of a Bard

Kevan Manwaring

BOOKS

Winchester, UK
Washington, USA

CONTENTS

Dedicated to all those who have helped me along the Way

Prayer for Awen

Let the Awen descend, star-crowned, immortal.
From the citadel of the silver wheel,
From the dark secrets of the sky.

She comes through the torn edges of night,
Between the blink of an eye, a waking dream.
She comes unbidden, by her own volition –
Inviolate, invading my mind.
Bringing her rich dowry of words,
Wearing her dress of sound.

Three rays of light
Trepanning my mind.
Bringing me inspiration.

She walks into my head –
Pale, tall, and dark,
Or a fiery Spring maiden.
In the crackle between fingertips and
Keyboard, page and pen, plectrum and string –
Aether made manifest, elusive, mysterious.

Three rays of light
Trepanning my mind.
Bringing me Eloquence

O fickle, loyal, muse,
Grant me your grace.
Generous, callous,
Cruel and gentle,
Otherworldly, wild

And elemental.

Three rays of light
Trepanning my mind.
Bringing me wisdom.

O Goddess descend,
Guide my hand.
May I channel your beautiful truth –
A stream-bed of clear mountain water.
Let the Awen pour through me,
As tears of tender ecstasy.

Kevan Manwaring

Preface

It is hoped all who are interested in living creatively will enjoy this book as it has universal elements that require no previous knowledge or experience. Nevertheless, it explores living creatively along one particular path – what I call the Way of Awen – which although I see as being applicable to any form of creative expression or indeed belief system, within reason, for me manifests in the Bardic Arts based upon the British Celtic Tradition.

Expanding upon the foundation of *The Bardic Handbook*, this volume explores the transformations the initiate Anruth must go through to become a fully-fledged Bard. Mirroring the ancient Bardic Colleges, with their twelve years of training, *The Way of Awen* seeks to provide a comprehensive development programme (supplemented by residential workshops held at inspiring locations) for those dedicated to the path of the Bard.

Using the legend of the Welsh semi-mythic bard Taliesin, who undergoes metamorphoses after imbibing the Potion of Inspiration and is chased by the crone Ceridwen, we will examine in detail each one of these anthropomorphic stages – using them as metaphors for the stages of bardic development from Anruth to Bard.

The Bardic Handbook explored the first year of bardic training, as an Anruth from Gwion to Hare Grade (summarised in Chapter One). *The Way of Awen: journey of a bard* continues the training from this point onwards:

Grades 1-12 *Anruth*
- 1st Grade: Gwion
- 2nd Grade: Hare
- 3rd Grade: Greyhound
- 4th Grade: Salmon

- 5th Grade: Otter
- 6th Grade: Wren
- 7th Grade: Hawk
- 8th Grade: Cian
- 9th Grade: Black Hen
- 10th Grade: Elphin
- 11th Grade: Gwyddno
- 12th Grade: Maelgwn

Grades 13-20 *Bard*

- 13th Grade: Taliesin

Each grade will have a chapter dedicated to it, exploring the Taliesin legend and its associated symbolism in detail, connecting it to one's own bardic practice. The focus will be primarily on the many layers to each animal/character/stage of maturity – looking closely at the natural world and the lessons it can teach us.

The Way of Awen will differ from *The Bardic Handbook* by not offering practical activities – this is not a manual (the first book is complete in that respect). Instead it offers a more intuitive, experiential approach, based upon the authenticity of my own journey and response to the Awen. I will try to lead by example – by relating my own experience, as recorded in twenty years' worth of journals and notebooks – not as a blueprint, but as an invitation to embark upon your own bardic path. This is ultimately, the challenge that Taliesin offers us, as Michael Dames suggests in *Taliesin's Travels*: '...He implicitly challenges us to undertake our own version of his travels, no matter where we start from, or intend to go.'

Taliesin's thirteen year 'journey to Deganwy', a metaphor for the bard's journey to self-actualisation, is explored in microcosm – I recommended spending at least one week on each chapter/stage (a month would be better – ideally synchronised with a full lunar cycle) because the idea is to allow enough time for the paradigm of each to seep into your consciousness, so that you experience the world and engage with it as hare, greyhound, salmon, otter, wren, hawk, hen, grain of wheat … attuning, learning and 'shape-changing' through each – providing an accelerated self-learning programme. In an age of Climate Change, Peak Oil and geopolitical tensions we need validated bards working in communities now, not in several years time. Tomorrow maybe too late.

The first thing I recommend is that you buy yourself a journal to use throughout this journey. The Way of Awen starts as soon as you want it to. The page of life awaits.

Whether you wish to pursue a bardic path, would like to explore living creatively, or simply enjoy the Celtic legends, may your find the Way of Awen rewarding.

Kevan Manwaring, Bath, 2009/2010

Introduction

The Journey to Deganwy

I will set out on foot,
To the gate I will come,
I will enter the hall,
My song I will sing,
My verse I will proclaim,
And the king's bards I will cast down.
In the presence of the Chief,
Demands I will make,
And chains I will break –
Elphin will be set at liberty

Taliesin, Journey to Deganwy

Imagine the scene. A royal hall on a rugged headland in the wild north of Cambria. The court of King Maelgwn – feared for his harshness, his power-mongering and brutality. His twenty-four royal bards process before him to recite and declaim their honeyed phrases. Maelgwn's bards are renowned throughout the land. To afford the patronage of not one but two dozen bards (one for every hour of the day) shows real wealth. Traditionally, a bard had the best seat in the house (next to the host); a portion of the feast fit for the hero; rewards of silver and gold arm- and neck-rings... All vied for their honour, their praise and all feared their satire – said to raise boils on the faces of their enemies.

Today there is an atmosphere in court. Maelgwn's servants and vassals tread lightly around him, even more than usual, for someone had dared insult his bards – and to make it worst, it was his own nephew – Elphin! The King has had his insolent relative bound in chains, albeit silver ones (on allowance of his rank and blood) – and has summoned the bard boasted of. And now, the court nervously awaited his arrival.

A messenger nervously informed the surly Maelgwn that a boy waited outside. What did that matter to him? Send him to the kitchens, or have his guards beat him off the castle grounds. No, explained the dry-mouthed servant, the lad said he had been summoned – he was the ward of Elphin and Gwyddno...

Maelgwn realised then who he was. He made the young visitor wait outside in the lashing rain, despite having come many hard miles over the mountains. Make his young visitor wait and consider his place in the scheme of things, smiled Maelgwn grimly, swirling mead around the chased horn in his mailed gauntlet – silver and gold and steel catching in the firelight. To think Elphin boasted a mere *plentyn* could best his bards! To send a boy to defend his honour! His nephew's fate hung by a thread. He had always known Elphin was foolish, but his fortunes had increased over the years. He had become ... useful to Maelgwn.

Taliesin was forced to wait while the royal bards made their entrance. They passed him as he sat upon the rain-wet rock outside the gatehouse on the castle's eastern flanks. The keen-eyed youth would have normally enjoyed the view over the Conwy, but the grey day put pay to that, and he had other things on his mind. As the royal bards processed in their splendid robes with their pot bellies and neatly trimmed beards, Taliesin played upon his lips – blerwm, blerwm, blerwm – watching the old men, who laughed into their beards.

'Hardly fit to be a boy, let alone a bard...!' they mocked.

But when they went before their liege, all the royal bards could do was play upon their lips like babies.

Maelgwn glared and summoned in the stripling, suspecting gramarye. Word magic. The enchantment of awen.

Imagine standing before the court, thirteen years' young, all eyes burning into you, being asked to make an account of

5

yourself...

Taliesin did this and far more. He recited his extraordinary origins, his many lives, his vast and deep knowledge. He refuted the bards of Maelgwn. He claimed the Chair of Deganwy. He sang his song of the cosmos. Then he set a riddle that none could answer – summoning the elusive solution along the corridors of the castle... The wind blasted all but he; leaving the court breathless. All doubt extinguished, Taliesin banished his conjuring as easily as he had called it. A true windsmith.

Maelgwn relented – accepting Elphin's claim. His nephew was summoned from the gaol on the castle's heights – a lonely rock-hewn cell open to the elements, his only companion the carcase of a sheep that had fallen in.

Taliesin sang a cantrip that made the silver fetters fall from his master, then he went to bow – but Elphin made him stand before him – man to man. He was thirteen now – he had come of age. He had shown his mettle, past his test, released his master and thwarted the machinations of Maelgwn – who had sent his loathsome brother Rhun to test Elphin's wife's virtue only to be outwitted by the prescient Taliesin.

Elphin's boast was vindicated – Taliesin was indeed the greatest bard there. His ward had won the Chair of Deganwy, the first of many laurels. This moment was the start of his legendary bardic career.

Yet his personal legend had begun thirteen years earlier.

Deganwy was the end of the beginning, the result of a long and winding journey. Thirteen years ago he could not have achieved what he did that day. Fifteen years ago, he was no more than a sleepy village boy. To his humble origins we must return if we are to track how Taliesin accomplished such a feat of bardic prowess.

How did he begin upon the Way of Awen? Where does the fledgling bard start?

* * *

The Way of Awen provides not a strict curriculum, but an invitation for creativity – for truly, creativity is not about following instructions, it is about following inspiration. It's more about attitude and awareness than 'just' technical knowledge (*The Bardic Handbook* provides a comprehensive 'crane-skin bag' of techniques and exercises). This is different. Here I shall endeavour to explore the nature of creativity, using the legend of Taliesin as a framework and a framing narrative. The mercurial changes of Gwion/Ceridwen show the protean genius of the creative process – one idea sparking another and another, until the original catalyst is transformed beyond recognition. Art equals transformation. An artist is a chef of life – 'cooking' up the raw matter of existence in the cauldron of art, spicing it with experience into every conceivable variation, delighting the senses, making us see things as though for the first time. Making us open our eyes and pay attention. Awen: awake!

The Way of Awen will consist of three main ingredients:

1. Framing narrative – Taliesin's story
2. Essays on each animal/stages of maturity
3. Journal of a bard

The latter, gleaned from twenty years of journals and notebooks, will show how I have personally followed the Way of Awen. I feel this is the only legitimate way of showing the validity of what I am offering – an invitation to walk the Way of Awen. Perhaps you already are, and you will find this book a clarification or confirmation. The key thing is authenticity: Fidelity to who we are, what we believe, what colours our dreams, fires our desires, our fears and hopes – the authentic self of conscious being, which the Way of Awen helps us to awaken.

Creativity is our god/dess-given potential. By honouring it we are honouring and taking part in creation. Matthew Fox, in *Creativity: where the Divine and the Human meet*, says:

I do not know any area of human potential more important if we are to be sustainable species again. Creativity, when all is said and done, may be the best thing our species has going for it. It is also the most dangerous.

Creativity is a double-edged sword. It comes with responsibility: to the audience; the viewer; the reader; the art and to yourself – your creative self. It is not an easy option. It is not the path to riches. Want to be rich and famous? That is the wrong motivation, likely to lead to to frustration and disappointment. Material success is only what 'society' (the media's construct of it anyway) values. The Way of Awen is a process, not a destination. Like walking along a woodland path, the very act is edifying in itself. A path of health, sanity, happiness, connection with the natural world and one's community – true wealth.

I believe dis-ease is caused in communities because people do not honour their creative selves. They are not living in their own story. They spend their lives exerting themselves for others, marginalising their dreams – something to put off until retirement. And so folk bifurcate themselves, keeping their secret self out of waking life – thus they sleepwalk through their precious time on Earth or only lead a half-life. Certainly we cannot all 'live in the clouds'. We need to use the rational left-side of our brains to get by in the world, to do practical things, to engage with the consensus reality. But that's only half the story. Khalil Gibran, author and artist of *The Prophet* said: *'Whosoever does not spend his days in the theatre of dreams is a slave all of his days'* (from 'The Queen of Imagination'). This is mirrored by Blake's powerful declaration: *'I must create my own system or be enslaved by another man's. My business is not to reason and compare. It is to create.'*

If we do not dream hard enough we end up living in someone else's dream.

And so this book attempts to empower the reader to fulfil

their creative potential. Only you can say what that is. The Taliesin story offers a key and a gateway. It's up to you to go through it. As a catalyst, a challenge, a 'Call to Adventure', I offer my own distinct modality of creative living, drawn from embodied experience. This is not something created out of abstraction, but out of being alive.

I am on my own journey of the bard– it is my life-path, and I can only offer you what I know: what it is to live the Way of Awen every day.

If it inspires you to commence your own journey, it would have succeeded.

I believe awen should be for all, not just the bards. Everyone can benefit from tapping into their creative self and being around others who are doing the same. A buzz of creativity is mutually empowering. We create our dreams, heal our communities, and honour our complete being.

So, let us begin our 'year of living creatively' (the actual timespan is up to you – from a few weeks to a lifetime). Be warned. It may change you (as all true journeys should)! To become Taliesin Penbeirdd, the boy from Llanfair Caereinion, Gwion Bach discovered that: *'To make yourself, it is also necessary to destroy yourself.'* (*Voss*, Patrick White). Basically, you have to be prepared to change.

When I perform a story I liken it to holding onto a dragon's tale – seeing where it leads you. To receive awen is an act of surrendering. Realization comes through release. In my poem Dragon Dance, I say: *'Dance the dragon, let the dragon dance me...'*

Are you ready for the dance?

Chapter 1

The Books of the Fferyllt

The tale of Taliesin began, in all likelihood, as an oral narrative –
as did the bulk of the source material compiled and published in
1848 by Lady Charlotte Guest and called the *Mabinogion*. Strictly
speaking outside of the official books that comprise it (the Four
Branches: Pwyll, Branwen, Manawyddan and Math) the *Hanes
Taliesin* (The Story of Taliesin), a 16th Century text and a 14th
Century volume *Llyfr Taliesin* (which comprises of 77 poems
attributed to him) was included by Guest, although later editions
have tended to omit it on grounds of scholarly inconsistency.
These unique tomes – small, fragile, priceless – have themselves
become books with a magical aura about them. Only academics
of the highest credentials are allowed to handle them – in holding
them one holds 'secret knowledge' akin to the magical book
Ceridwen was said to have had, the mysterious 'books of the
Fferyllt'.

**So she resolved according to the arts of the books of the
Fferyllt, to boil a cauldron of Inspiration and Science for her
son, that his reception might be honourable because of his
knowledge of the mysteries of the future state of the world.**
(Guest, from *The Red Book of Hergest*)

Whether this book existed or not seems unlikely – for druids did
not write down their secret lore – but we must remember that the
story we have today is a result of what *was* written down, in
however garbled a form, and that the sheer physicality of the
book and the act of reading has many magical resonances.
Alphabets and words have been considered sacred since the

earliest civilisations: hieroglyphs, runes, Ogham and other sacred alphabets spell out the magical origins of language. Anyone who understood them was probably perceived as having magical power – the aura surrounding books lingered until literacy became more widespread (through various Education Acts) and even today literacy may seem like a strange exclusive world to those not blessed with it.

In the story, no doubt embellished by tellers over the centuries of its existence, Ceridwen is depicted consulting a magical tome – an image that has become a cliché of a witch now with her Book of Shadows, appearing in popular culture (e.g. *Buffy the Vampire Slayer*; the Harry Potter film series; the BBC TV serial *Merlin*). They are called the 'books of the Fferyllt', and have been identified in the past as the 'Books of Virgil', because Fferyllt has been translated as a Welsh form of Virgil (or philosopher; scientist). In modern Welsh the word means simply chemist – but in the past this might have all kinds of associations. The further back you go, the more the worlds of science and superstition blend until you get alchemy. So, Ceridwen's magical texts may be books of alchemy. This would be appropriate, since by her arts she affects magical transformation. To 'boil a cauldron of Inspiration and Science for her son' sounds like the kind of arcane experiment an alchemist would undertake and the aesthetic is not dissimilar to the laboratory of the latter, with its alembics, phials, pestles and mortar and so on – the Medieval equivalent of Frankenstein's lab.

Yet the books of the Fferyllt have an interesting echo – for Virgil's story mirrors in a mythopoeic way Taliesin's. Living between 70BC-19BC, Virgil was the author of *The Aeneid* – a poet who gained legendary status after his death. In medieval Europe he is depicted as a magician with his own story-cycle of birth and deeds. Said to have been conceived after his mother drank a golden cordial, he was born with a gold star upon his brow – closely foreshadowing radiant-browed Taliesin in his conception, appearance and career trajectory. However tempting these links are, it seems unlikely a Welsh witch would be referring to classical texts about a Latin poet, assuming she had the books at all – which have never been proven to exist. It is possible that the name is just another example of Classical cultural filters – scholars rendering things in terms they are familiar with. Empires have done this – when the Romans invaded they shrewdly assimilated local worship, taking over sacred sites. At Bath, they discovered hot springs dedicated to the Celtic goddess Sul and seeing in her an echo of their own Minerva they rededicated the temple they raised to Sulis-Minerva and named the city *Aquae Sulis*. 'Virgil' might just have been a byword for anything esoteric and exotic – a word that conjured up power, a certain paradigm, in the same way 'Newton' once did, then 'Darwin' and 'Einstein', and now 'Dawkins' and 'Lovelock'. It becomes emblematic. And so, if the original word is a Welsh rendering of Virgil it may have been a shorthand for 'esoteric knowledge' in general. These might have been books on alchemy, but it seems more likely that Ceridwen's 'books' were nature itself – a book which every wise woman is able to read. She gathered her ingredients from the apothecary of Mother Earth.

Yet from the beginning one of the key themes of the story is introduced – that of education. Ceridwen wished to concoct a potion of inspiration for her son so 'that his reception might be honourable because of his knowledge of the mysteries of the future state of the world.' As we know, Afagddu disastrously fails to receive this. The story of Taliesin is, in effect, a Bildungsroman – 'a novel dealing with someone's formative years or spiritual education' – but it is an unwitting bit-part who becomes the focus and recipient, Gwion Bach. He is the raw material transformed by this alchemical process, set out in Ceridwen's secret books of alchemy. It is a rite-of-passage that 'goes wrong' – although perhaps Gwion Bach was destined to receive the awen meant for his ill-favoured step-brother. His name was on it all along.

The books of the Fferyllt could be seen as a metaphorical allusion – to either Ceridwen's arcane knowledge written invisibly in the 'book of Nature'; or to the alchemical process which Gwion Bach undergoes to become Taliesin – a 'book of changes', a Celtic I-Ching, detailing the cycles of life, death and rebirth – transformations Gwion will undergo while ill-favoured Afagddu remains the same, destined to remain in the shadows of his shining-browed half-brother.

(i) Afaggdu's Need

Afaggdu
Shadow is my skin,
I am night-in-the-day,
Dusk-lurker,
Gloom-hair –
I bear my own pall.
A puddle of inky peat
My footprints.
Black-plumed,
Bedraggled,
Ceridwen's sea-crow –
First-born forgotten son.
I known not the light of awen,
No shining brow for me.
Forever the darkness
Of my own ignorance.
Denied a sip from the cauldron
Brewed for me.
I would savour its aroma of magic –
Watch from the dark
As the village lad stirred,
The old man stoked.

All this effort, just for me.
I knew my mother's love,
If no one else's.
Then
The cauldron split, its hot broth spilt.
In a flash, my awen
Wasted.
I returned to the lightless place
The negative space
Of my life.
Taliesin's bane, curdled with envy.
My eyes always looking –
Green flames – from the edges
Of his world. I wait.

In times past there lived in Penllyn a man of gentle lineage, named Tegid Voel, and his dwelling was in the midst of the lake Tegid, and his wife was called Ceridwen. And there was born to him of his wife a son named Morvran ab Tegid, and also a daughter named Creirwy, the fairest maiden in the world was she; and they had a brother, the most ill-favoured man in the world, Afagddu. Now Ceridwen his mother thought that he was not likely to be admitted among men of noble birth, by reason of his ugliness, unless he had some exalted merits or knowledge. For it was in the beginning of Arthur's time and of the Round Table.

Taliesin's story starts with another's story – as is true of our own narratives, there is always a 'before-story' (what happened before we were born) and 'after-story' (what happens after we die). Stories have to start and end somewhere – to give them shape, and to make their telling viable (although the recital of some national epics, like the Altai Maadai-Kara cycle, can go on for hours, even days). Several narratives converge in the making of

Taliesin. Yet he is not unique in this respect. As individuals born into this world, we are the tip of a pyramid of genealogy, stretching back to distant ancestors and beyond, into the origins of life on Earth and the origins of the Earth itself. Many skeins weave into the making of our particular thread – right back to the birth of the universe.

Taliesin's extraordinary story begins in a seemingly mundane way, with a couple – Ceridwen and Tegid Foel (admittedly not the most 'conventional' of parents – one a witch goddess, the other a fairy giant) who do the most natural thing in the world and start a family. They have three children. The firstborn son, Morvran ('sea crow') seems something of a black sheep, as we never hear from him again, yet he seems a strange precursor to their second son, Afagddu, who shares a similar negritude, his name meaning 'utter darkness'. They have a daughter too, Creirwy, who is as fair as her younger brother is foul. The story describes the former as 'the fairest maiden in the world' and latter as 'the most ill-favoured man in the world'. We are in the Manichaean world of duality, of binary opposites. These extremes must be brought into balance.

If we consider that true beauty is a quality of the soul (it is someone's inner qualities that make them beautiful) and that 'ugliness' is just a symptom of a 'blocked soul' this makes Ceridwen's efforts to improve her son's lot not an early form of makeover, but an endeavour to bring out her son's true qualities. Yeats said 'education is not the filling of a pail, but the lighting of a fire'. Afagddu, for whatever reason, is a benighted soul, yet the spark is within him, waiting to be nurtured and drawn out – this is the inner potential in all of us, and in some ways we all start out life as 'Afaggdus', emerging chrysalis-like from our own ignorance. But it could also be said we begin life as 'Creirwys' too – pure souls, shining with our own innate, uncorrupted beauty. This is our natural state, and it is only the vicissitudes of life that dampen this, block it (negative signals from family, friends, school; formative and traumatic experiences). When Taliesin is discovered by Elphin, much later in the story, the hapless son of Gwyddno (in his own 'dark night of the soul') cries out: 'Behold, the radiant brow!' Taliesin's awen shines out from him – his fire has been lit, has been revealed, the fire that unfortunately for Afagddu, never gets kindled. He is the untaught pupil, the unwatered flower. His potential is not developed; it is well and truly arrested.

But it is not from want of trying.

Ceridwen, Afagddu's mother, is not without her art and cunning. Like any parent, she wanted to give her child the best start in life. What nature did not provide, she would compensate for – in a kind of early form of genetic engineering. If her son had 'exalted merits or knowledge' then it would not matter what he looked like. Perhaps her son was not merely 'ugly' but had what would be called these days special needs. She did not want her son to be disadvantaged by any perceived 'disability'. This was in a time before political correctness, equal opportunities or the Disability Act. If it was contemporary, Afaggdu's parents could have taken King Arthur to court for discrimination – but in truth this is merely a PC lens on a mythic story, which has its own rules. The Round Table of Camelot symbolises among other things healthy, holistic completeness – a blueprint of 'heaven on earth, of humans fulfilling their potential, rising to excellence, the apotheosis of the human project – and Afagddu is 'ill-made', incomplete, broken. He cannot join their exalted company until he has been 'completed' by other qualities – as a rounded education seeks to do, and as 'finishing schools' claim to finalise, although these days, a gap year and an internship seems to offer a more practical 'rounding off'.

Yet, should not both Afagddu and his mother be happy with his lot? 'Ugliness'/disfigurement/disability often goes hand-in-hand with some kind of exceptional gift. Myths and legends are rife with such figures – the crippled blacksmith, Hephaestus;

Odin with his one eye; Nuadu and his silver hand; Achilles' with his heel...

At one time, children born with a blemish were seen as 'special' – touched by the gods.

Ugliness in the metaphorical world of story is often a sign that 'all is not what is seems'. An enchantment is at work, or the hero is being tested in some way. The Frog turns out to be a Prince – if the princess is willing to overcome her churlish nausea and grant him a kiss. In the Arthurian story of 'Gawain and Lady Ragnall' the King is tested by a hag, who Gawain agrees to marry to save his king. Gawain is offered the choice – for his hag-wife to be 'fair by day and foul by night', or 'foul by day and fair by night'. He chooses to let his wife 'choose her own way' and thus emancipated, the enchantment is broken and she is revealed, in her beauty. When we can see people for themselves and stop projecting our fears and desires onto them, then they can truly shine.

Yet in the context of the Taliesin story, Afagddu's need is a real one – one that we all have, to rise to our potential, to be illuminated, to step out of the darkness of our ignorance, our fear, and become truly great. As Nelson Mandela once said: 'Our greatest fear is not that we are inadequate but that we are powerful beyond measure'. Many of us are too afraid to step up to the mark of our true potential, and instead we choose to live 'half-lives', in the shadow of what we really can be – Afagddus, lurking in the dark rather than dwelling in the light of our true potential. Too frightened to dream; to make them come true. We all need, at one time or another, to drink from the cauldron.

Yet what is the cauldron and what does Ceridwen brew in it?

(ii) Cauldron of Change

Then she began to boil the cauldron, which from the beginning of its boiling might not cease to boil for a year and a day, until three blessed drops were obtained of the grace of Inspiration.

Once she has gathered the ingredients, Ceridwen prepares the potion of inspiration for Afagddu in her cauldron. This is the most important example in myth of a Cauldron of Inspiration, but it is by no means unique. In the Celtic Tradition other cauldrons exist, and analogues throughout myth, legend and religion around the world.

The cauldron is an analogue for the womb in which life is 'cooked'. In the story it takes the symbolic 'year and a day', that is a full turning of the wheel of life – similar to the spiralling nine months of pregnancy. When the waters break (three drops escaping) the cauldron breaks and Gwion is 'born'.

In the Dark Ages, the mysteries of life were something that women seemed to have command over with their bodies that changed shape, with bellies and breasts that swelled and shrank. From the cauldron of the womb came new life, raw and screaming, miraculous and vulnerable.

The cauldron gives Gwion Bach the power of fith-fath, shapechanging, and so echoes the metamorphoses of pregnancy – both in the mother and in the embryo.

The cauldron's potion also bestows upon the accidental recipient the gift of prophecy – knowledge of the mysteries of the future state of the world. Thus endowed with the triple gifts of Inspiration, Prophecy and Shapechanging, akin to the paths of Bard, Vate and Druid, Gwion, our little Prometheus, scarpers – having imbibed Ceridwen's own qualities as a son does from his mother's genes. The mitochondria of awen now flows through his veins. But such stolen power comes at a price – as he will discover!

Other cauldrons exist in Celtic Tradition and they too come with their deadly price... In the story of Bran and Branwen – from the *Mabinogion*, the plot revolves around the fabled Cauldron of Rebirth, which ironically is the cause of much death (perhaps a sign of what happens when a gift from the Otherworld, one of the sacred hallows, is misused). The cauldron is described as formerly belonging to two giants who live in a 'burning house' on a lake – which echoes the connection with Taliesin and Tegid Foel, who is associated with Llyn Tegid. Much calamity is caused by this cauldron when it is gifted to the Irish wooer of Bran's sister, Branwen... Of the mighty war host who cross the Irish Sea on Bran's back to retrieve it and his insulted sister, only seven return – including Taliesin Penbeirdd himself. The Cauldron, whose resurrecting properties are exploited by the enemy, is split in two by Evnissyen, as Ceridwen's is by Gwion. When they make landfall back in Cambria Branwen dies of a broken heart, heartbroken themselves the weary warriors are consoled for seven years at Bran's castle at Harlech by the birds of Rhiannon; and then for another eighty year's on the island of 'Gwales' (possibly Grassholm) by Bran's head itself – resurrected, filled with song. Finally they achieve their destination – the White Mount – where Bran's head is buried 'facing France', to protect Britain from invaders.

The other main cauldron of Celtic Tradition is the Cauldron of Plenty, said to cook food for no coward, only offering the hero's portion to the bravest. This echoes the notion postulated by Jessie Weston in *From Ritual to Romance*, that the Grail 'may act simply as a feeding vessel', but through ritual this is transformed, via a secret rite: '...in which the worshippers partook of the food of life from the sacred vessels.'

King Arthur Pendragon himself goes on a a daring raid to the Otherworld, the harrowing of Annwn, to win the Cauldron of Plenty – his own Grail Quest – as recorded in a poem ascribed to Taliesin, *Preiddu Annwn*. Again, this fabled cauldron afflicts a deadly toll – of the three shipfuls who set sail, only seven return. The intrepid Prydwenauts (they sail in Arthur's ship Prydwen, 'fair-faced') have to run the gauntlet of seven otherworldly caers – like seven stages of consciousness, or rather pre-consciousness as they regress into the chthonic realms 'before birth'. These are akin to Plato's realm of Ideal Form, but far earthier, darker, messier and perilous. The final caer, from whence those in win the Cauldron, 'warmed by the breath of nine muses' (the nine daughters of memory themselves – identical, it seems, to the Greek Pantheon), is Caer Sidi, the revolving castle of Queen Arianrhod. This is this initiatory place of poets, as Taliesin declaims: 'I have sat in the perilous seat/Above Caer Sidi...' (Hanes Taliesin, 69-70).

These three cauldrons are mirrored by the Three Cauldrons as mentioned in a 15-16th century legal codex from Ireland, as Caitlín Matthews discusses in *The Encyclopaedia of Celtic Wisdom*: Coire Goriath, the Cauldron of Warming; Coire Ernmae, the Cauldron of Vocation; and Coire Sois, the Cauldron of Knowledge. These I deal with in detail in *The Bardic Handbook*, but in brief they relate to different parts of the body (basically stomach, heart, and head). Each must be nourished. It is important to replenish the well. As bards, this is essential; otherwise we run the risk of running dry, of burning out, or worse, channelling 'anti-Awen', tainted inspiration symptomatic of a diseased soul. Every year I return to places of power to 'replenish my cauldron' – especially places in Wales where the awen is close to the surface.

The Cauldron of Vocation is especially relevant to that of the bard – the poem associated with it has given me succour over the years:

The Nine Gifts of the Cauldron

The Cauldron of Vocation
gives and is replenished,
promotes and is enlarged,
nourishes and is given life,
ennobles and is exalted,
requests and is filled with answers,
sings and is filled with song,
preserves and is made strong,
arranges and receives arrangements,
maintains and is maintained.

Good is the well of measure,
good is the abode of speech,
good is the confluence of power:
it builds up strength.

It is greater than any domain,
it is better than any inheritance.
It numbers us among the wise,
and we depart from the ignorant.

Ancient Welsh

This cauldron is associated with the heart – the green chakra. On the Qabalistic Tree of Life the green path is the path of service, and this is the path the bard walks. He or she does not exist unless they serve their community.

The stone on Lucifer's crown (once the brightest of angels) was green and when he was cast out of Heaven his green stone fell to Earth, and is thought by some to be the actual Grail. When we consider the Grail Question 'Who does the Grail serve?' it relates back, mythopoeically to the green stone, the green chakra and the green path of service: Love.

When this power is misappropriated and abused, woe can befall the perpetrator and his world, as happened to Amangons – a mythical king who despoiled the maidens of the wells and stole their golden cups, with which they would traditionally refresh weary travellers. Amangons lives on and on, unable to die but unable to enjoy the gift of life which he has desecrated. He becomes wounded and his kingdom becomes wasted. The self-cursed monarch becomes the Fisher King, who ironically can only be healed by the Grail – a very symbol of what he had exploited, which now he needs more than ever, but cannot acquire at any price – for he has squandered the priceless gift of the land. Only if a youthful soul comes along, wins the Grail with his noble heart or pure consciousness (Parsifal/Perceval: 'pierce-the-veil') can the wounded king be redeemed. The corrupt soul needs the healing balm of forgiveness, the renewal of pure life, perhaps which only a child can bring to a world-weary soul.

In the controversial *Holy Blood, Holy Grail*, the authors (Michael Baigent, Richard Leigh, and Henry Lincoln) explore the idea that the Holy Grail is not a cup but a bloodline – Christ's no less – passed down by the 'vessel' of Mary Magdalene.

In Glastonbury, long associated with all matters Arthurian – you have Joseph of Arimathea, Jesus' apocryphal uncle, turning up, possibly bearing the sacred vessel (said to have caught Christ's blood on the cross, or have been part of the dinner service of the Last Supper). Medieval monks, strapped for cash, added fuel to the Arthurian fever in the town, sparking the tourist industry, by 'discovering' the grave of Arthur and Guinevere. In the Twenties, this reached it apogee in the Chalice Orchard Club: Wesley Tudor-Pole, Dion Fortune and Fiona Macleod whipping up a frenzy of esoteric speculation, to the point where a blue glass bowl – the kind of thing you'd expect to be awarded in some WI prize-giving – found in the Chalice Well was taken for the Grail itself.

Numerous Grails have been found across the world and no doubt more will come to light. The Grail Myth has led to countless sometimes wise, often foolish 'Grail Quests'. The cauldron represents a chthonic prototype and seems far more rooted and real, in a mythopoeic sense.

In Irish tradition a king-in-waiting had to ritually 'mate' with a mare (symbolic of the goddess of the land) and then gorge himself on a broth made from horse-flesh – cooked in a large vat or cauldron into which he himself had to immerse, in a weird combination of sauna and fondue. He had to imbibe the spirit of the horse to attain his kingship.

There are many customs associated with drinking, especially with toasting. The Anglo-Saxon word 'wassail' means 'May you be in good health'.

In Somerset around Old Twelfth Night (January 17th) the orchards are wassailed: cider poured on the roots, toast soaked in the wassail liquid (hot spiced cider) attached to the branches, and 'bad spirits' scared away by shotguns and loud noises. 'Good spirits' are welcomed in with offerings of song – traditional wassail carols, and the trees and everyone present are toasted with the Wassail Bowl, a version of the cauldron, living on in the Twenty First Century.

Tristan and Iseult drink from the Hanap, the love cup, made by Bronwen, her servant, to instil amorous feelings in her lady's heart towards King Mark on her wedding night. They drink from the forbidden draught and are smitten. From then on the fugitive lovers are caught in an inescapable net of consequence, compelled by matters of heart – of which the Cup symbolises (water; west; emotion). To drink from the cup is to assimilate the feminine, to 'open one's self up' to the intoxication of love:

Drink to me only with thine eyes,
And I shall pledge with mine,
Or leave a kiss but in the cup,
And I'll not ask for wine.
To Celia, Ben Jonson

The cauldron has endured by being shape-changing itself. From a crude cast iron pot found in a witch's cave, to chased metal of the medieval court and abbey, to the cup, the chalice – it continues to change, becoming whatever people want it to be. Weston's book, *From Ritual to Romance*, sparked renewed interest in it, influencing TS Eliot to write *The Wasteland*. John Steinbeck, whose first book was *The Golden Cup* went on to spend the last year's of his life on his own grail quest, working on a new version of *The Noble Acts of King Arthur and his Knights*, moving to Bruton, Somerset, to breathe the same air and walk the same earth as his legendary residents of Camelot. Witches adopted the chalice from the Christian Communion for their own ceremonies, often combining it with a plunging dagger – an athame – that 'charges' the vessel in a sexually symbolic ritual known as the Great Rite. In the late Eighties and early Nineties the Grail was adopted by Jungian analysts and mythographers to symbolise wholeness, completion, integration, with a perilous forest of books on the subject – like the scene in John Boorman's 1982 visionary master-piece *Excalibur* where the Grail Knight is confronted with several 'grails'. Amid so many versions, it is often perilously tricky for the seeker to discern the genuine from the false.

But Ceridwen's cauldron is undoubtedly the real deal – its concoction has the desired effect, but on the 'wrong' subject (perhaps the intended candidate all along). Like Sauron's Ring of Power, perhaps the Cauldron has a will of its own, and bestows its boon on whomsoever it chooses. Its ways are as mysterious as the goddess.

Gundestrup Cauldron

There is one cauldron that exists that is important in its rich iconography – which shows powerful primal combinations of man and beast, perhaps echoing the Taliesin legend, and is worth looking at here in detail.

A glory of Celtic civilisation, the 'Gundestrup Cauldron' is a richly decorated silver-gilt vessel thought to date from the *La Téne Period* of Celtic art in the 2nd or 1st Century BCE. It was found in a peat bog near Gundestrup in Himmerland, Denmark, in 1891. It is now kept in the National Museum of Copenhagen. Made of 14 plates, it was found dismantled (with one plate missing) in a dry section of peat bog, suggesting it was a ritual deposit. The style and technique suggests it could have originated on the shores of the Black Sea, an area of Thrace well-known for its fine metalwork, especially in silver-gilt. However, the images (one round base plate, 5 shorter inner plates, 7 longer ones facing outwards) are tantalising glimpses into the cosmology of the Celts, with larger figures dominating smaller humans, suggesting the relationship between gods and mortals. The tableaux are filled with strange monsters, zoomorphic images which echo the shape-changing chase of Gwion and Ceridwen, and shamanic iconography around the world.

The most reproduced image depicts a horned man, sitting cross-legged, holding a ramheaded serpent in one hand and a torc in the other – a horned god or shaman figure often associated with the Celtic deity Cernunnos. If he is the god, then he is one of a pantheon depicted, including a fierce-looking Taranis a thunder deity – with his wheel being held, or stopped, by a smaller horned figure. These fascinating windows into the Celtic world inspired many elements of my novel *Windsmith* (Awen 2006). I endeavoured to create a narrative around them as a way of unlocking their mystery and empathising with the paradigm of the people it represents in such an iconic way. All the images are worth meditating upon, but the one which most evidently concerns us here is what is referred to as plate (e), which illustrates some kind of death and resurrection ritual involving a cauldron. In the lower half, a line of warriors bearing spears and shields, accompanied by carnyx players march to the left. On the left side, a large figure is immersing a man in a cauldron. In the upper half, heading away from the cauldron, and probably having completed the initiation ritual are warriors on horseback. Later Celtic myth features resurrection themes based on immersion of dead warriors in cauldrons, and indeed our story here involves a hero who is 'twice-born' having emerged from the destruction-creation of the cauldron. But if we are to win the cauldron-grail, then a form of the Grail Question needs to be asked: To whom does this cauldron belong? What is the nature of its owner?

(iii) The Crooked Crone

His wife was called Ceridwen

Ceridwen's Song
They call me the Crooked One,
A bent-backed crone, in
The way they mock
All the wise women of the world.
The ones they fear.

Yet I was mother
Before I became hag.
Suckled two children from my dugs.
A daughter and a son –
As different as day and night.
One fair as the spring sun,
The other as foul as winter's midnight.
I loved them both, of course,
As only a mother can.
I wanted the best for them
And what fortune did not provide,
I would with my cunning art.
I gathered the ingredients
To brew a potion of inspiration

From barley, acorns, honey, bull's blood and ivy,
From the five trees of power,
To give to my son inspiration.
Imbue him with imbas.
His Utter Darkness I shall spark
With the shining brow.

With my cariad I shall give him cerddeu.
I shall brew for him with my love
The awen of the world.

Cerddeu: poems/Cariad: love

Ceridwen is the archetypal crone. She is known as the 'Crooked Woman' or the 'Bent White One', which could be related to her shape-shifting abilities, fith-fath, which are 'accidentally' passed on to Gwion Bach through the potion she concocts in her cauldron. This latter ingredient is a traditional part of the witches' regalia, to the point where now it has become a cliché, along with the very notion of the magical, but ugly crone (as though to suggest a woman's job is to be beautiful and submissive to men – and those who seek knowledge cannot be desirable – they have sacrificed their femininity). This caricature is perpetuated by a Dr Harrington, describing a famous witch said to dwell in Wookey Hole, who was turned to stone (like so many pagan presences in Christianised Britain) by what could be called moral petrification:

The Witch of Wokey, by Dr Harrington
Her haggard face was foul to see,
Her mouth unmeet a mouth to be;
Her eyne of deadly leer,
She nought devis'd, but neighbour's ill,
She wreak'd on all her wayward will,
And marr'd all goodly cheer.

As with so many depictions of witches it smacks of misogyny. The many women who were persecuted, tortured and executed as 'witches' were rarely wise women – just people that somebody with influence wanted out of the way, or merely vulnerable scapegoats – soft targets in times of religious xenophobia.

In the city of Bath, there is an alleyway called Slippery Lane, where local 'witches' were taken to the River Avon, just above Pulteney Weir, to be tried by dunking stool. If they drowned they were innocent. If they survived they were burnt or hung as witches.

Yet the witches are back! Since the partial repeal of the Witchcraft Act in 1951 there's been a growing interest in witch-craft with a wave of books on the subject, cresting in the New Age phenomenon of the Nineties. Thanks to mainstream portrayal in fashionable TV series and films like Buffy and Harry Potter, Wicca, as it has been branded, has never been more popular. When the job for the Witch of Wookey was advertised in the summer of 2009, over three thousand applicants applied for the position (including many 'serious witches' from the Glastonbury area), even though the job description included 'must be able to cackle'.

The Witch of Wookey's 'cauldron' was the very cave system itself, carved out by the action of rainwater on the Oolitic limestone rock, filtering down from the Mendips, over vast tracts of time.

The Corryvreckan Whirlpool, a natural phenomenon between Jura and Scarba, caused by powerful tidal flows, derives its Gaelic name Coire Bhrecain (Bhreacain's Cauldron) after a Scandinavian prince who fell in love with the local princess but failed the test set him by his future father-in-law. He was dragged to his death in the treacherous whirlpool. It is also known as the Cailleach's Washtub.

The Cailleach is the Scottish and Irish Hag of Winter. Her name means the 'hooded' or 'veiled one', which could echo Ceridwen's nomenclature. She is said to haunt the mountain fastnesses of the Highlands and is sometimes referred to as the Mountain Mother – a fearsome figure, best to be avoided. She seems akin to the Valkyrie, Morrighan and Kali – sisters of destruction, of dissolution, providing a necessary katabolic function in the world. As with Mother Nature herself, the Divine Feminine is the giver of life and the bringer of death.

Even that humblest of types, the washer women, the 'Mrs Mangles' of this world, are sisters of these archetypal presences. The Washer at the Ford was a terrifying figure seen on the eve of battle, washing the clothes of those who are destined to die – and so is a harbinger of death like the banshee and the fetch.

The cauldron is a vessel of transformation – like, to a lesser extent, any cooking vessel or oven (to which the women traditionally knew the 'mysteries' of more than men). Women have been bending over steaming pots and vats for millennia, tending the hearth, feeding, cleaning, washing. Ceridwen and her cauldron-sisters are mythopoeically related to the figure depicted on the plates of the Gundestrup Cauldron – showing the tall figure immersing the warriors. Athena was said to have similarly immersed Achilles in a vat of invulnerability; because she held him by one ankle, he was vulnerable on that one part of his body, his Achilles' heel.

In the boyhood of Cuchullain, a Northern Irish culture hero, the wild youth is possessed by a battle-frenzy – akin to the berserker rage of the Vikings – which only the cooling of three vats set up by the women of Emain Macha can assuage. The first one he is dunked in boils, the second one steams, and the third one soothes.

Three is commonly the magic number in many cultures. The triple-aspect goddess appears not only as maiden, mother and crone but often as three sibylline sisters: the Fates, the Nordic Norns, the Græae – with their one eye between them. Shakespeare took this trope and played with it in the 'Scottish Play', *Macbeth*, with the three witches:

*"When shall we three meet again in thunder, lightning, or in
rain?/When the hurlyburly's done, When the battle's lost and won"*
(Act I, Scene I)

In Celtic culture it was traditionally the role of a certain women
to train the men in the arts of war. Cuchullain, the Hound of
Ulster, is sent to Scathach ('the shadowy one') on the Isle of Skye
to learn the skills necessary for a warrior prince – the Salmon
Leap, the throwing of the Gae Bolg, chariot-riding and so on.
Scathach acts like Ceridwen, as an Initiatrix, yet it is in the Arts of
Love that her pupil receives final instruction. When Scathach
wages war on her sister, Aoife, an enchantress, Cuchullain is
restrained and prevented from entering the fray. He breaks free
from his bounds and plunges into the heat of battle. He is
matched by Aoife, who defeats him with her womanly wiles.

It is for another 'object of desire', Branwen, sister of Bran the
Blessed, that further conflict is caused – the heroine becoming a
Welsh Helen of Troy. This time it is the Cauldron of Rebirth
which must be won back from the Irish king, who is given it as a
dowry upon marrying Bran's sister – but when news arrives that
she is mistreated, Bran raises a mighty war-host, many of whom
he carries upon his back across the sea, to repatriate the Cauldron
and his sister – resulting in enormous losses on both the Cymric
and Hibernian sides. As with Ceridwen's cauldron, the ensuing
action results in the shattering of the vessel – but this time inten-
tionally, as Evnissyen, Bran's brother, the cause of the calamity,
makes amends by breaking the Cauldron of Rebirth which has
given the enemy an overwhelming advantage. But by then the
damage is wrought. Bran has been mortally wounded and his
sister dies shortly afterwards of a broken-heart.

In the *Preiddu Annwn*, another Cauldron, of Plenty, (that cooks
food for no coward) is kept within a series of magical fortresses
'Caers' in the Underworld and is 'warmed by the breath of nine
muses'. These seem to be sister, if not identical to, the nine Muses

of the Mount Parnassus – inspirer of poets. And so there is a deep connection between sacred cauldrons and otherworldly powerful women. The Cauldron of Plenty is kept ultimately within Caer Arianrhod – the initiatory place of poets. Arianrhod was said to have a silver wheel, and her caer is associated with the Corona Borealis – the Northern Crown, which in its very name echoes Taliesin's shining brow. Here Taliesin said he spent many lifetimes ('Three times in the prison of Caer Arianrhod'). Could he even be 'star-born'? He claims '...my original country is the region of the Summer stars.' Some would see an extra-terrestrial aspect to his 'shining' and uncanny knowledge. Ceridwen herself seems not unaware of astronomical cycles.

And she herself, according to the books of the astronomers, and in planetary hours, gathered every day of all charm-bearing herbs.

These are things which most herbalists would do anyway – sowing, pruning, gathering and preparing in accordance to lunar and diurnal rhythms – but to those not possessing the secret knowledge, such activity would indeed seem magical.

No doubt because of her pivotal role in the creation of Wales' greatest bard, Taliesin Penbeirdd, Ceridwen is the Patroness of the Order of Bards in Wales and looms large over its landscape. In her other guise, Henwen, the giant sow, her profile can be delineated by the Welsh coastline – a boar's head. Merlin in his 'wild phase', Myrddin Wyllt, talks to a 'little pig', from whom he receives knowledge. Pigs were said to be a gift from the Underworld (in the story of 'Pwyll of Dyfed' Arawn, Lord of Annwn, the Celtic Hades, sends a herd as a token of friendship).

With her 'books of the Fferyllt' Ceridwen the Alchemist acts as initiatrix to Gwion Bach and to all who decide to walk the Way of Awen. She demands everything and what is not given freely will be taken anyway – for to be 'twice-born' one must suffer a ritual death, and Gwion undergoes this 'soul-winnowing', showing us what we, as Anruths, must endure, if we are to be reborn as Bards.

(iv) A Man of Gentle Lineage

In times past there lived in Penllyn a man of gentle lineage, named Tegid Voel, and his dwelling was in the midst of the lake Tegid

The story describes Afagddu's father as 'a man of gentle lineage'. This suggests one of the Faerie Folk, as the 'Gentle Folk' were one of the euphemistic epithets given them. This would chime with the suggestion he was the father of the Y Tylwyth Teg, the Welsh Tuatha de Danaan, or fairy folk in Gwynedd, North Wales; siring the Plant Annwn, the 'children of the deep', undines or genius loci of the eponymous Llyn Tegid, AKA Lake Bala. Like Gwyddno, (who in one guise is the ruler of Cantre'r Gwaelod, the flooded 'lowest hundred' of Cardigan Bay) he has misfortune with wells – similarly losing his lands through neglect and inundation.

Tegid Foel

Who remembers me?
The absent father in your memory.
Before I became a cameo
I was Chief of Penllyn,
Five parishes to my name.
A city it is said
And a secret bride
By a magic well –
A fairy tale romance –
Until one day the fool forgot
The daily task

To cover the well – Ffynon Gawr.
Some say it was an itinerant minstrel
Distracted by a bird, so he says,
Lured to a hillside of dreams.
He awoke to behold
What his negligence had caused:
A lake where once there was none –
His harp afloat upon its surface.
At least they named it after me –
Llyn Tegid, it has a nice ring to it,
Doesn't it?
And some say I still dwell
Below its surface
With my mysterious bride
In my lost city.
And we have not been neglectful in our duties –
The waters are the playground of
Plant Annwn, the Children of the Deep.
It's whispered I may be the father of
Y Tylwyth Teg themselves! Fairy Godfather, perhaps.
How I had time to sire two
On that old witch,
Lord knows!
Like hot iron doused in blacksmith steam
Loins of the father
Cool in Bala's green depths.
Let its monsters in fathomless mystery keep.

Tegid Foel is the shadowy primogenitor of this tale – after his brief mention at the beginning he disappears from the narrative, becoming a kind of 'absent father' figure, an abstract patriarch. His paternal archetype reappears in differing forms later in the story: as Gwyddno, the long-suffering father of the hapless Elphin – who himself suffers a similar Bala-esque catastrophe due to neglected duties (he loses his 'sixteen cities' because a drunken steward fails to close a sluice gate); and as the 'dark father' figure of Maelgwn. These three men – Tegid Foel, Gwyddno and Maelgwn – could almost be the male equivalent of the triple-aspect goddess: the three faces or phases of Man. Could Tegid Foel be akin to the Lord of Day; Maelgwn; Lord of Night, and Gwyddno, with his associations with thresholds, Lord of Dusk? None are wholly 'good' or 'bad' – they all have negative and positive qualities. These are more clearly seen in the figure of Maelgwn, whose character is fleshed out compared to the other two – shadowy supporting figures – but there's no sense of moral judgement about them. They exist, in suspension, like flabbily spandexed Fathers4Justice, standing astride a tall public building, wanting rights for fathers, but failing to win deeper 'access' to the story and its young protagonist.

(v) Fair-Face

And also a daughter named Creirwy, the fairest maiden in the world was she

Creirwy
Fair-face I was named
But who looks below the surface
Of my beauty?
A harsh prophecy had I to live up to.
Ungrateful, some might mutter,
Considering my less-favoured brother –
But who spares a moment,
An iota of compassion,
For Creirwy?
Forever typecast
To be the beautiful one –
A maiden whose role

It is to be fair,
And nothing more.
No brains, no soul
In here.
I'm a mirror to your desire,
Doomed to be its object.
Yet what of mine –
Do I not look out?
Gaze if you must
But let me be more
Than just the receptacle of your lust.
Let me have my own story.
Beauty is a quality of the soul.
I am the pure seed in all.
I simply need water, sun and soil
To bloom to the flower of my potential.
If am allowed to grow, I will.
But you like to keep me, contain me,
Within this dress of thorns.

Ceridwen's daughter, Creirwy is called in the tale 'the fairest maiden in the world'. One would think a child of such magical lineage would inherit her mother's powers or be instructed in the Crooked Crone's arts, but no more is heard of Creirwy beyond this initial mention. It seems she is destined to be set in opposition to her ill-favoured brother, Afagddu, as one dualistic extreme. Between these binary opposites, like Scylla and Carybdis, the tale of Taliesin sets forth. We shall look at 'flower maidens' in detail when we consider Maelgwn's daughter, Eurgain – the maiden who stands at the other end of the story. Here, we shall consider Creirwy as a symbol of the soul – the soul-spark in its original state, pure and untainted by the world. We may come into this world in the utter darkness of unawareness, like Afagddu – benighted by a caul of ignorance that can take a lifetime or even lifetimes to emerge from – but we also contain this Creirwy element: the Divine Spark – our covenant and connection with the Source. Each of us has the potential to be as Taliesin – if we can discover and express our inner genius, let the brow shine. Creirwy's 'fair-face' is a hint of that, beauty being a quality of the soul. When it is blocked, for whatever reason (a difficult childhood, negative messages, trauma, low self-esteem, etc) then we appear 'ugly'. This is like a capped spring. It can be restored with love. Allowed to flow. Sometimes people bloom late in life. Old people can be so beautiful – an old man, comfortable in his features; an old lady with a halo of white hair. When people block this natural beauty – with too much make-up, perfume, plastic surgery, botox injections, wigs, clothes that are too young, too tight for them, etc, then they start to become ugly again. Cosmetic surgery often has the opposite effect to what people intend. And it is pertinent that Ceridwen does not use her 'arts of the books of the Fferyllt' to create a glamour of beauty for her son, but a potion of inspiration – for it is wisdom that will make him 'beautiful', not cosmetic compensation. Knowledge can be an aphrodisiac as much as power. Intelligence is attractive. Creirwy could be far more than just a pretty face, but in narrative terms she is simply a 'flat-character', a mask. The archetype of beauty. An ideal, but not, in this instance, an idol. She is not the 'object of desire' in this story – that role is played by the awen itself – and perhaps Creirwy resembles closest the classic Muse of the poets: the beautiful young maiden who must be wooed to be won. All such muses seem to be animas – the feminine aspect that is often projected onto others, but which we, in truth, all possess. We spend our lives seeking for this ghost-image – trying to find someone who will match up to it. Of course, they never do, because it is a self-generated illusion, an impossible pedestal. Yet Creirwy also represents 'cleansed perception' – she embodies the innocent soul embarking upon the journey of knowledge, and the right attitude that should be sustained throughout. In the words of William Blake: 'When the doors of perception are cleansed, man will see things as they truly are, infinite'. Fair-faced Creirwy teaches us to experience the world without tinted spectacles. With open eyes and open heart we set forth, and though we are bound to be hurt and disillusioned along the way it is, perhaps, a necessary desecration. Creirwy is sister to the Maidens of the Wells, who offered weary travellers a drink from their cups of gold. We are all refreshed by the bright fountain of their beauty. Our lives are richer for the Creirwys of this world, which otherwise would be overshadowed by utter darkness. Yet without her crepuscular brother, Creirwy's world would be too perfect, too light, too anaemic – like the popular New Age Fairy festivals: all whimsical wings and saccharine Victoriana. Only when Creirwy gains her shadow can she be whole.

If this was Creirwy's story, her tale might resemble Cinderella's or Snow White's. She is the cousin of all fairy story heroines – the virgin soul setting out into a hazardous world of moral choices and chancy thresholds. A maiden who must lose her virginity to gain knowledge. Every Eve must taste the apple to become a woman. Otherwise innocence remains as ignorance, and Creirwy would stay as 'in the dark' as her brother.

(vi) The Blind Servant

A blind man named Morda to kindle the fire beneath it

Morda is representative of all minor characters in stories who have unglamorous roles – the gatekeepers, the guards, the night watchmen – the blue-collar workers of mythology. Without such industrious 'flat-characters' the world of story, like the human world would fall apart – without the men who empty the bins, the school dinner ladies, cleaners, janitors, attendants, shop assistants, road sweepers, home-carers. The unsung of the world. The dogsbodies – destined to be kicked, to be kept down. On one level such *characters* (not the human beings) 'deserve' it – for they represent, in terms of a mythopoeic narrative, the Lower Self. They will stay in their unenlightened state until they aspire to the Higher Self, and try and fulfil their potential. Sometimes such lives are wasted, not through mere circumstance (for many have risen to fame, fortune or greatness, despite humble origins) but through a lack of effort and ambition. A chronic lack of self-belief. A cowardly acceptance of one's lot – that one does not deserve a better life. A lack of courage to live one's beliefs, to follow one's dreams. A soul-laziness.

Sometimes this dormant aspect can be positive, a kind of service to the Higher Self/Higher Cause – either inside or out. There is the touching story of Odysseus's loyal hound, Argus, who waited for his master to return for twenty years – ten years at Troy and ten years' odyssey getting home. The dog slept on a dung heap, ('there lay Argus, full of vermin') but never gave up hope. After two long decades, when all hope seemed lost, his master made it back to Ithaca just in time to save his wife Penelope from the suitors she had held off for as long as she could. When the dog finally saw his beloved master back, (though Odysseus was in disguise his senses did not deceive him) he greeted him and, vigil complete, expired.

Amidst such sufferers of life's slings and arrows there are worthy men and women who stoically beaver away without any recognition or reward.

Jean Giono's beautiful eco-classic, *The Man Who Planted Trees*, (1954) describes such a man:

> *For a human character to reveal truly exceptional qualities, one must have the good fortune to be able to observe its performance over many years. If this performance is devoid of all egoism, if its guiding motive is unparalled generosity, if it is absolutely certain that there is no thought of recompense and that, in addition, it has left its visible mark upon the earth, then there can be no mistake.*

Giono's fictional hero, Elzéard Bouffier, is a Morda-type – stoically going about his life's works – planting thousands of trees in sub-Alpine Provence, Southern France – in a humble unannounced way. He knows he will not live to see the full fruits of his efforts – it is an offering to the future.

As poets, this is all we can do – sow our seeds of wisdom, scatter pearls of truth and beauty, and hope for the best.

In a letter to Thomas Butts, 22nd November 1802, William Blake (an artist and poet who met with little success in his lifetime) describes how he labours under 'Another Sun':

This Earth breeds not our happiness.
Another Sun feeds our life's streams,
We are not warmed with thy beams

Dylan Thomas, who was on his own dark journey, wrote how he burnt the midnight oil working on his 'craft or sullen art' for little gain – labouring for love:

In my craft or sullen art
Exercised in the still night
When only the moon rages
And the lovers lie abed
With all their griefs in their arms,
I labour by singing light
Not for ambition or bread
Or the strut and trade of charms
On the ivory stages
But for the common wages
Of their most secret heart.

Metaphorically speaking, few live in the sun. Many live in the shadows. Morda represents the underclass, the unseen, who keep the wheels of the world turning, symbolic almost of the 'blind' or invisible forces that operate nature and the cosmos – the infinitely complex mechanism of the universe, ruled over by Einstein's blind watchmaker.

When the devastation of the cauldron is discovered, Ceridwen, enraged, puts out one of Morda's eyes.

In Norse mythology Hod, the blind god of darkness, inadvertently slays Baldur, his sun-like brother, through the nefarious agency of Loki. All things in the nine worlds have sworn not to harm Baldur, Odin's son, all except mistletoe – so slight a plant, a mere parasite, it 'didn't matter'. Loki discovers this and forges a spear from it, with which Hod slays his brother by accident. This seems to be a solar myth, acting out the death and rebirth of the sun at midwinter in the Northern Hemisphere. The blind agency of Morda seems a necessary force of the cosmos. Morda's ruined eye can be spied in the black holes and dark matter of the heavens – the negative spaces of the universe.

And in the kingdom of the blind, as the Bible tells us, the one-eyed man is king. Perhaps like other culture heroes Morda has made a sacrifice of part of himself and gained the secret knowledge.

Yet his fate is also a salutary parable – showing what happens when you become set in your ways, like a scholar or scientist blinkered by their obsession, to the detriment of their health, social life and sometimes sanity.

Sometimes you have to bypass logic to access wisdom. The intuitive flash can strike upon the solution when the methodical approach can fail, or simply take too long. Nowadays 'brain-storming' activities are common, but certainly since the Age of Reason a linear approach has been favoured until quite recently, indicative of a dominant patriarchal paradigm. The Celtic Tradition prefers a more cyclical, feminine, spiralling approach, as its stories attest.

Morda is akin to Finnegas in the story of Fionn and the Salmon. The hermit spends twenty years trying to catch the

Salmon of Wisdom. Then young Fionn comes along and it is caught straight away. Fionn is charged with overseeing its cooking, and ends up imbibing the hermit's longed-for wisdom. And yet this seems to have been part of the great plan. Finnegas is symbolic of all those who lay the foundations for the future. On the shoulders of giants, it has been rightly said, we stand. Without their diligent work, the painstaking scholarship and research, experimentation and verification, there would be very few 'break-throughs'. As many scientific discoveries have proven – you need the intense saturation in a problem before the 'Euraka!' moment. Arthur Koestler said: *'soak, and wait'*. Only when the mind is sated with all available material can the subconscious work its magic and come up with the solution, the sonnet, et cetera, 'in a flash'. This is exactly what happens with Gwion Bach, our young 'research assistant', the hapless sorcerer's apprentice:

And one day, towards the end of the year, as Ceridwen was culling plants and making incantations, it chanced that three drops of the charmed liquor flew out of the cauldron and fell upon the finger of Gwion Bach. And by reason of their great heat he put his finger to his mouth, and the instant he put those marvel-working drops into his mouth, he foresaw everything that was to come, and perceived that his chief care must be to guard against the wiles of Ceridwen, for vast was her skill. And in very great fear he fled towards his own land.

Morda loses his eye like Odin on the World Tree – yet the secret knowledge has got away. Morda, the Lower Self, must be sacrificed if we are to soar. Gwion is the 'gleam in his grandfather's eye' – the double-helix of DNA, escaping into Nature with the encoded 'information', the stolen fire. Morda suffers in the ashes, like the slag left over by a casting, or the residue left over in the alchemical process – while the young Prometheus, our erstwhile firebrand, makes good his escape. Ceridwen seems to know who's to blame, yet still she punishes poor old Morda – the story's fall guy – implacable in her wrath. Sometimes it takes something extreme to make us pay attention and truly 'see', to awaken us from stagnant patterns of behaviour.

Thereupon came in Ceridwen and saw all the toil of the whole year lost. And she seized a billet of wood and struck the blind Morda on the head until one of his eyes fell out upon his cheek. And he said, "Wrongfully hast thou disfigured me, for I am innocent. Thy loss was not because of me." "Thou speakest truth," said Ceridwen, "it was Gwion Bach who robbed me."

But now let us turn our attention to the young offender himself, Gwion Bach.

(vii) The Awen Thief

And she put Gwion Bach the son of Gwreang of Llanfair in Caereinion, in Powys, to stir the cauldron

Gwion Bach
I did not know it was destiny
When the old witch came a-knocking,
Asking for help –
Gainful employment, she said.
A year's graft
For a bed, grub, a shirt on my back.
I was just one extra mouth to feed
In a house with too many sticky siblings
Crying for the best crust.
To be honest, I was glad to leave
It was my ticket out of there –
From a family in which I felt I never belonged.

The others teased me – said the witch would
Gobble me up. I was for her pot,
Not its stirrer. Of course,
They were greener than witch's hair.
Off I went to her lair, without
So much as a backward's glance
At my Ma. I would never see her again,
As her little Gwion.
As Taliesin I would return to Llanfair
She would not recognise me, shining-browed
Bard of Kings with the gift of tongues.
For now, I had to eat humble pie,
Or at least cookà it –
Stir-the-pot, that's me –
Watching the spoon
Go around and around. The heady fumes of
The witch's brew making me drowsy…
A moment's lapse,
A sudden splash,
And my small world
Changes.

Gwion Bach follows in the hapless footsteps of fool figures throughout myth, legend, folklore and fairy tale. He is brother to every Jack who fails to sell his mother's cow at market – coming home with three 'magic beans', like the three drops which splash onto Gwion's hand. His Irish cousin is the young Fionn MacCumhail himself, who is asked to cook the Salmon of Wisdom which Finnegas the Hermit has finally caught not long after the arrival of his young pupil. Like Gwion, Fionn is given simple but strict cooking instructions: to ensure the fish does not burn in its cooking. Inevitably, the taboo is broken – blisters appear on the salmon's flesh, to burst them he uses his thumb and is scalded by the hot juice. To soothe his thumb, Fionn places it in his mouth and instantly receives the 'forbidden wisdom' meant for Finnegas. From then on, whenever he wishes to receive wisdom, the hero of Erin simply chews his thumb – a surrogate nipple connecting him back to the Divine Feminine.

Gwion as 'the fool who breaks the rules' is a necessary force – sometimes, adults who have been programmed to see what they are meant to see, act in the way they 'should' act, fail to notice what is obvious to a child, as in the fairy story of The Emperor's New Clothes. Every child has, potentially, the cleansed 'doors of perception' of Blake, who saw angels in the trees of Peckham Rye, London as a boy. This is the innocence of perception of the Holy Fool, which Cecil Collins explores in *The Vision of the Fool* (Golgonooza, 1994). As Parsifal/Perceval's name suggests, the fool-knight 'pierces-the-veil' and achieves the Grail. In the Grail Tradition the fool is the Freer of the Waters – the one who asks the Grail Question and heals the wounded king, and thus, the Wasteland itself. Gwion is an inadvertent 'freer of the waters' (by making Ceridwen's cauldron split in two and spill its contents) but paradoxically at the same time the creator of a (local) wasteland, with the poisoning of the stream where Gwyddno's horses drink:

And the cauldron burst in two, because all the liquor within it except the three charm-bearing drops was poisonous, so that the horses of Gwyddno Garanhir were poisoned by the water of the stream into which the liquor of the cauldron ran, and the confluence of that stream was called the Poison of the Horses of Gwyddno from that time forth.

Gwion represents youthful energy – the impulse of life. He is a kind of Jack-in-the-Green figure; a green boy. Dylan Thomas' *'the force that through the green fuse drives the flower'* – the fructifying urge of creation. Each of his 'deaths' gives rise to a new life; in the way that energy is recycled via the cycle of life (one thing dies to provide something else with life – a fallen tree trunk provides home for fungi; a carcase protein for prey, for scavengers, for parasites).

In JRR Tolkien's *The Lord of the Rings*, the 'death' of the One Ring provides life for Middle Earth – it triggers the cataclysmic eruptions of Mount Doom: rivers of lava cascading down its flanks like hot semen – symbolising the freeing of the waters. The nexus of death has been fertilised by the casting of the 'seed' into its womb. In a similar way in *Star Wars* (George Lucas, 1977) Luke Skywalker symbolically inseminates the Death Star with one well-aimed shot, finding its mark – a tiny shaft – like the winner in the race of competitive spermatozoa. This Imperial egg is 'fertilised' and explodes in a dazzling ball of light. Death is 'killed' by Life.

Gwion symbolises healthy curiosity, purity of consciousness, youthful exuberance. The child in us who is nourished from the cauldron of legend.

We all need the Gwion-energy. Without it, without joy, the capacity to play – experiment in a trial-and-error way, as well as generally 'purposeless' foolery – something in us withers and dies.

(viii) Fith-Fath

Animal transformations and magical metamorphosis occur in many myths and legends around the world. Ovid's *Metamorphoses* is filled with tales of shapechanging. This fith-fath, as the Irish druids called the art, features prominently in the tale of Taliesin.

In the British and Irish Traditions there are a plethora of examples. In the magical Scottish ballad of 'Tam Lin', the heroine Janet must hold her fairy-bound man as he changes into an adder, an ask, a red-hot iron, an eel, a dove, a swan and a naked man (which could be a metaphor for the evolution of the embryo into the foetus into the new born child – a folk analogy for pregnancy). 'Tam Lin' features four and twenty maidens playing chess – a similar court scene to Deganwy, with Maelgwn's twenty-four bards; and in the story of Arthur and Owain playing gwyddbyll with ravens as go-betweens betwixt board and battle-field. These could be seen as hours of the day or, in the latter case, the consciousness of the combatants – shamans duelling on the psychic plane. The symbolism may have carried over from Norse tradition – the All-father Odin had two ravens, Hugin and Munin: 'thought' and 'memory'.

Similar tumultuous and passionate transformations occur in another Scotish ballad, 'The Twa Magicians', in which each fith-fath of the fleeing woman is outmatched by the amorous male: 'turtle: dow'; 'eel: trout'; 'duck: drake'; 'hare: greyhound'; 'grey mare: gilt saddle'; 'het girdle: cake'; 'ship: flood'; 'silken-plaid: green-covering.' This protean brinkmanship could be interpreted as lively love-making – preceding the pregnancy imagery of 'Tam Lin' – and echoed by the boxing hares of March, when the females 'fight off', or test the tenacity of the males. If the male persists, staying the distance and weathering the storm, he eventually gains her maidenhead. An exhausting game of scissors-paper-stone!

In 'The Twa Magicians', this shamanic foreplay is made explicit in the final consummation:

> 'She turned hersell into a hare,
> To rin upon yon hill,
> And he became a gude grey-hound,
> And boldly he did fill'

Another British ballad, 'The Coal Black Smith' offers a similar dizzying predatory sequence of fith-fath: fish–otter; hare–greyhound; fly–spider; quilt–coverlet. Were these ballads a form of mnemonic about the foodchain and wheel of life? Or do the similar tropes and sequences allude to a magical initiatory tradition? Certainly RJ Stewart – musician, author and esoteric teacher – leans towards the latter.

In the folk-song 'If All Those Young Men', this erotic aspect is echoed further – 'Young women they run like hares on the mountain. If I were a young man I'd soon go a-hunting' – often with an exchange of gender, as the sexes take turns to be the hunter and the hunted.

Rapid transformations occur in the Greek myth of Aristaios the Apiarist and Proteus – Proteus was the remorseful beekeeper's ancient elusive cousin – a slippery fellow by all accounts, who gave his name to all things protean, as truth often is (Proteus was an oracle who shape-changed to avoid giving a straight answer, wriggling out of direct questions like a modern day politician).

Shape-changing can lead to unfortunate consequences, as many folk tales attest – in which a character in animal guise is wounded by mistake. In the land of story, one can never be sure what one is eating – and there are many taboos against certain foods.

Cuchullain had a taboo against eating the flesh of a hound – his namesake. On the eve of his final battle three old women offered him a meal. He also had a geas against refusing hospitality, and so he partook of their meal, only to discover it was hound. He died the next day. The formidable trio seem to have been a form of the Fates in disguise, perhaps appearing like the hooded threesome, the *Genii Cucullati*.

In Australia, Aboriginal tribes-people have a taboo about eating the flesh of their respective totem. Native Americans hold similar beliefs.

Taboo about eating the flesh of the hare – Kerry folk tradition warns against it, saying it is 'eating one's grandmother'. Indeed, if the local wise-woman had a habit of turning into one, as is the popular belief regarding witches and hares, then this would indeed be an unfortunate thing to do.

When such multiple shape-changing occurs in anamorphic poetry (e.g. The Song of Amergin; The Song of Taliesin) could this encode an animistic one-ness with life on Earth? Or even a shamanic cosmogony? Literally, this is ec-static poetry – out of body utterances – as the poet-shaman slips out of his own anthropogenic shell and enters the bodies of animals. This paradisal state – as embodied by the wild man in myth (e.g. Enkidu in the Babylonian epic of 'Gilgamesh') – is a one-ness with life, which is unfortunately shattered by the corruption of civilization (when Enkidu is seduced by a prostitute the animals shun him; when he destroys a sacred tree and kills its guardian, he sickens and dies). The myth of the Golden Age suggests humanity once lived in total harmony with nature. Poetry at its best can, briefly, returns us to the state of consciousness. Novelist John Cowper Powys in his Celtic opus *Porius* (Overlook 2007) said Taliesin's verse:

'left upon the mind a feeling of paradisic obscurity, the ecstatic sufficiency in fact of pure sensation about which it is impossible to say anything except what is implied in those childish proclamations so often repeated: "I was," or "I was there," or "I was with," or "I saw." (p374)

This 'ecstatic sufficiency' is state of Gaia-consciousness, an at-one-ment with all life. It is a communion which many poets, especially the Romantics, have sought to recreate ever since. John Clare, so-called Peasant Poet of the Fens, said, incarcerated in Northampton Lunatic Hospital and Asylum: '*I long for scenes where man has never trod…*'

Eliade suggests this ecstasy is synonymous with metamorphosis:

Like death, ecstasy implies a "mutation," to which myth gives plastic expression by a "perilous passage"
(Shamanism: archaic techniques of ecstasy, p482)

The entire story of Taliesin illustrates this perfectly, with the ensuing shape-changes and pursuit as the perilous passage leading to death and rebirth.

Eliade goes on to suggest the universal motifs in legends could be of *'ecstatic origin'* – that is originating or 'borrowed' from the *'narratives of shamans describing their journeys and adventures in the superhuman worlds'*. (ibid p510)

Further, he postulates that 'the pre-ecstatic euphoria constituted one of the universal sources of lyric poetry' (ibid, p510).

Perhaps in the mercurial changes of the Taliesin story we see a depiction of the trance-like state which the poet goes into when inspired: these rapid transformations, one dazzling flourish being outdone by the next, seem akin the synaptic firing that occurs in the creative process, when we have a 'brainstorm'. The ions of our neurons fire across the hemispheres of the brain – an internal thunderstorm – resulting in flashes of inspiration, Eureka! moments. And the agile, witty shapechanging sequence that follows is akin to the metaphors a poet pursues.

When psycho-geographer author Iain Sinclair, in *Landor's Tower* (2002) writes: 'The beginning of language is ecstasy' he hits the nail on the head. He seems to be alluding to the liminal state in which acts of creation occur. David Jones, Welsh artist and poet, called this the 'space between', which went on to inform his shamanic epics about modern warfare and the 'past inhabiting the present', *In Parenthesis* (1937), and *The Anathemata* (1951).

This strange space is where the fire in the head occurs. It is the cauldron of creativity. Art creates fith-fath through imaginative transformation of materials. All artists are 'Ceridwens' in this respect, changing and being changed by the dance of art – a dance of materials, their qualities, and the artist's muse, of nature and nurture. The river and the river bank, wave and particle, swept along by the exhilarating processes of creation.

The shaman, in his healing 'performance' invites in the help of spirit-guides, often in the form of animals, which he will embody, imitating 'animal cries or behaviour', as Mircea Eliade explains:

> *The Tungus shaman who has a snake as a helping spirit attempts to imitate the reptile's motions during the séance; another, having the whirlwind as syvén, behaves accordingly Chukchee and Eskimo shamans turn themselves into wolves; Lapp shamans become wolves, bears, reindeer, fish; the Semang hala can change into a tiger, as can the Sakai halak and the bomor of Kelantan.*
> (ibid p92-93)

The shaman turns himself into his animal spirit to receive its help. Eliade notes that: "Animal language" is only a variant of "spirit language". In the Welsh story of Culhwch and Olwen, Culhwch enlists the help of Gwythyr, master of tongues, who is able to commune with all animals. With the help of the animal guides they meet – the Black Bird of Cilgwri, the Stag of Fernbrake Hill, the Owl of Cwm Cawlwyd, the Eagle of Gwernabwy, the Salmon of Llyn Llwyd – they achieve their quest, which initially involves the finding and releasing of the divine child, Mabon ap Modron, imprisoned behind the 'walls of Gloucester' like a repressed or damaged aspect of the Self – a missing soul-part.

In the story, upon discovering the destruction of the cauldron and the ruination of her (apparent) plans, Ceridwen uses her own art of fith-fath, turns herself into a sleek greyhound.

And she went forth after him, running.

Both predator and prey now embody 'the books of Fferyllt' – alchemical changes – through a dazzling progression of transformations, as though the Alchemist herself was trying to change the 'lead' of Gwion Bach into the 'gold' of the Penbeirdd.

But first that 'lead' – the raw material of Gwion Bach – must become as quicksilver, as swift as the mountain hare.

For this to be achieved, the child must 'die'. Eliade points out that:

The presence of a helping spirit in animal form, dialogue with it in a secret language, or incarnation of such an animal spirit by the shaman (masks, actions, dances, etc) is another way of showing that the shaman can forsake his human condition, is able, in a word, to "die." (ibid, p93)

This is akin to actors' training, part of which involves the breaking down of the ego by various activities so that the actor can become an 'empty vessel' for the characters they hope will 'possess' them. Therapists and spirit mediums undergo a similar training, working through their 'stuff' before being able to help others. In the case of the shaman, this process is more extreme – they are taken into the Underworld, often at adolescence, suffering an extreme illness which threatens to destroy them. They are 'tested', pulled apart. The Self is obliterated and replaced by a diamond body. This is an essential process, if the shaman is to be able to endure the many return journeys to the Underworld on behalf of their patients. They are the classic wounded healers (as Nietzsche said: 'that which does not destroy us makes us stronger'). Having gone to 'Hell and back' and survived, they are now in a position to help others. They have become psychopomps – but to begin with they require the help of existing ones. Eliade again:

From the most distant times almost all animals have been conceived either as psychopomps that accompany the soul into the beyond or as the dead person's new form. (ibid, p93)

This is the rites of passage that Gwion Bach must undertake if he is to become a 'shaman'. There is a sense in which Gwion Bach dies at the point the cauldron bursts – and everything that follows is a psychopompic journey: a series of afterlives.

Gwion embodies his animal spirits – he must assimilate their qualities to have the full knowledge of the shaman bard, as the poems ascribed to Taliesin Penbeirdd testify: a vast knowledge of life, perhaps gleaned from several lifetimes. To be reborn first he must 'die'. But help is at hand:

> *The role of the animal spirit in initiation rites and in myths and legends of the hero's travels in the beyond parallels that of the dead man's soul in (shamanic) initiatory "possession." But it is clear that it is the shaman himself who becomes the dead man (or the animal spirit, or the god, etc), in order to demonstrate his real ability to ascend to the sky or descend into the underworld.*
> (ibid, p95)

Before he can 'fly' the initiate must be prepared to go down into the earth and experience the cycle of life intimately, and that is what we will do now, following in the tracks of Gwion Bach. Having supped at 'the ecstatic font of poetry', the boy from Llanfair must now be prepared to undergo katabolic 'mutations'. His soul depends on it.

The chase is on.

Chapter 2

Hare

And he saw her, and changed himself into a hare and fled.

The Song of Gwion Hare
Boss-eyed bosky moon-boxer,
I high-tail it from Ceridwen's lair,
Over the hills and hollow ley,
Jink-jinking all of the way
To give my pursuer the slip,
Though she will
Snap at my heels soon enough –
As relentless as death,
As inescapable as my shadow.

Heart beating its tattoo of flight,
Legs thrumming like a drummer boy's sticks.
Through cwm, over bryn, cefn, coed,
The gaps between the awkward spaces,
Through a hedge backwards, this way, that –
A mad man's mind.
Method to my erratic path.
Yet always, her hot breath at my heels.

Driven by the fire in my
Stream-lined head, an arrow of fur,
Long ears swept back,
Best paws forward. Coney foot, bring me luck.
Ablaze with awen,
The world transformed

Into a landscape of scent and sound.
Predator and prey. Forage, territory and fate.

I must turn and face my foe.
Run through the fire
And be transformed.
Let the fith-fath change me.

That which is fixed, dies.

The hare, fleet-foot and fecund, crops up throughout British folklore. A hare was said to inhabit the moon. The notion of the 'Mad March Hare' refers to the 'boxing' hares seen around the time of the vernal Equinox – as male and female contest territory and mating rights – and perhaps this is why it is thought to be a symbol of sexuality. The hare is said to be the only creature that runs towards, rather than away from the fire – a symbol of initiatory transformation, apt for our hare-hero (although Gwion the hare flees one fire – and its repercussions). He is surely fleeing out of the frying pan, into the fire – as what awaits him is even more katabolic. You cannot escape change. All you can do is approach it in the right attitude.

Saying 'white rabbit' three times on the first day of the month was said to bring luck. Alice, at the start of her *Adventures in Wonderland* (1865), spots a white rabbit while in a half-waking/half-sleeping state (wondering whether to make the effort to pick daisies to make a chain on a dreamy summer day). This one seems to be in a hurry. Anxiously he checks the time – a dapper pocket watch on a chain – and cries in dismay: '*Oh dear! Oh dear! I shall be too late!*' Her curiosity piqued, Alice follows this hasty fellow down the famous rabbit hole – which soon becomes a very deep well – and her dream-like underworld journey begins in earnest. In all her shape changing and encounters with magical animals, her journey could be said to run parallel with Gwion

Bach's. Of course, she does not become a bard (disturbingly the real girl she is based on, Alice Liddell, seemed to be Charles Dodgson's muse) but as an every-girl figure, to Gwion Bach's every-boy, she serves a similar purpose – drawing the reader/listener in. Before we know, we are down the rabbit hole too.

Lore of the Hare

The Hare
In the black furrow of a field
I saw an old witch-hare this night;
And she cocked a lissome ear,
And she eyed the moon so bright,
And she nibbled of the green;
And I whispered 'Shsst!' witch-hare,'
Away like a ghostie o'er the field
She fled, and left the moonlight there.
Walter de la Mare

Hares have always been thought of fey, flighty creatures. You have only to catch a glimpse of their eyes to see the lunacy there, and hares have had a long association with the moon; indeed the hare is said to live there and can be glimpsed with a bit of imagination amongst the lunar Rorschach Test of craters and seas. The moon affects the tides, and the highest are the Neap Tides, every equinox – the Spring tide often highest due to rivers swollen with winter-melt floodwaters. The animal is sacred to the Norse Spring Goddess Eostre, who was said to be hare-headed, and gave her name to oestrogen, the female hormone which has ended up in some rivers and seas, due to sewage pollution, giving rise to sex-change fish – modern day fith-fath. Hares are associated with fertility and unbridled sexuality – one could say it has something of a reputation. Robert Graves, in *The White*

Goddess, rather colourfully speculates:

> *The hare was sacred, I suppose, because it is very swift, very prolific – even conceives, Herodotus notes, when already pregnant – and mates openly without embarrassment like the turtle-dove, the dog, the cat, or the tattooed Pict.*

Graves claims the Ceridwen-Taliesin chase-sequence is in seasonal order, (ibid p400) with the hare in the autumn coursing season, although there was a strict hunting ban on hares in England, which was only lifted on one day: May-Day – which interestingly chimes with the time-frame of the story (Elphin discovers the leathern bag in the coracle at his father's weir on May Eve, so, strictly speaking, the chase should have happened at least nine months earlier, around Lammas (31st July/1st August) celebrated as Nos Gwyl Awst in Wales. This ancient fire festival was the traditional start of harvest, and the 'grain of wheat/black hen' sequence could allude to this. Working backwards from this, we might be able to find other seasonal correspondences suggesting a possible ritual calendar:

- Hare – Greyhound: Samhain (31st October)
- Salmon – Otter: Imbolc (1st February)
- Wren – Hawk: Beltane (31st April – 1st May)
- Grain of Wheat – Black Hen: Lammas (1st-2nd August)

Hare customs cluster around Easter, not surprising since its original connection with Eostre – giving rise to the bastardised and somewhat surreal image of the Easter Bunny bringing its basket of eggs. In 17th century Southeastern England there is evidence of a custom of hunting a hare on Good Friday, and in 18th century Coleshill there was a manorial custom in which young men tried to catch a hare on Easter Monday. They would have a hard time of it, since a brown hare can run up to speeds of 45 miles an hour. There is the possibility that Boudicca released the hare before battle not for divinatory purposes, but to bring dismay to the ranks of the legion as they flailed wildly at the jinking hare – like the later Easter chase, a test of their swiftness and agility.

If hares are the superbikes of British fauna, then rabbits, their slower gentler cousins, are mopeds. Rabbits are Norman Johnny-come-latelys, but even brown hares weren't introduced to Britain until the Roman period (2000 years ago, or perhaps a little earlier). Mountain hares – whiter, with shorter ears – are the only native species and are now only found in Scotland and parts of the Peak District. It is possible the Romans introduced hares, for sport, as well as sustenance – for they observed no taboo against eating their flesh. Perhaps it was a statement of power – having observed the reverence for hares in the natives (Boudicca's use of one before battle) they took it on themselves to eat their enemy's sacred animal.

Hares are mainly nocturnal. They forage at night, and sleep by day – perhaps giving rise to their association with the moon.

They sleep in 'forms' – hollows scooped out of the earth, a kind of earth-cauldron – rather than burrows, allowing them to up sticks and flee swiftly.

Hares don't mate for life. They are often solitary, (just after birth the abandoned leverets move apart from the original 'nest', and are weaned individually by the mother hare, who returns only once a day at sunset) and it's rare you see a drove of hares, unlike their sociable cousins, the rabbits in their warrens. Rabbits are suburbanites, hares are chancy travellers. They have ants in their pants. The males move about, perhaps explaining the well-observed Spring rite of 'boxing hares' – when females fight off the unwanted attention of roving males, or to make them prove their mettle, tenacity and genetic 'fitness'. Females only suckle their young once a day, towards evening – and the common belief is hares are born with their eyes open. So Gwion hits the ground running, alert and agile. This is evolutionary survival. Hares commonest predator is the fox, and so it is clear why even the young leverets need to be able to scarper when Reynard is abroad. This is partly why hares prefer open land, which is normally arable land – explaining their late introduction to the British Isles (until land started to be cleared for agriculture, the habitat would only have been suitable for mountain hares). They evolved in the grassland steppe of Central Asia and moved west with early Neolithic man as he cleared the primal woodland with his stone and bone tools.

In a Welsh legend a Saint Melangell, originally from Ireland, ended up in a remote corner of North Wales, at Pennant Melangell, by Llangynog – it was said she sheltered fleeing hares in her skirts. This seems a strangely sexual image for an Irish nun, considering the hare's status as fertility symbol. Could this be a remnant of a more ancient practice? Certainly the church bears evidence of earlier usage – its raised lozenge shape a sure sign it was a Bronze Age sacred site, and the ring of yew trees attest to its longevity to. (Peter Please, *Travelling at Home*, 'Shelter Queen – St Melangell', p 95-96)

On one of the corbels of Kilpeck Church, in Gloucerstershire – famed for its shamelessly exhibitionist Sheela-na-gig – there's an almost cartoonish hare and dog, straight from Looney Tunes. It offers a delightful touch of idiosyncratic whimsy to this most interesting of sacred nexus points – even official interpretation boards in the church grounds refer to the 'leys' it is meant to be on, being one of those surveyed by leyhunter pioneer Alfred Watkins. A Norman motte and bailey stands cheek by jowl; an Iron Age henge encompasses it; ancient trees loom over it – a palimpsest of history.

Hare is seen as a trickster in many cultures. It appears in African folk tales as such, and these stories were imported, along with African slaves, to America, where they formed the basis of the Brer Rabbit stories. That 'wise guy' Bugs Bunny is a Twentieth Century animated version of this elusive fellow.

Here's a fecund example of the Old English art of kenning –

the Saxon penchant of referring to things laterally, in elliptically poetic ways (for names were believed to have power. The poet displays dazzling swiftness of wit, embodying the frenetic creativity of his chosen subject – the raw, in-the-moment, seat-of-the-pants, wildness: awen incarnate.

The Names of the Hare

The man the hare has met
will never be the better of it
except he lay down on the land
what he carries in his hand —
be it staff or be it bow —
and bless him with his elbow
and come out with this litany
with devotion and sincerity
to speak the praises of the hare.
Then the man will better fare.

This opening section could be referring to an ancient form of divination. Boudicca herself released a hare just before entering into battle – it's jinking a way of interpreting its outcome. The hare was similarly worshipped by followers of a chthonic British woodland deity, Andraste. This curious poem seems to insist on a placatory gesture to this ancient Briton (rabbits are Norman interlopers), if he wishes to change his luck.

So, then follows the most astonishing list of hare-kennings – an impressive 'splitting of hares':

'The hare, call him scotart,
big-fellow, bouchart,
the O'Hare, the jumper,
the rascal, the racer.

Beat-the-pad, white-face,

funk-the-ditch, shit-ass.

The wimount, the messer,
the skidaddler, the nibbler,
the ill-met, the slabber.

The quick-scut, the dew-flirt,
the grass-biter, the goibert,
the home-late, the do-the-dirt.

The starer, the wood-cat,
the purblind, the furze cat,
the skulker, the bleary-eyed,
the wall-eyed, the glance-aside
and also the hedge-springer.

The stubble-stag, the long lugs,
the stook-deer, the frisky legs,
the wild one, the skipper,
the hug-the-ground, the lurker,
race-the-wind, the skiver,
the shag-the-hare, the hedge-squatter,
the dew-hammer, the dew-hopper,
the sit-tight, the grass-bounder,
the jig-foot, the earth-sitter,
the light-foot, the fern-sitter,
the kail-stag, the herb-cropper.

The creep-along, the sitter-still,
the pintail, the ring-the-hill,
the sudden start,
the shake-the-heart,
the belly-white, the lambs-in-flight.

The gobshite, the gum-sucker,
the scare-the-man, the faith-breaker,
the snuff-the-ground, the baldy skull,
(his chief name is scoundrel.)

The stag sprouting a suede horn,
the creature living in the corn,
the creature bearing all men's scorn,
the creature no one dares to name.'

This impressive list was perhaps a bardic test of memory, or even membership – oral password mnemonics – acting in the same way as slang, cultural codes of belonging, specific to particular social groups. The poet who composed, or comprised this list has certainly embodied its wild, inexhaustible skill. Like the Native American who reverently eats one of his 'brothers', who imbibes its spirit and takes on its characteristics. This last stanza echoes that:

When you have got all this said
then the hare's strength has been laid.
Then you might go faring forth—
east and west and south and north,
wherever you incline to go—
but only if you're skilful too.
And now, Sir Hare, good-day to you.
God guide you to a how-d'ye-do
with me: come to me dead
in either onion broth or bread.

(translated by Seamus Keaney)

Robin Williamson does a spine-tingling version of this on his album, *The Iron Stone* (ECM 2006), and is recommended listening if you wish to tune into the spirit of the hare.

Can you relentlessly pursue a metaphor as far as it will go? Use the spirit of the hare in your writing, in your art. Keep on going into you exhaust every nuance, every aspect of that which you 'track'. Become it.

In your performance dazzle the audience with your daring skill, the assured rapidity and wit of your delivery.

In life, sometimes we need the hare's alacrity, but one must be careful not to become the cousin of Aesop's hare from his famous fable of the tortoise and the hare. More haste, less speed. Don't jump the gun, but when the situation is clear and demands action, act swiftly and wisely.

WB Yeats seems to allude to ancient divinatory practices in his poem, 'The Collar-Bone of a Hare':

I would find by the edge of that water
The collar-bone of a hare
Worn thin by the lapping of water,
And pierce it through with a gimlet, and stare
At the old bitter world where they marry in churches,
And laugh over the untroubled water
At all who marry in churches,
Through the thin white bone of a hare.

A true poet sees the world through the 'collarbone of hare' – a lateral, perceptive perspective. Yeats sounds bitter and mocking here, perhaps hurt by the world, by matters of the heart (or of conventional love). The hare-soul flies in the face of convention, jinking through life to avoid its 'slings and arrows'. Yet no matter how fast or far you run you can never outrun the repercussions of your actions. Gwion's karma is in pursuit – four legs and a nose on his scent, fangs bared, slathering, snapping at his heels: the Greyhound.

Chapter 3

Greyhound

But she changed herself into a greyhound and turned him.

Song of Greyhound

This new dog's got old tricks –
The fith-fath he has fled with.
Long dog now am I,
Deadly Sirius,
Death at his heels,
Snapping, slavering.
A knife thrust forever forward.
Fangs bared in tight death grin,
Eyes on fire,
I will never blink,
Never lose sight of my prey.
As swift as a wisht-hound,
Running through the sky,
The night is my road,
Harrowing souls who stray
Into the wild-wood.
There is nowhere you can hide,
Little hare,
No hollow or shadow.
Your scent leaves a ribbon of bright noise
My nose follows with ease.
I am drawing near,
I can taste your fur
On my fern tongue.
Little Gwion, you'll make a tasty morsel,

Replace the potion you have stolen,
The awen usurped,
The triple drops of inspiration – a pound of flesh
To replace the potion,
The awen usurped,
Drops of inspiration,
Stolen from my son.
From my son.
Hare-thief, there's no taboo
That will stop me eating you.
Maw of darkness devour you
In one gigantic
Gulp.

With her own powers of fith-fath, Ceridwen the Crooked One, turned herself into a sleek greyhound bitch and gave chase, following the hare's scent into the wild.

Ceridwen could not have picked a better predator to seek her absconded prey. The greyhound was bred for coursing game and hunting – its powerful long legs, sleek aerodynamic body and deep chest are designed for speed: it can match the hare's remarkable top speed of 45 miles an hour, attaining that velocity in three strides.

The greyhound has keen eyesight, (one of its names is: 'sight-hound') ideal for hunting in the open. It is believed they were introduced to the British Isles in the 5th or 6th Century from Celtic mainland Europe (contemporary with the historical Taliesin, making them the cutting edge of hunting technology of the time) although it would appear Picts of what is now Scotland had large hounds similar to the deerhound before then.

The greyhound appears in iconography throughout human history. They are connected to the Lurcher breed – known as long dogs – and possibly originating in Egypt, where one seems to be depicted upon a frieze (a bas-relief depicting a smooth-coated

Saluki, a Persian Greyhound, or Sloughi was found in an Egyptian tomb built in 4000 BCE). Modern greyhounds may be in fact related genetically to herding dogs, but there seems little doubt that these 'long dogs' were important in Egyptian mythology: as the image of jackal-headed Anubis – the Egyptian psychopomp – attests. Anubis is associated with mummification and the afterlife. He is referred to as both 'He who is in the place of embalming' (the head embalmer would wear an Anubis costume) and 'He who is upon his mountain', alluding to the fact he is often depicted on top of tomb-monuments, guarding the dead. This could have a mundane origin. The canine is strongly associated with cemeteries in ancient Egypt, as dogs and jackals often haunted the edges of the desert where the dead were buried, although this tradition – a hound guarding the dead – manifests throughout Western culture in folk song and story. The hound appears in myth and legend as a guide and guardian.

In the 17th Century folk ballad 'The Three Ravens' a hound guards his fallen master along with a 'his haukes' and a leman – a fairy lover in the form of a fallow doe – thus preventing the carrion birds from having their feast:

Downe in yonder greene field,
There lies a Knight slain under his shield,
His hounds they lie downe at his feete,
So well they can their Master keepe

This image of the hound and/or other animals guarding the body of the fallen lord, often between streaming blood and tears, haunts Western folk-imagery, as in the analogous variant, 'The Twa Corbies', and the Medieval Christmas Carol, 'Down in Yon Forest'. Such songs seem to serve as psychopompic dirges, sending the recently deceased soul on its way with the necessary blessings and accoutrements for the afterlife. Without these, the naked soul is in great peril, as is emphasised in the chilling ballad from Northern Britain, 'The Lyke Wake Dirge', which relates a litany of harsh karma:

> *If ever thou gavest hosen and shoon,*
> *Sit thee down and put them on;*
> *If hosen and shoon thou ne'er gav'st nane*
> *The whinnes sall prick thee to the bare bane.*

This relates back to Anubis' role, who weighed the hearts of the dead against the feather of truth in the eschtalogical Court of Osiris, where the deceased has to make account of his or herself. Anubis would escort souls there, a kind of bailiff of the afterlife, and became thought of as the 'guardian of the veil', the gatekeeper of the Underworld.

With the necessary funerary rites attended to, and with the attendance of mourners, singing the soul on, and sometimes, otherworldly servants (hounds and horses buried with their master, as at Sutton Hoo; or even servants and wives slain or sacrificed to accompany their master) the soul will be ensured a good afterlife. As the balladeer of 'The Three Ravens' heartily oaths:

> *God send euery gentleman,*
> *Such haukes, such hounds, and such a Leman.*

Hellish hounds sometimes guard not the dead, but the Land of the Dead itself, most famously Cerebus – three-headed threshold guardian of the Hellenic Underworld, Hades, who echoes Anubis' role.

The Irish mythological hero, Cuchullain, became the Hound of Ulster after accidentally killing the guard dog (likely an Irish wolfhound) of Culann the smith. The young Setanta, as he was originally called, arrived late for a feast there – fresh from a hurling match – and finding himself deprived entrance, he made his way in by force, using his red bronze hurley stick to deadly effect. When he discovered what he had done – slain his host's best guard dog – Setanta offered to replace the hound. Culann refused the noble gesture, but granted the fierce youth his new name, Cuchullain (Cu: hound) and status as 'threshold guardian' and, eventually, the champion of his people – by dedicating his wild energy to a higher cause and following the path of service.

Otherworldly hounds gambol through British folk-legend. They are normally white, with red ears (symbolic of salt and blood perhaps – the two streams again). In the story of Pwyll, Prince of Dyfed, from *The Mabinogion*, the lord comes across a mighty stag run to ground by such a pack. He drove off the uncanny canines with his own pack and they finished off the mighty beast – the consequences of which he has to spend a year and a day making amends, for the phantom pack belonged to Arawn, Lord of Annwn (the Welsh Hades). Pwyll has to exchange places with this Lord of the Underworld and defeat his demon enemy in his place, to pay the blood-price of his rash action. Arawn with his pale hounds seems one and the same as Gwynn ap Nudd, who was said to ride out with his Gabriel Hounds, collecting the souls of the dead. Glastonbury is near enough to Wales to share the same mythological 'water-table' – the streams of Annwn flow through them both. These unearthly hounds have also been called Wish-Hounds or Wisht-Hounds. This aerial pack seem of the same pedigree as the 'wind-dogs' said to fly at the winged heels of Hermes, the Greek God of communication.

Black Shucks and other phantom dogs lurk around the lonely places of the British Isles. Black cats seem more prolific these days, but there's a long tradition of their canine cousins inhabiting the wild edges of the land. Arthur Conan Doyle exploited this 'rural myth' in the Sherlock Holmes case of *The Hound of the Baskervilles*.

A black dog is said to appear shortly before someone dies.

Cambridgeshire bard, Nick Drake's eerie, heart-renching song, 'Black-eyed Dog' was written and recorded shortly before his death at a tragic young age.

However, it is the 'greyness' of the greyhound that defines them, as distinctive from other hounds. The name is thought to derive from the Old English 'grighund'. 'Hund' is undisputably the antecedent of the modern 'hound, but the etymology of 'grig' is less clear. It does not necessarily mean grey – linguistically, it is not connected – and greyhounds have a wide variety of coats: grey isn't the default – indeed they were bred in the Medieval period for different 'liveries', as branding by the hunting aristocracy – making them more easily identifiable in amidst the thrill of the chase (as seen in the Pwyll and Arawn story). Deer- and wolf-hounds are more commonly grey in colour, and perhaps the name was originally a generic one for them. There is a possibility that 'grey-hound' may actually mean 'fair dog' – and the idea of the 'fairy dog' is echoed throughout folkloric evidence. Grey-hound may have derived from the proto-Indo-European root 'g'her', which means to shine or twinkle. This could be connected to the Old Icelandic *gryja* 'to dawn', and *gryjandi* 'morning twilight'. The greyhound seems to be, by name, a dweller of the twilight, of the shadow-realms, the between-worlds. This seems to chime with its Egyptian funerary ancestor, Anubis. And yet in Old Irish *grian* means 'sun'. Could the greyhound be in fact a 'shining hound'? If so, what better creature to harry the future 'shining brow'?

In *The Odyssey*, Odysseus's dog, Argus, touchingly remembers his master after twenty years:

As they were talking, a dog that had been lying asleep raised his head and pricked up his ears. This was Argus, whom Odysseus had bred before setting out for Troy, but he had never had any enjoyment from him. In the old days he used to be taken out by the young men when they went hunting wild goats, or deer, or hares, but now that his master was gone he was lying neglected on the heaps of mule and cow dung that lay in front of the stable doors till the men should come and draw it away to manure the great close; and he was full of fleas. As soon as he saw Odysseus standing there, he dropped his ears and wagged his tail, but he could not get close up to his master. When Odysseus saw the dog on the other side of the yard, dashed a tear from his eyes without Eumaeus seeing it, and said:

"Eumaeus, what a noble hound that is over yonder on the manure heap: his build is splendid; is he as fine a fellow as he looks, or is he only one of those dogs that come begging about a table, and are kept merely for show?"

"This hound," answered Eumaeus, "belonged to him who has died in a far country. If he were what he was when Odysseus left for Troy, he would soon show you what he could do. There was not a wild beast in the forest that could get away from him when he was once on its tracks. But now he has fallen on evil times, for his master is dead and gone, and the women take no care of him. Servants never do their work when their master's hand is no longer over them, for Zeus takes half the goodness out of a man when he makes a slave of him."

So saying he entered the well-built mansion, and made straight for the riotous pretenders in the hall. But Argus passed into the darkness of death, now that he had seen his master once more after twenty years.

(Homer, *The Odyssey*, Book 17)

Argus, as well as embodying lifelong loyalty, could symbolise that part of us which Jungians would call the Lower Self – wallowing in self-misery on the dunghills of life, flea ridden and unloved, but with some dim memory of a greatness that may return. When, finally, the Higher Self returns to claim its throne, the Lower Self dies.

Arthur's dog, Drudwyn, loyally sits by the side of his wounded master – echoing the haunting ballad 'Down in yon

Forest' and the Corpus Christi carol, which mirrors its symbolism:

And yn that bed ther lythe a knyght,
His wowndes bledyng day and nyght

The redemptive sacrifice of the solar-king heals the land. In this mythic ecosystem, the wound and the hound seem indivisible, as Michael Moorcock's 1981 grail-novel *The Warhound and the World's Pain*, captures in its title.

Drudwyn plays a pivotal role in the tale of Mabon and the Oldest of Animals, from 'Culhwch and Owen' in *The Mabinogion*. Twrch Trwyth, a monstrous boar is ravaging the land. Only one hound can catch it – Drudwyn – and only one person can handle that hound, Mabon: the ancient divine child who was 'stolen from between his mother and the wall when only three nights old'.

In Snowdonia, North Wales, a tourist industry has developed around the suspect legend of Beddgelert, (as historian Ronald Hutton has proven in 'How Myths are Made' *Witches, Druids, and King Arthur*, Hambledon & London, 2003), which is now the name of the village. 'Bedd' means grave, and 'Gelert' is the name of the loyal hound, hence 'Bedd Gelert: 'Gelert's Grave', which you can visit on a small tourist trail around the stunningly located honeypot.

The story, in a nutshell, is as follows: Prince Llewellyn ap Iorwerth went on a hunting trip and left his infant son in the charge of his faithful dog Gelert, an Irish wolfhound. On his return, the Prince was greeted by Gelert – to his horror he noticed his hound's muzzle was soaked in blood, and his son was nowhere to be seen. Assuming the worst, Llewellyn attacked the dog, and it fell to the ground gravely injured. However, within minutes he heard a cry and stumbled through nearby bushes to find his son, safe in his cradle. Beside the cradle lay the body of a giant wolf covered with wounds, the result of a fight to the death with hound Gelert. Llewellyn strode back to his faithful dog and watched it die from his actions, stricken with remorse. He built the grave in honour of his loyal hound, and it stands, to this day in a beautiful meadow below Cerrig Llan and consists of a slab lying on its side, and two upright stones – looking suitably ancient, like one of the many Welsh 'standing stones' erected by wily farmers keen to attract or trick visitors for their own amusement or gain.

Even the local website acknowledges: 'The truth is that this story was made up by local traders some time ago in an attempt to lure Snowdon's visitors to their village. It appears the place name actually refers to Gelert, a sixth century saint from the area. This legend was well known by the time George Borrow visited Beddgelert in 1854 as part of the journey through the country, as recorded in his 1862 classic Wild Wales.

There is something about the death of animals in stories that affects us more than human fatalities. Perhaps it is because of their 'innocence'. Such a tale was intended to tug at the heart strings, and despite its falsity is repeated with effect to this day.

A classic 'shaggy dog story', but a highly emotive one which attests to the power of story and the willingness of people to believe in a good tale. As a footnote, or paw-note, Gelert now gives his name to a Welsh manufacturer of camping and walking gear, following in the footsteps of the Tolkien-inspired Rohan outdoor suppliers.

There's countless tales of heroic canines – regurgitated in popular form in the 'Lassie' series – there's something reassuring about such stories, perhaps telling us our covenant with nature is not entirely broken.

Recently a German shepherd dog called Trakr, which sniffed out survivors at Ground Zero, in the immediate aftermath of 9/11, is to be cloned, much to the delight and pride of its owner, James Symington.

Some sleeping dogs are not left to lie.

In a curious incident of art mirroring life the popular robotic canine from the long-running Sci-Fi BBC TV series, *Dr Who*, K-9, was resurrected in the revamped series after a long campaign by fans.

Yet cosmic canines are nothing new under the sun.

The Dogon Tribe of Africa claim ancestry from Sirius, the Dog Star, the constellation of Cannis Major, which sits at the feet of Orion the Hunter. Man's best friend – written in the stars.

The hound totem teaches us loyalty, attention to detail, and determination. A budding bard needs this diligence and dedication to make headway on their path.

And if the hare represents the 'fire in the head', then the greyhound tells us that we must pursue it relentlessly. Don't let the Muse slip away!

Chapter 4

Salmon

And he ran towards a river, and became a fish

Song of the Salmon
I am long-memory,
The oldest of animals
Though newly born
By my stolen art.
I slipped free of death's jaws,
Shed my fur, my moonwarm blood,
Came to the waters for rebirth.
Sliding through a glassy world,
Hidden to the human eye.

Escaping by
The skin of my teeth,
Drawn by instinct
Back to the source
By urgent need
To seed the soil that sired me.

Leap the waterfalls,
Run the gauntlet of rapids,
The fangs and talons of predators,
Ever pushing forward.
One slip and
I'll be swept back.
A ocean of questions searching
For their river answer.

To push the liquid envelope,
Or surrender to
The flow.

Scales glitter,
Scallops of sun,
Ripples snag
And run.
Irresistable river
Sweeping away all
Stagnant currents.
Life force spent,
Minerals of mortal remains
Delivered to a cold bed,
I yield
To her deciduous embrace.

Traditionally the poet's fish – because it is meant to eat of the hazelnuts that fall from the five hazel trees said to grow by the Well of Segais that is 'under the sea', according to Irish legend (a metaphor for deep inspiration) – the salmon is the embodiment of wisdom. Its wise reputation might be for a more prosaic, but no less impressive reason: it crosses oceans and finds the one river where it was spawned, returning to its source with extreme effort. The salmon's ability to recall the particular watercourse of its origin suggested to the ancients it held the longest of memories – and thus was the oldest of animals.

This is illustrated by the story of Culhwch and Olwen from *The Mabinogion*. All the animals are asked where Mabon is, stolen from between his mother and the wall when three nights old. None can remember except the Salmon of Llyn Llwyd, who takes them to where Mabon is imprisoned – the seekers riding upon his back: an image echoed in famous panels of the Gundestrup Cauldron. The mighty salmon takes its passengers up the Severn estuary, which it swims up every tide. The Severn has the second highest tidal range in the world (up to 15.4 metres) and has a famous tidal bore, that can reach up to 7.5 metres high at certain times of the year. Travelling 25 miles between Awre and Gloucester, and reaching up to 10 miles an hour, it carries many salmon in its wave, (although these days mostly surfers) thus suggesting a factual basis for this aspect of the legend – as the wise salmon predict and use the incredible tidal energy to their advantage. The Severn Bore is enjoyed by thousands of people who, correctly gauging the optimum time and location, line the banks. It brings out an innocent delight in the natural wonder of the world. Thus it is with wisdom we release the golden child within.

The salmon plays a key role in the story of young Fionn MacCumhail. He goes to the hermit Finnegas to learn of wisdom. The old man had been trying to catch the fabled Salmon of Wisdom from the sacred river Boyne for seven years. With Fionn's arrival it finally happens. Delighted, Finnegas prepares a fire and instructs Fionn to supervise its cooking, making sure it doesn't burn. Fionn does his best, but the salmon develops a blister: it bursts, scalding his thumb (some say he burst the blister with it) and what did he do? Place it in his mouth, of course. In a flash, he received all the wisdom of the world, mirroring the fate of Gwion Bach. And like the embryonic Taliesin, the young Fionn goes on to fulfil his destiny, rising to greatness, growing to fill his legend.

Other characters from Irish mythology claim in their anamorphic utterances to have been a salmon at some point in their career, including Amergin, in his famous song, (the first wave in *The Book of Invasions*), Tuan mac Cairill, follower of Partholon – Erin's Noah (the second wave), and Fintan mac Bóchra (in his colloquy with the super-annuated Hawk of Achill).

What can the salmon teach the budding bard?

Follow your instincts. Hone your memory. Return to the source. Travel, but always remember your roots.

Via the salmon story, we connect with the hazel tree, which is intimately connected to water, intuition, feelings, and the feminine. Yeats' described how Wandering Aengus 'cut and peeled a hazel wand'. A druidic hazel rod, dating back to the Celtic Iron Age was found on Anglesey, last outpost of the Druids. Carved and deposited with intention, it seems likely to have been considered of ritual significance. Hazel rods are used for divination, for dowsing water, and seem ideal for finding springs of inspiration. It certainly worked for Aengus. From his hazel rod he caught a trout, which transforms into a 'glimmering girl', the Muse. And yet she slips away: 'She called me by my name and ran and faded in the brightening air...' She becomes the classic 'one that got away', and in many ways embodies the Awen itself.

Salmon are anadromous: they are born in fresh water, migrate to the ocean, then return to fresh water to reproduce. There is a rare exampe of a purely fresh water salmon – the exception that proves the rule – but the majority walk between the worlds. They know the universal ocean and the particular in the stream of their origin. They swim the world's currents but manage to find their way back home – exerting enormous effort to return to the exact stream of birth (if they are not eaten by predators first), mating, spawning and dying soon after, in a hazardous process of reproduction called semelparity: basically, they have one chance to pass on their genes. Their bliss is their oblivion.

The salmon's odyssey takes four years and they can travel through three thousand miles of ocean to return home – many more miles can be added to this, depending on how far up river they were spawned (the furthest salmon have been known to journey upriver is three thousand miles in NW America). The annual salmon run brings a much-needed influx of protein-rich food after the rigours of winter and the lean pickings of spring. On their journey back to their source, the salmon feed the wolf, bear and eagle – often in spectacular fashion (the catching of salmon proves a kind of rites of passage in itself for the young cubs – only with patience, persistence, and skill can it be achieve – the very act teaches 'wisdom'). And in their death their decaying bodies provide nutrients for their eggs, laid on the river bed, (eggs which also provide a delicacy for certain species of bird) and also for the forest itself – bringing valuable minerals from the sea, their final cargo. And so the salmon is a key-stone species, whose presence is pivotal to a whole eco-system.

Zoomorphic tales explain how animals came to look the way they do, in the same way topographical tales relate the shape of the land. In Norse mythology, when Loki, god of mischief and strife, tricked Holdur the blind god into killing Baldur, god of beauty and light, Loki jumped into a river and transformed himself into a salmon in order to escape punishment from the other gods. When they held out a net to trap him he attempted to leap over it but was caught by Thor who grabbed him by the tail with his hand, and, says the story, 'this is why the salmon's tail is tapered'.

Gwion the salmon swims for his life, but is pursued by Ceridwen in the form of an otter-bitch. Ahead, in the landscape of his story, there's a waterfall to high for even he to leap over. It looks like he is doomed to suffer the same fate as Loki. If only he was swimming at Conwy Falls, near Betws-y-Coed, where a salmon ladder had been gouged out of the rock, to allow the returning salmon to make it up stream. But with a final burst of effort, using the ladder of his art, (fith-fath) Gwion manages to slip away, leaping out of the water and transforming into a tiny bird...

Chapter 5

Otter

And she in the form of an otter-bitch chased him under the water

Song of the Otter

Water-dog, wave-dancer,
I am – the river,
My circus ring.
Sleek-head, ripple-eye,
The wet flames of my fur,
The dripping snout of my muzzle
Hiding a grin of fangs.
I am the comedian of death,
Fate's fool,
I shall hunt you down,
Be your shadow,
Never ceasing.
When the time is right,
I shall pounce, seize you in my jaws,
And you'll not stand a chance.
You'll be mine –
Hook, line, and sinker.
And yet,
I am a child of joy,
I know the secret of play.
Like the soles of Saint Cuthbert,
Your feet I'll dry
And await your blessing.
With my only coat,

Your harp I'll keep from harm.
Fill me with red gold, Hreidmar's eldest,
The blood-price of the magician's son.
Watch me dance in the brightening current
And you'll forget your woes.
Yet once my teeth are in you,
There's no escape.
Cold-hearted kelpie,
I'll drown you in my element.

My river shall be your grave.

The otter, being amphibian, (with one exception, see below) is a walker between the worlds. It knows the chthonic depths, which it navigates with ease, and it knows the pleasure of the warm sun on its fur, rolling on a soft riverside with its playmates.

Their very name sums up their *isness*: deriving from the Old English word otr, otor, or oter. This and its cousin words in other Indo-European languages grew from a linguistic root from which stemmed the English words *water, wet* and *winter*.

An otter's den is called a *holt*. Male otters are *dog-otters*, females are *queens* and babies are *cubs* or *pups*.

The otter is considered a pest by fishermen – because it is the more effective hunter – but fortunately it is protected now and although its population in the UK is low, it is starting to appear, a strong indicator of a river's health. In early summer 2009 otters and beavers were released into the wild at the Slimbridge Wetland Centre in Gloucestershire.

British otters were victims of what Rachel Carson called the 'Silent Spring' in her seminal book on environmental degradation. In the British Isles they occurred commonly as recently as the 1950s, but became rare in many areas by the 1960s due to the use of chlorinated hydrocarbon pesticides (organo-phosphorus insecticides) and as a result of habitat-loss and water pollution (they remained relatively common in parts of Scotland and Ireland). Population levels attained a low point in the 1980s, but are now recovering strongly. The UK Biodiversity Action Plan envisages the re-establishment of otters by 2010 in all the UK rivers and coastal areas that they inhabited in 1960. Roadkill deaths have become one of the significant threats to the success of their re-establishment. Now, up to 13,000 are estimated to exist in coastal areas, estuaries and stretches of fresh water with suitable cover. The holt acts as a kind of 'bat cave' to these super-heroes of the waterways – lined with grass, usually on stream banks, with an underwater entrance, they enable access to hunting and protection from predators.

The sea-otter (*Enhydra lutris*) is the only aquatic variant, found off the Pacific coast of North America although ranging as far North as the Bering Strait and Kamchatka and as far south as Japan and is known as a key-stone species. It was nearly hunted into to the brink of extinction because of its highly waterproof and thus highly-prized fur: their remarkable pelt has two hundred thousand strands of hair per square centimetre of skin. So few sea otters remained that the fur trade had become unprofitable by the time the 1911 Fur Seal Treaty gave them protection.

Their survival was critical, as later ecologists discovered: the sea-otter hunt sea-urchins, who diligently keep the marine forests of kelp in check – which the otters use to 'baffle' fish and slow them down in pursuit, but too much and this becomes untenable. Without the otter's presence as predator in the foodchain, urchins run amok, the kelp runs rampant and chokes the sea of its life. Deprived of precious sunlight the photosynthesis of plankton cannot occur. Carbon dioxide cannot be absorbed and converted into oxygen. The sea becomes dead. The eco-system collapses.

The 'fake Indian' from Hastings who called himself Grey Owl defended the North American beaver from intensive hunting – which he wrote and talked eloquently about. Whatever one thinks of his 'authenticity' his actions were of merit. He was a real fake. Like stories themselves, Grey Owl's white man lies told a greater truth.

The otter has acquired its own layers of mythology and folklore. The otter is considered an important totem animal to some Native American tribes. In Zoroastrian belief, the otter is believed to be a 'clean animal' belonging to the highest rank of divinity, the Ahura Mazda, the Uncreated Creator (God) and thus taboo to kill. In Norse Mythology the myth of the Otter's Ransom is the starting point for the Volsunga Saga. It tells of how the dwarf Ótr, living up to his namesake, habitually took the form of an otter until one day in that form he is slain by Loki. The tale is full of the protean trickery of otters, and shows how everything is connected and every action, however small, is with consequence. The blood-price, or eric, for the death of Ótr, is a bag of gold made from his skin, but the hide magically expands, the more is put in it (like the bottomless bag from the story of Pwyll and Rhiannon). Such species are, basically, priceless and irreplaceable. No amount of human ingenuity could mirror something as elegant and complex as an otter. They are designed to perfection. Their eyes and nostrils are high on their head, to enable them to breathe and peek just above the surface of the water and scan the immediate vicinity – as do seals, in what is called 'spy-hopping'. They have strong lungs and can stay under water for up to four minutes, travelling up to 400 metres before resurfacing. They can reach speeds of up to 12 km an hour and can outrun a man on land. The males (dogs) have large ranges – up to 20 km of river, and daily travel long distances patrolling their territory.

The number three seems to be the magic number for otters. Their cubs take 63 days to gestate. Up to three in a year can be born. They are blind for the first 35 days. They are suckled for the first six months, protected by the mother, who has to persuade them to take to the water – which takes up to three months.

That which terrifies them becomes their ally.

They have valves in their ears that protect against water pressure and their big whiskers, called 'vibrassae' probably act as antennae in dark water, enabling them to navigate obstacles and find food.

The otter tells us to play, to enjoy being in the naked moment. Their collective noun expresses this: a *pack* or *romp* of otters. They are very sociable creatures who seem to delight in their element – they dance with it. Yet there is a purpose to the play – they are very effective hunters.

Spend time observing them, in the wild if possible (as wildlife film-maker Simon King was fortunate enough to do in his Shetland Diaries) – or at places like Slimbridge. Learn from them and try to assimilate the energy of the otter into your life, into work, into relationships, into creativity.

For now, the story moves on apace. Gwion, having imbibed the lessons of one element, leaps into another – taking wing into the air.

Chapter 6

Wren

Until he was fain to turn himself into a bird of the air

Song of the Wren
All the birds of the forest
Gave me their plumage –
Except flower-face,
Cursed of the sun.
I am the smallest
But I soar the highest.
Through my cunning
I became king.
Yet that crown places
A prized price on my head.
Sunbird,
They hunt me at midwinter –
Those wren boys,
Grubby fingers reaching into my round nest,
Into a wren house
King–for-a-day
And then cruelly slain,
As I must die so that the true king
Within all can live.
Cave-dweller, eaves-dropper,
Doomed to dwell in a gilded cage.
Counting the numbered days
Until my destiny's sharp edge.
I must perish for my people.
The smallest must

Become smaller.
With gramarye from cauldron-wrung,
Wrench my quintessence
From the thin air.

The Wren is a tiny, round, brownish bird. It is often thought of symbolically as the female equivalent to the robin – an erroneous assertion as they of a different family – and yet it probably rounder and 'plumper'. For such a small bird it has a remarkably powerful song – ten times louder, weight for weight than that of a cockerel, and a sweet one too, described as a 'gushing burst of sweet music, loud and emphatic.' Perhaps that is why it would make a good candidate for the unnamed 'bird' that Gwion the Little turns into on his way to becoming a bard. All the other animals in the fith-fath sequence are named except for this one, and I have used artistic license to choose one that seemed appropriate. The wren 'fits the bill'.

A common visitor to gardens across Britain, this tiny, energetic bird rarely stops still for long – and this twitchy energy perhaps also qualifies it as an obvious feathered fugitive. It is a nervy raider – stealing from the garden's 'cauldron' and then making a dash for it. Its very short rounded wings allow it to manoeuvre between the hedgerows with ease – although it does make it look almost un-aerodynamic. And yet it is remarkably successful – the commonest UK breeding bird – with breeding pairs numbering in the region of eight and half million.

The wren is one of the smallest birds, but apparently paradoxically is known as the King of the Birds because it won the contest to see who could fly the highest. One day all the birds got together to find out who could fly the highest. Everyone expected the mighty eagle to win and he certainly flew higher than all the other birds who, one-by-one, fell back. He returned in triumph, expecting to receive the crown – but then, to his astonishment, from his back emerged wren, who had been hiding there all along. Standing on the eagle's back with its surprisingly long legs, it had just pipped the eagle to the post, and so became the avian monarch.

This story shows how the wren uses its bright intelligence (some would say cunning) to succeed – and the story of 'stolen prestige' echoes that of Gwion and Afaggdu. The Wren, like Gwion Bach, is the classic young pretender. The upstart who steals the show.

For a 'sun-bird' it is surprisingly associated with darkness – it was thought to dwell in caves and dark alcoves, hence its scientific name, *Troglodytes troglodytes*. In fact it is generally in winter it holes up in old nests or orifices, sometimes in a group. The male builds several nests, but it is the female who selects one to line and inhabit.

In the story of 'Math, Son of Mathonwy' from the *Mabinogion*, the infant (and yet unnamed) Llew Llaw Gyffes casts his needle, with which he was stitching the queen's shoes, between the bone and sinew of a wren which had alighted on their boat (Gwydion had transformed a pile of seaweed into one, along with some kelp/cordovan). The throw mirrors, in miniature, the spear that is cast at Llew himself (transforming him into an eagle) and the one he then casts at Gronw, his would-be assassin, in return.

The wren was said to have gained its scruffy plumage because it flew too close to the sun when the birds set out to bring fire back for humankind. The robin scorched its breast red, but the wren lost all of its feathers, and so the other birds offered their own feathers – one from each bird, except owl: another interesting echo from Llew's tale (his wife, Blodeuwedd, flower-face, was turned into one).

Because of its kingly status in Ireland, and later Christian gloss, it was traditionally hunted and sacrificed at midwinter instead of the King – the ban from hunting it was lifted on St Stephen's Day. The wren boys would scour the stark hedgerows for it – when captured, it was placed in a specially made cage, the

Wren House, before being slain. Its cruel fate echoes the Fool-King in many pagan ceremonies and festivals, who is king for a day, given every luxury, and then slain. This midwinter fate is evoked in folk songs 'Who Killed Cock Robin' (a political satire of Robert Walpole, but based upon an earlier ritualistic ballad) and 'The Cutty Wren'.

The Wren also features in the legend of Saint Stephen, the first Christian martyr, who supposedly was betrayed by the noisy bird as he attempted to hide from his enemies. Traditionally, St. Stephen's Day (26th December) has been commemorated by Hunting the Wren, wherein young wrenboys would catch the bird and then ritually parade it around town, as described in the traditional Wren Song: *'The Wren, the Wren, the king of all birds, St. Stephen's day was caught in the furze. Although he is little, his family's great, I pray you, good landlady, give us a treat.'*

More tangentially, linguistic echoes are worth noting for the way they 'line the nest'. Sir Christopher Wren is the renowned architect some of London's famous monuments – the builder of bold nests, the famed dome of St Paul's Cathedral mirroring the roundness of his namesake! And in the modern era, the WRNS are the Royal Navy's female wing.

The wren, like the robin teaches us to be bold. To have a stout heart and claim what is ours (and sometimes even what isn't!) – transcending our fear to speak up for ourselves. Paradoxically, it also teaches us discretion – to achieve our aims sometimes it is better to act swiftly and discreetly, without drawing attention to ourselves. It is not a 'show-off' bird, but through its circumspect raiding, it gains what it desires – falling under the radar of the more aggressive birds. And yet it can be fierce in defence of its nest, as all nature's creatures can – as this fairy tale from the Brothers Grimm describes: One day bear and wolf are out walking. The bear, upon hearing the sweet song of the king of the birds wishes to see its 'palace'. The wolf advises against this. The bear goes ahead, and is surprised to see such a pitiful nest, filled with gawky chicks. He shares his opinion with wren. His insult leads to a war, in which the wren typically uses cunning to win – and the bear is forced to apologise.

Try to spend time observing the wren – set up a bird feeder in your back garden and buy a pair of binoculars. Watch it carefully. Try to learn from it. And for a while work with its energy. Follow the 'way of the wren' in daily life. Honour it on St Stephen's Day. Write a poem about it. Perform a wren dance – follow the awen. When you have assimilated all you can from the King of the Birds, thank it, and like Gwion, move on. Ceridwen, his relentless initiatorix, is hot on his tail and about to undergo her own spectacular fith-fath.

Chapter 7

Hawk

She as a hawk, followed him and gave him no rest in the sky

Song of the Hawk

I will catch you with my fierce gaze alone –
Stare of flames, freezing you in mid-flight.
Spitting feathers,
My shriek splits the sky.
Wind-hover,
I am mistress of the air,
The calm at the storm's raging heart.
Eye of the tempest,
Nothing escapes my lightning-gaze.
You cannot hide, little bird,
The slightest movement, and I shall strike.
My fatal blow, the last thing you'll know.
My talons, the reaper's sickle.
My beak will break your neck.
Why fear? You won't feel a thing
When you're dead.
I have a whole autumn
In my feathers.
I wear the forest's shroud,
Sharp shadow,
The last thing you'll see.
I am the birthmark on the sun's face.
I come to blot out your light,
I will take away life's burden,
Death's friend, come to take your hand.

Let me free you
From your tiny parcel of soul.

The story names the form in which Ceridwen pursues Gwion the 'small bird' in the sky as a hawk, but does not stipulate which kind. At least this gives us a starting point. Birds whose main survival strategy is hunting and killing other creatures are classed as birds of prey. They are also called 'raptors'. The owl belongs to one group of sky-hunters, the rest are grouped as diurnal birds of prey because they tend to hunt during the day. They are more dependent on eyesight than owls, though again there are exceptions. The hawk belongs in this latter category.

The word 'hawk' has now become synonymous with war-mongering politicians, as opposed to pacifist/peace-promoting 'dove' types. Yet ironically it has been man who has been the aggressor when it comes to the story of the hawk:

> *Birds of prey generally have been hit hard by human activities, from persecution to chemicals to agricultural changes, and it has taken decades of dedication, conservation and campaigning to help many species recover. Some still face significant threats.*
> (Hawk and Owl Trust)

The hawk, as with virtually all animals, kills out of need, not out of greed. It hunts to survive and to feed its young. A sleek killing machine it may be, but this is the way evolution has designed it for maximum efficiency in the perpetuation of its species. And, as a result, has created the most magnificent of all birds. So, which raptor amongst this fierce company would be the likeliest persecutor of Gwion? Could it be the Hobby, who captures dragonflies, swallows and martins and whose long narrow wings and short tail makes it very agile and acrobatic? Until the end of the 19th Century hobbies were confined to England south of a line from the Severn to the Humber. There were occasional records as far north as Yorkshire and even Perthshire. Now they breed throughout southern England, the north Midlands and the eastern counties to the Scottish border, south-east Wales and south-east Scotland, and so they could qualify.

A buzzard, the most common bird of prey, although it can feed on small birds, is more likely to grab a rabbit, and it's hard to imagine it pursuing a wren – it would be like a Lancaster Bomber going after a model aircraft.

The dashing Goshawk is a large, but secretive woodland bird of prey and was largely confined to Scotland, but has started to appear in conifer plantations in Wales – but this doesn't seem likely to have been the predator Ceridwen would adopt.

The Red Kite, with its distinctive triangular tail, seems the ideal choice – so emblematic of Wales, with its ruddy plumage echoing the hue of the nation's flag, and where its largest population is still to be found, thanks to a successful rebreeding programme: 'one of the major conservation success stories of recent times'. (Hawk and Owl Trust)

Red kites were widespread in the Middle Ages particularly in towns and cities were their important role as a scavenger led to them being protected by royal decree. But by the 16th century they were classed as vermin and their decline began. By the 1870s they were confined to Wales and by the beginning of the 1900s only a few pairs survived there. Wardening by committed volunteers, including those from the Hawk and Owl Trust, prevented complete extinction.

Their original habitat and distribution seems perfect for our purposes: wooded upland valleys in Wales and well-wooded farmland in the lowlands. The original population is still confined to mid Wales. It has an added frisson of fear, for being primarily a carrion bird – with echoes of the Morrighan and the Valkyries. Yet they will catch small mammals up to the size of rabbits and young hares, a variety of birds, as well as insects and earthworms.

Their breeding habits echo the Ceridwen-Gwion chase sequence: *'Display flights occur over the breeding site in March and April when the pair circle high in the sky, chase each other and grapple with their talons.'* (Hawk and Owl Trust) This combative foreplay might be mirrored in the 'love chase' of Ceridwen and Gwion. Death and Love often go hand-in-hand together – the ruthless dance of Thanatos and Eros.

It is said that beauty is in the eye of the beholder. In the hawk's case this seems especially apt. Hawks are widely reputed to have visual acuity several times that of a normal human being. This is due to the many photoreceptors in the retina (up to 1,000,000 per square mm for *Buteo*, medium-sized wide-ranging raptors, against 200,000 for humans), an exceptional number of nerves connecting these receptors to the brain, and an indented fovea, which magnifies the central portion of the visual field.

There is a fierce intelligence in those eyes. In February 2005, the Canadian ornithologist Louis Lefebvre announced a method of measuring avian "IQ" in terms of their innovation in feeding habits. Hawks were named among the most intelligent birds based on his scale.

The One Who is Above

The hawk is a bird with strong mythological significance. It crops up in many legends, ballads, and folklore. In the British ballad 'The Three Ravens', the hawk is one of the three guardians of the fallen body of the knight: *'God send euery gentleman, Such haukes, such hounds, and such a leman.'* It seems to be performing a psychopompic function, along with the hound. In Egyptian mythology Horus, 'the one who is above', the son of Isis and Osiris, has the head of a hawk. His hieroglyphic name means 'falcon'.

Horus is, predictably, a Sky god, the protector of his people. Horus was told by his mother, Isis, to protect the people of Egypt from Set, the god of the desert, storms and chaos. Horus was also seen as a Sun god. Since Horus was said to be the sky, he was considered to also contain the sun and moon. Indeed the sun was said to be his right eye and the moon his left, and that they traversed the sky when he, a falcon of vast size, flew across it. Thus he became known as Harmerty: Horus of two eyes. Later, the reason that the moon was not as bright as the sun was explained by a tale, known as the Contestings of Horus and Set, originating as a metaphor for the conquest of Upper Egypt by Lower Egypt in about 3000 BC. In this tale, it was said that Set, the patron of Upper Egypt, and Horus, the patron of Lower Egypt, had battled for Egypt brutally, with neither side victorious, until eventually the gods sided with Horus.

As Horus was the ultimate victor he became known as Harsiesis, Heru-ur or Har-Wer ('Horus the Great'), but more usually translated as Horus the Elder. In the struggle Set had lost a testicle, explaining why the desert, which Set represented, is infertile. Horus' left eye had also been gouged out, which explained why the moon, which it represented, was so weak compared to the sun.

It was also said that during a new moon, Horus had become blinded and was titled Mekhenty-er-irty ('He who has no eyes'), while when the moon became visible again, he was re-titled Khenty-irty ('He who has eyes'). While blind, it was considered that Horus was quite dangerous, sometimes attacking his friends after mistaking them for enemies.

The Eye of Horus became an important Egyptian symbol of power. Horus had a man's body and a falcon's head. Horus fought with Seth for the throne of Egypt. In this battle one of his eyes was injured and later it was healed by Isis. This healing of the eye became a symbol of renewal. Horus united Egypt and bestowed divinity upon the pharaohs who were viewed as incarnations of Horus in life.

Interestingly, Horus was occasionally shown in art as a naked boy with a finger in his mouth sitting on a lotus with his mother. In the form of a youth, Horus was referred to as Neferhor. This is also spelled Nefer Hor, Nephoros or Nopheros meaning 'The Good Horus'. This image echoes both Gwion Bach and the young Fionn MacCumhail, soothing their awen-scolded fingers, imbibing wisdom.

Horus was also said to be a war god and a hunter's god; since he was associated with the falcon. Thus he became a symbol of majesty and power as well as the model of the pharaohs. The pharaohs were said to be Horus in human form. Falconry has been the especial province of Arabian princes ever since.

Hawk of Battle

In the 10th Century Anglo-Saxon poem, 'The Battle of Maldon', a disastrous encounter between the Saxons and a party of raiding Danes at Maldon on the Blackwater in Essex is described in haunting detail. Near the beginning there is a brief account of a young man, knowing that battle is at hand, sends his valuable hunting falcon into the woods for its protection and so that he will not have any encumbrances when the time comes to fight. *Tiercel* (a falconry term meaning a male Peregrine falcon) by Andrew Eason (Bristol 2001) is an illustrated poem inspired by the Saxon original:

> *He loosed from his hands his beloved hawk,*
> *let it fly to the woods and went to the fight.*

The poem describes the battle that ensues from the falcon's point of view:

> *I see between the rushing boughs the state of war.*

Ironically, this bird associated with war is let go before the fight, 'sought of groves of peace', but it cannot deny its true nature:

A killing bird/familiar to men's hands/seeks out the hidden warmth of prey

Nature is indeed red in tooth and claw. Birds of prey are killing machines of the air. Yet they kill mostly out of need and have raised it to an artform. There is an elegant efficiency about a bird of prey's hunting – a Sword of Damocles dropped from above, administering a swift coup-de-grâce.

Hawk of Achill

The ancient Irish poem, 'The Hawk of Achill' is one of the key bardic texts, which deserves to be studied and meditated upon in full – the current scope of this book does not allow us to print this lengthy colloquy here in its splendid entirety. It involves the shamanic conversation between one-eyed Fintan the Bard and the Hawk of Achill, who discover, by relating their life histories, that they are exactly the same age – an incredible 6515 and furthermore, the hawk was the one who plucked out Fintan's eye! (Like Odin, who lost his eye while languishing on Yggdrasil, the World Ash, for nine days and nights, to return with the runes, the Elder Futhark.) There is further mythic cross-hatch: Odin retrieved the runes from Mimir's Spring at the base of Yggdrasil, while Fintan communes with the Hawk of Achill at a frozen river mouth or waterfall. Within the long colloquy, in the form of gnomic stanzas, there is much lore and revelation including a sequence with a magical branch, which seems uncannily like the silver branch wielded by other ambassadors of the Sidhe, and bards who had travelled to the Otherworld and back.

Both Fintan and the Hawk have lived for a long time, as super-annuated as Methuselah, and both expire at the end of the sequence – perhaps suggesting the Hawk is Fintan's totem or soul-bird, sharing a dual-destiny. However, the Hawk seems to be more than this – being present at many great battles and delighting in plucking out eyes and snatching limbs of fallen heroes – which suggests he may be Death itself (omnipresent and perennial). Yet there is a fascinating correspondence between Bards and birds in more than name alone. There is the *tuirgin*, the shamanic feathered cloak of the vision-poet. Bards were said to speak the legendary Language of Birds. In 'The Hawk of Achill' Fintan boasts at one point: "I am able finely to converse with thee in bird-language". This skill is also possessed by the bard Gwythyr, Interpreter of Languages who, in the Tale of Mabon and the Oldest of Animals, is able to converse with the Blackbird of Cilgwry, the Owl of Cwm Cawlwyd and the Eagle of Gwernabwy, among other totem beasts. The 'Language of Birds' is sometimes another name for the Ogham tree alphabet – said to have been inspired by the legs of crane in flight. And, of course, the Crane-skin Bag is part of a bard's sacred regalia. But perhaps this correspondence is not at all surprising when we consider that both bards and birds share the same element (air) and furthermore, are the masters of it. Air, wind, breath and speech are all connected; wind is seen as a cipher for the Holy Spirit, or the Divine itself in several cultures.

'The Hawk of Achill' preserves a great deal of mythic history, and perhaps was used as a mnemonic for doing so. Spend some time with this poem. It may seem obscure to begin with but with persistence and a poet's intuition it begins to unlock its secrets.

As an exercise try writing a dialogue with your own totem. See what wisdom can be channelled in this way.

Hawk of May

We cannot conclude our discussion on hawks in legend and folklore without mention of Gwalchmai, AKA Gawain, the Hawk of May. The nephew of King Arthur Pendragon is famed for his passion and integrity. He often steps into the fray in lieu of his uncle, taking a more active role, and could be seen as the active principle of Arthur's Round Table (each knight an aspect of the Self). He offers himself in the place of Arthur to marry the hag,

Lady Ragnall, to save his liege from shame. When offered the choice whether she should be fair by day, or foul by night, or vice versa, Gawain wisely says she should choose herself – and thus he discovers what 'women truly want' (the riddle set by Morgen): to choose their own way – and thereby breaks the enchantment placed upon her appearance. This mirrors the young knight's adventure with the Green Knight – who appears before the Court one midwinter, challenging the King to play the Beheading Game: one stroke with his axe, if he is willing to accept the same blow a year hence. Gawain accepts the challenge and is forced to travel North through bleak fells to discover the green chapel where his doom awaits. Three days before his appointment Gawain arrives at a castle where a merry Lord Bertilak bids him welcome. A Lord of Misrule figure, Bertilak sets a game for his guest. Every day the Lord goes out hunting and upon his return they will exchange their respective winnings. Every morning, after her lord's absence, the lovely Lady Bertilak comes to Gawain's chamber and tempts him. He admirably resists, only accepting (at first) a chaste kiss upon the cheek. This he realises with horror he now has to give to the lord upon his return. The following morning one kiss becomes two from the fair Lady of the house. One kiss, two: one on each cheek. Each of these Gawain offers to Bertilak in the evening. The third day, the lady kisses the young knight full on the lips and offers her green garter, which has magical properties – she tells him to wear it and it shall protect him against his foe – Gawain keeps this final gift to himself... The next day he sets off for the Green Chapel, which is close by, down a drear gorge, a literal 'dead end'. There the Green Knight awaits, sharpening his axe. Gawain takes his fate like a man – and bows to receive the blow. The first stroke falls. The knight flinches, and the Green Knight mocks his cowardice. Chastened, Gawain does not flinch a second time – and receives only a nick to the neck. Saved by the green garter – but given an admonishing scar to show he was not entirely blameless. In 'shame' he returns to Arthur's court and recounts his adventure, but the King sees only virtue in his integrity. There after the knights all wear a green sash to show their own fallibility – and thus, the Order of the Garter is born, which exists to this day (although not from an unbroken lineage of course). Gawain has a shield upon which is a pentagram – which the poet says 'represents the five Christian virtues', although it is a well-known pre-Christian symbol of protection. Gawain is one of the most fully rendered and fullyrounded of Arthur's knights – in comparison to the extremes of Perceval or Lancelot. His pentacle is a symbol of earth in magical tradition, and his association with May also gives him a connection to earthy sexuality and rootedness. He is a 'knight of the world'.

Passionate and precise, keen-eyed and committed, fierce and focused. All of these qualities Gwion has to assimilate before he can move on to the next incarnation. Until he accepts them – all points of the pentagram – they will always pursue him. Like Gawain, he has to embrace the solid physicality of life and face his destiny. Ceridwen, his raptor-reaper, has finally caught up with him. It is time for him to be harvested.

Chapter 8

Cian

And just as she was about to stoop upon him, and he was in fear of death, he espied a heap of winnowed wheat on the floor of a barn, and he dropped among the wheat, and turned himself into one of the grains

Song of Wheat
Listen
Amongst glistening ears of wheat –
Hear my tiny heartbeat,
A mouse's feet,
Hiding on this threshing floor
From Ceridwen's impeccable wrath.
I have been hot-blooded and cold.
Scale and feather and fur –
Many skins have I shed
To escape the Crooked One's fury.
Will the chase never end?
Stillness now is my best friend.
Hide in plain sight,
One of the crowd.
A poet's fate I would fight,
Give me mundanity,
Run-of-the-mill respite.
Yet I am Henwen's tears –
With my body bread can bake,
Beer can brew.
Transformations never end,
Only you.

Gwion turns himself from a small bird into a germ of wheat to escape Ceridwen's wrath – within an inch of his life he made himself smaller and slipped through her talons down, down, down onto the threshing floor of a nearby farm – there to hide amongst the grains. The story has travelled from May Eve, when Elphin made his discovery at his father's weir, to the start of the harvest – from Beltane to Lughnasadh – suggesting the chase is a cyclical one reflecting the turning of the wheel, the life-force as it manifests throughout the seasons ('the force that through the green fuse drives the flower' as Welsh bard Dylan Thomas expressed). Here we have come to the rich field of harvest rites. Brighid has become Demeter.

An ear of wheat was a symbol of the Eluesinian Mysteries as enacted at Delphi – a symbol of the rebirth that comes about through sacrifice. We must give of ourselves for the greater good. At this time the bright god of growth is slain in his prime. Llew, Baldur, Osiris, Sir John Barleycorn – he is known by many names.

There is no escaping this fate.

Even Orpheus, grieving for his Eurydice high in the mountains, cannot slip the net though he has renounced Dionysus for Apollo. The gods are jealous. The wine-deity sent his Bacchanae after him – wild women who tore him to pieces when he would not join in their sensual frenzy. He had gone to one extreme (turning away from the world, from women, from the needs of the flesh – virtual self-mortification) and the Bacchanae were the other (driven crazy by bodily lusts). The two collided, resulting in Orpheus losing his head (torn off in the attack, it floated down the Hebron on his lyre to, of all places, Lesbos – that which you avoid...) and the wild women being turned into trees (withered, juiceless and bark-skinned – perhaps a symbol of old age, of the physical cronedom that awaits all women). The poet was 'harvested'.

Death is very much in the air at this time. The glint of the sickle in the corn. The days have an added poignancy as they start to get shorter. We must savour every drop of sunlight – as rich and golden as mead. There is an easing of pressure, of pace – after the harvest is gathered. First we must sweat in the sun, even work through the night, under the fat harvest moon. A collective effort, to bring the harvest home. The stooks of wheat stacked in the shorn fields, raw stubble like Ysbaddaden's beard after Culhwch had managed to give his future father-in-law a haircut: with the scissors and comb gleaned from between the ears of the porcine king Twrch Trwyth. In the Welsh story of Henwen – another giant boar – wherever she fled she dropped various symbolic offerings, amongst them a grain of wheat. A symbol of potential, of how our every action, our every word, creates an effect – wherever we find ourselves. Through the katabolic winnowing of the goddess Gwion is reduced to his bare essence – his soul-seed. As this germ-sperm he 'impregnates' the crone-goddess, making what is barren fertile once more. The black hen is very much a figure in the same lineage as the Morrigan, Cailleach, and Kali. Death is made fertile.

Returned to his primal essence, Gwion 'dies', to be reborn again: as a twice-born, shining-browed, bard – Taliesin.

Lughnasadh is the name of the Celtic fire festival related to the funeral games of Lugh, a sun god who dies at this time of year. In Saxon parts of Britain the festival was known as Lammas, or 'loaf-mass'. A sacred loaf was made from the first or last sheaf of wheat. Corn dollies were made, mirroring the Bridey dolls, Bride's bed and Bride's cross made at Imbolc. This is the promise of the Spring Maiden made manifest – as she blooms into her full potential: the maiden becomes mother. Demeter is the quintessential harvest matriarch – she wanders the fields, searching for her lost daughter, her grief shrivelling the fields in her wake. Yet, her daughter has tasted forbidden fruit – three pomegranate seeds from her dark captor, Hades; her own fruit of the harvest – and must spend three months of the year below ground. The

Spring maiden must wear the colours of winter. Her innocence has been 'defiled' – or rather, she has reconciled her Shadow self. The 'virgin' and the 'whore': two patriarchal pigeon-holes, categorising – and thus attempting to restrict – women's sexuality.

In the story of Llew Llaw Gyffes from the *Mabinogion*, Blodeuwedd, the bride made of flowers by Math and Gwydion, betrays her husband and orchestrates his assassination so she can run off with his rival, Gronw. This apparently heartless act may have been part of a bigger pattern – the consort of the goddess 'changing guard' from the solar Oak King (Llew, in the form of a golden eagle hides in an oak tree) to the shadowy Holly, (Gronw's spear shaft is hewn from holly) symbolising not a woman's fickleness but the turning of the year from its bright to dark half, from its waxing to waning tides, as days shorten and nights lengthen. In winter, it feels like the Earth's golden lover has forsaken her or exchanged places with his darker rival. The Goddess is perennial; her consort, seasonal – rising and falling with the sun through the year.

I feel more connected to this festival than any, perhaps because it falls less than three weeks before my birthday – a time when I always feel a sense of my own mortality. This year, the festival had intense resonance, for the week before I had scattered my father's ashes and planted a tree for another 'father figure', Tim Sebastian. Both were Barleycorn-esque figures, larger-than-life characters who enjoyed a few too many beers! Both died before their time – Tim at 59, Dad at 69. I commemorated what would have been Tim's 60th last year, and my Dad's 70th last month, a week before the Bardic Camp where I performed 'Grim Reapings: bloody tales for harvest tide'. My performance had an extra depth and edge to it because of the raw reality of its subject matter. My life is transformed into my art – and like the grazes acquired during the slog of harvest, raw scratches against the skin from the sharp stubble, the process of harvesting was painful. What can be gleaned from life's fields?

Lughnasadh, like all of the festivals, makes us reflect. It is time to take stock. Decide what to keep, what to cut. We must work hard now to gather in enough to see us through the harder months ahead. Life seems easy now, in the fat of summer, but lean winter awaits. The grain stores must be filled.

What sacrifices are you prepared to make for your harvest?

Chapter 9

Black Hen

Then she transformed herself into a high-crested black hen, and went to the wheat and scratched it with her feet, and found him out and swallowed him

Song of the Black Hen
There is no hiding from me.
I am Carrion's Queen,
Valkyrie, Kali, Cailleach, the Morrigan.
The Washer at the Ford.
I will strip away all that is non-essential.
I will find your weakest point
And tear you apart.
And yet,
I only have your best
Intentions at heart,
I want you
To show your truth.
I shall only snatch you
If you stray from your path,
If you lose your centre,
Lie to yourself.
I am the black mirror of
Your soul's dark night.
The ravenous maw,
Your worst fear made manifest.
The smouldering mother
Who devours her young.
A raw hole of need –

Never fulfilled.
Black Annis, Baba Yaga,
There's no escaping my hunger.
Let me eat you, obliterate you,
Test your strength.
If you are strong, you will endure.
Denial is only another dying.
Death only takes from you
What you refuse to give.
Release
Into the serenity
Of surrender.
Come to me, my sweet.
Let me cut the chaff
From your wheat.

There comes a time in everyone's life when it feels like it is all falling apart (or being ripped away). This katabolic process is embodied in the goddesses Hel, Kali, Cailleach, the Morrigan, Black Annis, Baba Yaga, the Washer at the Ford and the weaving Norns. In the Taliesin story Ceridwen embodies this energy – the vengeful crone chasing Gwion's soul through death-like transformations – this reaches its apogee in the figure of the black hen. The fact she is black should be symbolic enough – associated with night, death, oblivion, unknowing. Gwion hides on the threshing floor in the form of a grain of wheat. Here he reaches the final stage of his 'soul-winnowing'. There is nowhere else to go – except face up to his fate. His karma has pursued him relentlessly. There's no escaping it. Until he turns and face it – 'face the music' – he will never find peace.

Ceridwen the Black Hen's capture of Gwion is an inevitable as death – which catches us all in the end. The third Moirae (from the three Fates of Greek Mythology) was called Atropos, which means 'inexorable' or 'inevitable', literally 'unturning'. She was the cutter of the thread of life – choosing the manner and timing of each person's death. When she cut the thread with 'her abhorrèd shears', someone on Earth died. Her Roman equivalent was *Morta* ('Death'). From her name we get the word atrophy.

In alchemical terms this is the stage of 'nigredo' – of blackening, before the gold is achieved. It is the classic dark night of the soul, when the cloud of unknowing descends. We have to encounter and endure hope-loss-ness, despair, fully – before we can experience the uplifting rapture of 'rebirth'. The darkest hour is the one before the dawn.

This year I have had to deal with the sudden death of my father. This came on the top of three other bereavements within the space of four years. All good friends, and each of their deaths was devastating – but the last one was certainly the 'knock-out punch'. It left me nakedly aware of my own mortality – of my own status as 'the next in line'. Although I wasn't very close to my father, and didn't depend upon him for support of any kind it still felt as though the sheltering sky (to use Paul Bowles' powerful metaphor) had been ripped away. It all fell on my shoulders. There was no one left to turn to – I had to shoulder life's burden without any sanctuary if I faltered. My mother still lives, but she understandably devastated and I had to be strong for her. Indeed, my main concern was about her than my father – he had gone beyond suffering, I believe. My mother was the one who was grief-stricken and very ill. This could have been the 'straw that broke the camel's back' but somehow she has bounced back, which shows her strength of spirit.

And I had to as well.

And yet, when a death occurs of a loved one, one is challenged to the core in what one believes: where do you think that person goes? Does something of them live on? What remains? How we choose to enact our rites of passing is the real test of fire. Often though we have to consider others. And the compromises can be agonising – especially if one thinks the memory of the departed isn't being honoured (e.g. a Christian funeral for an atheist). But I believe such ceremonies are more for the living than the dead. It provides a fulcrum for the grief – and enables us to move on, to find closure, even if that process may still take years. Without it, we may not get a proper chance to say goodbye – to lay our ghosts to rest, for an unexpected bereavement brings up all the things we felt about that person; all the things we wished we had said or done; all the mistakes; lost opportunities and moments of pain. The dead do not become perfect with death – despite the immolations, the bland tributes – and neither do we. Our faults, our failings, are shown. And then it seems too late to do anything about it.

The forces of decay – the entropy at the heart of existence – are always present and will overwhelm us if we let them. Living is a constant act of will, of pushing forward against all odds. This endless struggle can feel exhausting at times – and it is perhaps understandable why so many people suffer from depression or even want to give in completely. The appearance of the black dog was said to be a harbinger of death – as indeed it did for Nick Drake, whose spine-chilling song 'Black Eyed Dog' is a cri-de-coeur of a soul at the gates of oblivion (he tragically overdosed shortly after recording it). The premature death of talented, shining souls seems to be painfully common in the artistic arena – too many amazing singers, musicians, poets and painters have died before their time: Jim Morrison; Janis Joplin; Jimi Hendrix; Brian Jones; Keith Moon; Sandy Denny; Ian Curtis; Kurt Cobain; Freddie Mercury... the list grows every year. Sublime songsmith and singer Jeff Buckley, who sang his own version of the psychopompic carol, 'Down in Yon Forest' on his only album, 'Grace', drowned in a swimming accident – following his father, Tim Buckley, into an early grave. Was he too lured by the eerie 'Song of the Siren'?

And yet art is a Weapon of Mass Creation in the war against death. With it we can counter the forces of entropy, of despair.

Every joyous act of life does this, whether it is witnessed by others or not. They don't have to be grand gestures. Anything that awakens the senses, makes us feel glad to be alive is an effective counter-blow. But it is not reactive living – it is pro-active.

The Black Hen hunts us all down. Challenges us all to change. If we don't, she will make us anyway. And if we don't 'bend', then she'll break us. Smash us to smithereens. She is the Dark Goddess, on our tail to teach us truth. Her job is to break down any illusion. To test our strength, our resolve, our integrity.

What are we willing to surrender? Whatever we hold onto too dearly, she will take from us. No sacrifice is too high. She is here to teach us about attachment, about immutability. That which is fixed, dies. We will all be 'digested' eventually, back into the earth, back into the cosmic soup – so it is wise to adjust to this and approach dissolution with grace, rather than with terror. Our deepest fears are often fear of being changed. Yet, as is so often said, if we don't change, we don't grow. We stagnate, we stop living – and that is the only death. A refusal to join in the dance of life. The Black Hen is not there to destroy us, but to liberate us.

The Boy in the Bag

And, as the story says, she bore him nine months, and when she was delivered of him, she could not find it in her heart to kill him, by reason of his beauty. So she wrapped him in a leathern bag, and cast him into the sea to the mercy of God, on the twenty-ninth day of April.

Song of the Twice-born

The sea is my cradle, my mother –
I rise and fall to her swell and swirl,
Her briny breathing.

From the crack in my leather bag,
Sodden with salt spray,
I see the exclamation of sky and wave –
Blue, white, turquoise.

I hear the keening of gulls –
One landed on my tiny craft,
My planet coracle,
And pecked at the caul
Ceridwen had placed about me –
Her act of kindness,
Slipping out past her cruel demeanour.
It broke her to let me go,
But I know she had to –
Afaggdu's eyes, dark daggers
He would plunge into me
Given half the chance –
And I forgive her.
It was an act of love,
An act of Goddess.

And now I dance in the chaos,
Beyond the ninth wave, the tenth,
In the lap, lap, lap of the gods.
Through night's belly.
My brow, my beacon –
A frail light in the vastness,
A taper in the tempest.

And yet
Even the darkest night shall pass, when
What rough dreams from our eyes we shall rub.
Ragged flags of hope fluttering in the dawn,
I have been Gwion,

I tasted the cauldron,
And now I am Twice-Born.

Beyond the Ninth Wave

When the as yet unnamed Twice-Born is cast by Ceridwen beyond the ninth wave, wrapped in a leather bundle and placed in a coracle – a small, round wicker-framed craft covered in hide once common in Ireland and Wales – he joins a select fleet of similar heroes, adrift in mythic waters.

There is something very Biblical about such imagery. In Exodus Moses was placed in a basket and cast upon the waters:

> *The Pharaoh had commanded that all male Hebrew children born be killed by drowning in the river Nile. At this dark time, Jochebed, the wife of the Levite Amram, bore a son and kept him concealed for three months. When she could keep him hidden no longer, rather than deliver him to be killed, she set him adrift on the Nile River in a small craft of bullrushes coated in pitch.*

According to Koran, she is commanded by God to place him in an ark and cast him on the waters of the Nile, thus abandoning him completely to God's protection and demonstrating her total trust in God. In the Biblical account, Moses' sister Miriam observed the progress of the tiny boat until it reached a place where the Pharaoh's daughter Thermuthis (Bithiah) was bathing with her handmaidens. It is said that she spotted the baby in the basket and had her handmaiden fetch it for her. Not unique, this birth legend is in many respects similar to the 7th century BCE Neo-Assyrian version of the birth of the King Sargon of Akkad in the 24th century BCE who, being born of modest means, was set in the Euphrates river in a basket of bulrushes and discovered by a member of the Akkadian royalty who reared him as their own.

It is perhaps not surprising to find so many examples of this kind of foundation myth, considering we are all borne in a watery vessel (buoyant in amniotic fluid within our foetal sack), 'benighted' and at the mercy of the God/dess – the 'divine' parent who carries us and upon whose life we depend. But there are echoes relating back to the dawn of humankind, even the whole planet. In the Christian Genesis, the face of God was cast upon the waters at the dawn of Creation:

> *And the earth was without form, and void; and darkness was upon the face of the deep. And the Spirit of God moved upon the face of the waters.* (Genesis 1:2)

This is in many ways akin to the dark night of the soul, also known as a 'Belly of the Whale' experience, after another Biblical story, Jonah and the Whale. This has become synonymous with a period of uncertainty and soul-searching. Joseph Campbell, mythographer, identified this as one of the key stages of the Hero's Journey, which he discerned by his extensive study of world myths and legends. This has now become a common trope in Hollywood movies, thanks to the popularising of Campbell's ideas by Christopher Vogler in *The Writer's Journey* (Pan 1999), in which he applies the Hero's Journey to story structure in screenplays. As Campbell found, there are many other examples of this motif in world cultures. In Egyptian tradition, the slain body of Osiris is floated on the Nile. It washes up amongst the reeds, and there, red-faced Set, in the guise of a serpent, tears it apart and scatters it limb from limb.

Orpheus is similarly dismembered, by the wild Bacchanae and his head is cast in the Hebron, where it floats, atop its lyre – still singing (like the head of Bran the Blessed) all the way to the shores of Lesbos. As the foremost poet of the Mediterranean Orpheus of Thrace, holds a similar status to Taliesin, his Welsh counterpart (similarly accompanying his liege on a perilous quest – as Taliesin did with Arthur in 'Preiddu Annwn' – Orpheus was one of Jason's Argonauts).

Gilgamesh must cross a Sea of the Dead to meet the Noah-type figure Utnapishtim (using two staves to punt his craft across the deadly waters – one for the journey there, the other for the way back).

Arthur journeys into the underworld of Annwn aboard his ship Prydwen, and takes his final journey to Avalon after the calamitous battle of Camlann aboard a Ship of the Dead – usually depicted as crewed by a black-clad Morgen and sometimes nine similar Morrighan-like dark figures; but in the *Vita Merlini* it is a psychopompic boatman, Barinthus, who is Arthur's ferryman – a Celtic Charon – who, with Merlin and Taliesin, takes Arthur to Avalon to heal of his grievous wounds.

There are many examples of these 'Ships of the Dead' around the world. When Baldur is slain inadvertently by his brother, the blind god Holdur, he is placed in a long ship, which is set alight as it sails into the west. At Barradule on the Isle of Man, where Gaelic and Nordic influences converge, there is a Viking 'stone boat' (burial cairn shaped like a longship) pointing towards the sunset. Such solar boats seem symbolic of the journey of the sun into the west – over the horizon – where it appears to die every night and then is reborn. In Egyptian mythology, Osiris, Lord of the Dead, is said to sail through the twelve gates of the body of Nut every night, to emerge in the morning, reborn. Spirit canoes exist in traditions of the Philippines and North America. Celtic Saints undertook perilous journeys 'into the west', immramas, recorded in chronicles, e.g. the Voyage of Bran, Brendan or Maeldun. Coleridge's Ancient Mariner, cursed for having slain the albatross – which he is made to wear about his neck by his fellow crew who, one-by-one, perish – languishes in the Doldrums, becalmed in a sea of slimy things. It is only when he learns the harsh lesson – accept his guilt of his environmental crime – that he can move on from this state of stasis.

And so, this Twice-born is in good company. And, like all of these heroes, finally he is able to move on. His small craft is caught in a weir belonging to a man – Gwyddno – whose horses his unfortunate actions had once poisoned – his karma has brought him full circle to where he must acknowledge his deeds, take responsibility for them, and live with the consequences. It is time to face the music. His wyrd is waiting.

Chapter 10

Elphin

And at that time the weir of Gwyddno was on the strand between Dyvi and Aberystwyth, near to his own castle, and the value of an hundred pounds was taken in that weir every May eve. And in those days Gwyddno had an only son named Elphin, the most hapless of youths, and the most needy. And it grieved his father sore, for he thought that he was born in an evil hour. And by the advice of his council, his father had granted him the drawing of the weir that year, to see if good luck would ever befall him, and to give him something wherewith to begin the world.

Song of Elphin
Hapless am I,
Good-for-nothing no good boyo,
So my father says.
I cannot even catch a fish
In his salmon-weir –
Sticking out into the ocean,
Like a licked finger in the wind –
Hoping for a change in fortune,
A winning tide,
To take our run of bad luck
away.
Here I am
On May Eve
When a young man like me
Should be making merry in the greenwood
With a bonny maid

Gathering flowers, dipping head in dew.
Instead, my wyrd is to sit

Waiting for something to bite.

What do I want from life?
What riches are waiting to be mine?
If fishes were wishes,
Which would I catch –
Fame? Fortune? Power? Like my Uncle Maelgwn?
A warm bed and a hot woman would do me now.
I cannot stomach
The prospect of returning to my father
Empty-handed.
It would just confirm his opinion of me,
A failure.
What will I amount to?
What is my destiny?
Is my story out there, in that wild chaos,

Waiting to be caught?

To be hauled in, landed, gutted, cooked?
If only more than my thoughts
Snagged on the basket-rack
Of Sarn Cynfelyn.

Elphin, son of Gwyddno Garanhir, represents the unfulfilled potential in all of us. He won the rights to fish at his father's salmon weir on May Eve, where it was possible to catch a hundred pounds' worth of the poet's fish (substantial wealth at the time). And yet nothing was 'biting'. In this respect he is akin to Finnegas, the hermit of Irish legend, who waits patiently to catch the salmon of wisdom. The hermit waited a long time –

twenty years in some versions – to no avail. Elphin has a reputation of being a 'bit of a waster': 'the most hapless of youths, and the most needy'. He's the classic mopey teenager – sleeping half the day, lounging around, doing nothing much at all – undisciplined, unfocused talent. It is an awful time adolescence – living in a limbo, the pressure of expectation, the frustration of hopes, a feeling of powerlessness, raging with hormones, with unchannelled energy. It used to be called existential angst, and for some it doesn't go away. Yet this is his defining moment – here at the salmon weir is where he finally meets his destiny, when he receives his aquatic inheritance. When it comes, it is an enormous relief – finally, a direction, motivation and a place in the scheme of things. Time, at last, to begin, to be-in the world.

I remember feeling like Elphin throughout growing up – a feeling of restlessness, of not fitting into my skin, which reached crisis point as I came of age. I kept a detailed journal throughout that time and it provides an invaluable record of my 'Elphin-state' – 1991 – my 'gap year' from my Fine Art degree, the year I found my Celtic muse, started writing poetry and embarked upon my bardic path in earnest (see **Taliesin's Apprentice**). This stage of uncertainty, of not fitting in your skin, followed by a late flowering is identified in Icelandic culture in the figure of the Kolbitar – young men who sit so close to the fire it's as though they eat the coal – literally Coal-biters. They are the classic dreamy introverts, not fully in their bodies, not happy in their lives, feeling like strangers in their families. But all that time in dream-space can pay off later on, as they utilise the imaginative faculties they have honed to create art and entertain others. JRR Tolkien, as a young man at Oxford, started a group called the Kolbitars – whose sole purpose was to read out Icelandic Sagas in the original language. Since a young boy Tolkien had had a passion for the Nameless North, as he called it. This daydreaming would one day manifest in *The Lord of the Rings* – a project that took twelve years to complete, but a lifetime to dream into being. Tolkien did not merely 'begin the world' – he created his own. He had found his calling. When that falls into place, the unfulfilled youth – lost in the dark night of the soul – suddenly is galvanised into action. They have a purpose. Whether they achieve it depends on numerous factors: tenacity, skill, luck, fate... but they can at last set out on the Hero's Journey. They have had the Call to Adventure – Elphin is about to receive his – but whether they Cross the Threshold, it is up to them. They must act.

But before this defining moment life can seem unbearably monotonous and unfulfilling. Some do not make it passed this stage. Their brief lives end in tragedy. One has to realise there is a life out there waiting for you – but you cannot wait for it to turn up. You have to go out there and find it.

The Drawing of the Weir

And the next day when Elphin went to look, there was nothing in the weir. But as he turned back he perceived the leathern bag upon a pole of the weir. Then said one of the weir-ward unto Elphin, "Thou wast never unlucky until tonight, and now thou hast destroyed the virtues of the weir, which always yielded the value of an hundred pounds every May eve, and to-night there is nothing but this leathern skin within it." "How now," said Elphin, "there may be therein the value, of an hundred pounds."

The chief problem of the Kolbitar is being able to define what it is they want to achieve. What do they want to do? The modern equivalent is choosing which subjects to study at school – pupils are expected to make decisions at a difficult age that will affect their future. The pressure is intense. The GCSEs (or whatever equivalent system is used) they choose will affect which university they get to – if at all – and what career awaits them. How can they possibly know at puberty what they will be happy doing as an adult? And yet the Kolbitar's choice is more critical – it is about one's soul calling. Seldom do people make career choices that reflect this – thus a clear disengagement with the whole process. Jumping through academic hoops for jobs they aren't really interested in. It's starting from the wrong way around. Rather than making the child fit the world, let the world fit the child. Dream big. It should start from inside – what in your heart of hearts do you want to manifest? The naming of names is critical. Half the battle of dealing with an illness is diagnosing it correctly. Once you have named your demon, you can deal with it.

After his Cloud of Unknowing, just at the point when he was going to turn back empty-handed. Elphin catches something out of the corner of his eye. A 'leathern bag' caught in the weir. It doesn't look promising. The weir-ward, one of those disparaging voices that is always eager to point out your failings, takes delight in commenting on Elphin's ill-luck: 'now thou hast destroyed the virtues of the weir'. The weir-ward is one of those people who love to moan. Whose cynicism is a consoling fiction – which everything in life confirms, whether it actually does or not, so that they can't see good fortune when it actually occurs – for that will puncture their paradigm. Fortunately, Elphin can – and he quickly wades out to pull in his unexpected catch. Without hesitation, he opens it and beholds a 'radiant browed' babe. In a flash, his dark night of the soul has ended. This is the flash of inspiration which comes after a prolonged period of uncertainty. There are many examples of this – of scientists and artists who have 'stumbled' upon a solution after reaching an impasse in their research: the 'Euraka!' moment. Elphin's variant of Copernicus' bathtub is the salmon weir. In his drawing of the weir, Elphin is, in effect, drawing lots – his choice will affect his destiny. Fortunately the gods smile upon him that day. His wyrd changes at Gwyddno's weir – a kind of field of potential, from which he plucks inspiration. His destiny finds a name.

The Naming of the Bard

Well, they took up the leathern bag, and he who opened it saw the forehead of the boy, and said to Elphin, "Behold a radiant brow!" "Taliesin be he called," said Elphin.

The naming of things is a very bardic act. 'In the Beginning,' says Genesis, 'was the Word'. 'The Word was God.' Language and creation is connected. To be able to define a thing is to bring it into existence. A linguistic framework goes some way to helping a thing to manifest. A deity exists if we have a name for them – for around that name it accumulates an accretion of belief and it gains a reality. Adam was said to have named all living things in the Garden of Eden.

To discover the true name of something is an act of magic, of potency. To be a name-maker perhaps even more so. Often this role was performed by an elder of the community. Native American tribes would look for signs in nature at the time of birth – a flight of birds, the splash of a fish, the sounds of creatures in the night. New names may be given at later stages, to mark a change in status – usually a move into maturity. This is not only common in First Nation cultures. When we marry, names and titles can change. We acquire 'names' when we get job – teacher, sales assistant, receptionist, police officer, executive, director, doctor, president – titles which 'define' us, so much so that when some are made redundant or retire they find it difficult to carry on. Their sense of identity is so wrapped up in their job they feel at a loss without it. Their name and their role are indivisible.

Setanta became Cuchullain – the Hound of Culann – and later, the Hound of Ulster, the 'threshold guardian' of a nation. His name and destiny are indivisible.

In the *Mabinogion* there is the story of Llew Llaw Gyffes, the child of Arianrhod who, shamed by the manner of his birth, places a geas upon him – that he will receive no name. But Gwydion, Arianrhod's brother and the boy's uncle, contrives through his magical trickery a way for Arianrhod to inadvertently name her son. Disguised as shoemakers in a small boat, they arrive at Arianrhod's castle – offering their services. The queen orders a pair of shoes from them. The first pair is finely made but too small; the second pair too big, and so she comes down to the quayside to have a fitting. As she steps aboard the boat a wren alights upon the prow. The boy takes his needle, with which he has been sowing the cordovan leather, and casts it at the bird – striking it between bone and sinew. The queen is impressed by the shots and cries out: 'behold the Lion of the Steady Hand!' in her native tongue and that his how Llew Llaw Gyffes got his name, for that is what it means. Another geas Arianrhod places upon Llew is that he will have no mortal wife, and so Gwydion and King Math fashion for him a 'wife out of flowers', whom they called Blodeuwedd, 'flower face'. Unfortunately, she lacks human morality and sleeps with another, arranging for her husband's assassination. For her infidelity she is turned into an owl by Gwydion and so lives up to her name: 'flower-face'.

Authors generally fall into two camps – those who like to use illustrative names (Dickens, Rowling) and those who prefer characters with nondescript nomenclatures.

John Cowper Powys in his Brythonic epic *Porius* says: '*some names are beautifully congruous with what they depict; others are disjointed, arbitrary, accidental.*' If we are lucky, we are given a name by our parents that captures our spirit well. Sometimes, we are less fortunate. Names can become self-fulfilling prophecies – each one has different levels of 'confidence', even 'luck', encapsulated in it. Parents all over the world, in wildly different cultures, like to give their children 'lucky names'. Hence the swathe of baby names reflecting popular culture – the Kylies and Liams, Beckhams and Obamas – illustrating the parents' tastes or displaced lifestyle aspirations, but also a subconscious wish that some of the luck of the original 'owner' rubs off on the child. If one is given a less fortunate name then one has to work harder to break free of the negative patterns surrounding it. Ultimately our luck is what we make it. Not all owners live up to their names, while many with humble names rise to prominence through their own merits. A name may contain the seed of destiny but it is up to its owner to fulfil its potential. A given name is like a river that carries you to the sea – the sea of adult life. How you fare in the wide ocean of life is down to your wits.

That wily old Greek sea captain, Odysseus, gave his name to his story, *The Odyssey*, which has come to mean any protracted journey – often involving frustrated attempts to return home. It would seem evident the title came after the name, but the two have become entwined in popular culture. The hero's name was synonymous with his destiny – like having a protagonist called 'Journey'. Certainly the gothic anti-hero *Melmoth the Wanderer* (Maturin, 1820) fits that bill. Yet Odysseus gives his name to his Cyclops captor, Polyphemus, as 'No-man', who blindly swears revenge upon his anonymous – and thus protected – attacker.

Names have power. The fairy story 'Rumpelstiltskin' hinges upon this one fundamental principle.

It is clear if you know the true name of something or somebody you have influence over them – as Elphin, by naming Taliesin, discovers.

The Consolation of Elphin

And he lifted the boy in his arms, and lamenting his mischance, he placed him sorrowfully behind him. And he made his horse amble gently, that before had been trotting, and he carried him

as softly as if he had been sitting in the easiest chair in the world. And presently the boy made a Consolation and praise to Elphin, and foretold honour to Elphin

The newly-named Taliesin starts earning his keep straight away. A babe of no more than a few days old (he was cast upon the waters on 29th April) he hits the ground running – bardically speaking – coming out with several long, esoteric poems. A child prodigy, to say the least. But it is interesting that Taliesin's first poem is one of consolation. This is a function that poetry has filled for a long time, although it is by no means its only one. People often turn to poetry at times of emotional crisis or flux: for rites of passage such as birthdays and weddings, although funerals tend to be the commonest time. Even those who have never penned a poem before find themselves having a go at times of bereavement, or, turning to others who have expressed universal sentiments of loss – taking consolation in the way their deep pain is articulated, but also the bittersweet joy of having known that lost loved one. Poetry can be a way of honouring – the historical Taliesin composed eulogies to his lord, Urien ap Rheged. Maelgwn's twenty-four sycophantic bards composed poems for their patron. Writing a poem for a loved one – perhaps for their birthday – can be a wonderful way of honouring them.

The act of reading or hearing poetry can be consoling in itself. Sitting down somewhere quiet and reading a poem can be soothing, as can listening to poetry being recited – either in performance, or the radio, or on a recording. Poetry therapy has taken off in the States and is starting to catch on in Britain, but it has been around for a long time. Now you can buy 'chicken soup' anthologies to suit every difficult occasion: to help cope with times of separation, loss or tragedy (such volumes became very popular after 9/11). Poetry can be renewing, it can rekindle a sense of hope. Poems can provide a 'moral compass'. Some provide balm for the soul. We turn to them, again and again, over the years, for guidance and reassurance through difficult times. It is like taking a draught from a cool, clear well.

In reciting his consolation to Elphin, Taliesin is using poetry in the same way that the shaman uses song – and indeed, at their root, the two are deeply connected. Taliesin's gnomic phrases are in many ways shamanic utterances, saturated with esoteric knowledge beyond his brief life. The baby Penbeirdd – an old soul in a young body – helps to sing Elphin's soul back home. Gwyddno's hapless son has finally found his destiny – his wyrd caught in a salmon-weir. From now on, his luck will change. He no longer needs to be a Kolbitar. Life has bitten him. It is time for him to take responsibility. The child is now the man. The son must become the father.

The real consolation of Elphin is, in essence, that he has found his soul-song. Taliesin performs a similar psychotherapeutic function for Merlin, helping to restore his sanity after the trauma of war. The shaman-bard sings his patient's soul back home. Where there is woundedness, division, disease, he creates healing wholeness.

Chapter 11

Gwyddno

Then came Elphin to the house or court of Gwyddno his father, and Taliesin with him. And Gwyddno asked him if he had had a good haul at the weir, and he told him that he had got that which was better than fish. "What was that?" said Gwyddno. "A Bard," answered Elphin. Then said Gwyddno, "Alas, what will he profit thee?" And Taliesin himself replied and said, "He will profit him more than the weir ever profited thee." Asked Gwyddno, "Art thou able to speak, and thou so little?" And Taliesin answered him, "I am better able to speak than thou to question me." "Let me hear what thou canst say," quoth Gwyddno.

Song of Gwyddno Garanhir
I am always waiting,
The anxious father,
Poised like my namesake
– Craneshanks –
Casting my thin shadow
On the waters of the deep.

Watching. Waiting
For my useless son
To return from the weir.
Even when fortune lands in his lap
That boy lets it slip through his fingers.
A wealth of salmon awaits him –
A hundred pounds in his nets.
Prodigal fool, when will he return?

My crane bag is full of
The sea's vast treasures.
Cantre'r Gwaelod is my kingdom,
The Lowest Hundred –
Sixteen cities under my name –
And now under the sea,
Thanks to that drunken dotard Seithennin.
Curse the one who failed in his duties –
Unsluiced, the waves rolled in,
Like a stampede of ghost-horses,
And covered my plain,
Where I had stood, perpendicular,
On my spindly heron legs.
And now they mock me
With thrones of feather and wax.

Yet who can withstand the tides of fate?

The southerning birds
Write their druid secrets on the sky
And my soul flies with them.
My luck has left me.
The sovereign of the sun
Slips into the purse of night,
But I am ill-fortuned upon this cruel coast.

Arianrhod, turn your caer
Towards me.

In the story of Taliesin, Gwyddno represents the positive father archetype, compared to the absent father of Tegid Foel and the 'bad father' of Maelgwn who we'll come to next. He is the long suffering father, who has to shoulder the burden of the 'slings and arrows of outrageous fortune' – the loss of his horses due to the cauldron-spill, a hapless son, the lack of a salmon catch, and ultimately, the devastation of his sixteen cities – Cantre'r Gwaelod, the Lowest Hundred. The *'sigh of Gwyddno'* was a byword for misfortune. It was said to have been heard when his kingdom was flooded:

Seithennin, stand thou forth
And behold the billowy waves:
The sea has covered the plains of Gwyddno.
'Seithennin', Taliesin

Of course, this infamous sigh, rich in sibilance, could have been the sound of the sea itself, the sound caused by a marine transgression. Cardigan Bay, the site of this legend, was indeed flooded at some point – probably the end of the last Ice Age – as evidenced by the fossilised forest near Borth exposed at low tide. Gwyddno's weir is not a river-weir, but a salmon-weir – similar to the salmon racks still used to this day along the Severn Estuary. The one associated with him juts out into Cardigan Bay just below Borth and is called Sarn Cynfelin. It is a ridge of gravel and rocks, again exposed at low tide. Several of these can be seen leading into the brine – one is said to stretch for miles towards Ireland – and one can see how the legend of the lost caers came about. It would be easy to mistake these weirs for walls.

Other associations connect Gwyddno with the sea: he is known as Gwyddno Garanhir – 'crane-shanks' and he is identified with the spindly fisher (adding another bird in the Taliesin menagerie). A local custom survives to this day: makeshift thrones are fashioned and whoever can stay upon theirs the longest as the tide comes in, 'wins'. Thus, Gwyddno is a kind of Welsh Canute – who commanded the tide back, not out of arrogance, but to show the limitations of even a monarch's powers.

Gwyddno is connected, through the Taliesin legend, to horses – and watching the white-capped waves roll in to Cardigan Bay, one could see this as a poetic association. Taken literally, it tells us that Gwyddno was (once) a wealthy man, an Ozymandias figure. The modern day banker, executive or politician watching the City's financial institutions collapse is the equivalent.

Horse legends proliferate in the *Mabinogion*: in 'Bran and Branwen', Evnissyen (the Welsh Loki) mutilates the Irish king, Matholwch's, horses (an act echoed in the Peter Schaffer play, *Equus*). Rhiannon is especially associated with horses and may have been at one point a horse-goddess akin to Epona (she first appears riding a swift white horse, and – falsely accused of murdering her children – she is forced to wear a bridle and carry people to court, telling them her story); Gwydion conjures horses and hounds out of toadstools and gives them to Pryderi in exchange for his magical swine.

In Irish myth a rash boast leads to an unusual horse-race. The indelicate Crunnchu mac Agnoman boasted his wife, the other-worldly Macha, was a faster runner than the king's own horses. The King, hearing this, summoned Macha, who was forced to make good her husband's claim. She asked for the race to be postponed, for she was with child. The King refused her requested and so Macha uttered this geas: 'Then the shame that is upon you will be greater than that upon me, and a heavier punishment upon you.' She then succeeded in outrunning the horses and, at the finishing post, gave birth to twins – the ultimate 'Lady's Day'. At her birth pangs everyone present endured similar loss of strength. Macha, the triumphant mother, then pronounced this curse: that until the ninth generation the men of Ulster would experience the weakness of a woman in child-bed for five nights and four days when their enemies were attacking them. An early blow for Women's Lib! Ever afterwards the setting of the race was known as Emain Macha (The Twins of Macha) outside Armagh in Northern Ireland. It is interesting that

Gwyddno experiences a similar set of misfortune at Taliesin's 'breach-birth' (the splitting of Ceridwen's cauldron) – his horses dying. This is karmically redressed by the bard when Gwyddno accepts the twice-born culprit, now Taliesin, as his foster grandson. From that point on, his fortunes change.

Gwyddno relates symbolically to all legends of fathers: Daedalus and Icarus; King Lear and his three daughters; Phaethön and the Lord of the Sun (with his four powerful horses); Zeus and his many amorous exploits; Odin (the All-Father with his eight-legged steed Sleipnir) and his equally colourful adventures; Fionn of the Fianna (father of Oisín); and even King Arthur; with his own ill-favoured offspring (Mordred, begat upon his half-sister, Morgen).

Now let us turn to the story's final paternal presence, completing the 'triple aspect' – the 'bad father' archetype as epitomised by Maelgwn, Gwyddno's brother, Elphin's uncle and soon-to-be Taliesin's challenger.

Chapter 12

Maelgwn

And forthwith Elphin gave his haul to his wife, and she nursed him tenderly and lovingly. Thenceforward Elphin increased in riches more and more day after day, and in love and favour with the king, and there abode Taliesin until he was thirteen years old, when Elphin son of Gwyddno went by a Christmas invitation to his uncle, Maelgwn Gwynedd, who sometime after this held open court at Christmas-tide in the castle of Dyganwy, for all the number of his lords of both degrees, both spiritual and temporal, with a vast and thronged host of knights and squires. And amongst them there arose a discourse and discussion. And thus was it said: "Is there in the whole world a king so great as Maelgwn, or one on whom Heaven has bestowed so many spiritual gifts as upon him? First, form, and beauty, and meekness, and strength, besides all the powers of the soul!" And together with these they said that Heaven had given one gift that exceeded all the others, which was the beauty, and comeliness, and grace, and wisdom, and modesty of his queen; whose virtues surpassed those of all the ladies and noble maidens throughout the whole kingdom. And with this they put questions one to another amongst themselves, Who had braver men? Who had fairer or swifter horses or greyhounds? Who had more skilful or wiser bards—than Maelgwn?

Song of Maelgwn
Some call me cruel,
But try and wear a crown
And see how easy it is to control.

One must mete mercy
With severity.
Otherwise no one knows
the boundaries.
And things fall apart.
Someone has to be in charge.
From the hard rocks of Deganwy
I rule the wild fastness of Wales.
In uncertain times
People look to a strong leader.
To rule wolves you have to be
Fiercer, mightier, wilier
Than the pack.
What is the point in having fangs
If you don't bare them occasionally?
A growl without a bite.
And yet I am not uncultured.
Let it not be said I am a brute,
A savage thug,
My court hosts famous feasts –
Four and twenty bards eat at my table.
Poetry, harp, song
Fill the hall every night.
Am I not then, patron of the arts?
Let the Three Strains win over their hearts,
Their minds – and then they are mine.
Distracted from the ugly mundanity
By the minstrel's glamour.
Keep the people happy with fool tales and festivals
And they'll endure the harshest yoke.
Impress the guests with generosity
Keep the nobility sweet, on your side,
Give them the illusion of liberty.
Your friends close, your enemies closer.

And you'll rule the fools
With a velvet fist.

Maelgwn is the ultimate authority figure in the Taliesin story – he represents the 'bad father' archetype, and epitomises all those who wield power cruelly and are corrupted by it. The history of the world is littered with such tyrants. Maelgwn is not in the same league as Attila the Hun, Adolf Hitler, Jospeh Stalin, Pol Pot, Chairman Mao, General Pinoche or Saddam Hussein – he's a minor hoodlum, a local heavy. From the heady heights of Deganwy Castle it is easy to see why someone would get delusions of grandeur – Maelgwn truly was lord of all he surveyed from that strategic point on the tip of North Wales. He ruled with an iron hand, until his like were replaced by a 'bigger fish', Edward Longshanks and his 'ring of iron' – an enclosing shield of Norman castles around the coast and English-Welsh of Wales to quell further Cymric rebellion. One of these can still be seen over the river estuary from Maelgwn's stronghold, clamping onto Conwy with a vice-like grip – completely controlling this important river crossing.

Maelgwn was said to have forced poets and harpers to swim across the Conwy river to see who would be best to play – the harps were ruined, but the poets had their material in their heads and so could perform unhindered.

A good story doesn't work unless it has a good villain – and in the Taliesin story Maelgwn is forced to play the 'villain of the piece'. And yet he acts as an initiator – forcing Taliesin out of the woodwork to make his bardic debut. If anyone acts with folly it is Elphin, but even he, with his rash boast, is perhaps contributing to a larger pattern. As Shakespeare wrote:'there is special providence in the fall of a sparrow'. Taliesin was destined to make his journey to Deganwy and Elphin's boast provided a suitable catalyst – so that Taliesin's actions seem heroic rather than boastful as well. He has a noble motive – his words will liberate Elphin – although many of his utterances come across as boastful, it has to be said. When Taliesin claims virtual omniscience and omnipresence he is on one level expressing a global or even cosmic consciousness – and is 'ego-less' – but on another level he is simply following in the tradition of his Nordic counterpart who gave his name to bragging, Bragi – who drank the Skaldic Mead (a brewery of Ceredigion is called Bragdy, Welsh for malt house – but the root seems similar). Taliesin, the young upstart iconoclast, refutes the utterances of Maelgwn's twenty-four bards as false or shallow – only he has the secret knowledge, the true voice. His awen is drawn from a deeper source, a purer stream. Taliesin represents the earlier form of bard, rather than the bastardised travelling minstrels – the medieval equivalent of pub-singers – who have a stock repertoire of classics, but do no add to the cannon. They are not torch-bearers.

Now at that time the bards were in great favour with the exalted of the kingdom; and then none performed the office of those who are now called heralds, unless they were learned men, not only expert in the service of kings and princes, but studious and well versed in the lineage, and arms, and exploits of princes and kings, and in discussions concerning foreign kingdoms, and the ancient things of this kingdom, and chiefly in the annals of the first nobles; and also were prepared always with their answers in various languages, Latin, French, Welsh, and English. And together with this they were great chroniclers, and recorders, and skilful in framing verses, and ready in making englyns in every one of those languages. Now of these there were at that feast within the palace of Maelgwn as many as four-and-twenty, and chief of them all, was one named Heinin Vardd.

A true bard works act a shamanic level, he is a priest-performer – bringing real magic and even healing with his song-dance. This is evident whenever one sees a 'legend' perform; someone who doesn't only plays their instrument, they dance with it.

Maelgwn is the quintessence of the male authority figure – against whom a whole generation have railed against, perhaps rightly, but ultimately to their deficit. A lack of respect of authority in youth culture, running feral in schools and on estates, is a symptom of this. After a century of bloody conflict the old patriarchy needed challenging, needed breaking down – but not to the point of blocking any masculine energy – which creates the 'absent father' syndrome. It is like bringing up a child with only one parent – however well this is done the child is always going to be hamstrung from the deficit. A child needs both to be balanced – otherwise they risk becoming 'mummy's boys' or 'daddy's girls' – in what could be called the Parsifal Syndrome (when the young protagonist, reared in isolation by his mother, beholds three knights riding through the forest it awakens something within him – the male energy his life was lacking, his destiny denied). If this connection with the opposite gender does not occur in childhood all the rage built up may end up being directed at all men or all women accordingly – because of the negative signals they received from not having the other parent present. Looked at in a more tolerant light – rather than seeing Maelgwn and thus all men/all authority as the root of all evil – the father/king archetype can be reclaimed. Some people appreciate someone who takes charge. Someone has to make decisions, to have the final say – otherwise things might never get done. Group discussion can only get things so far, but unless there is a consensus, someone has to decide. Think of all the great engineering works – magnificent buildings, bridges, tunnels, harbours, airports, roads, viaducts, canals and so on – none of them would have been achieved if people argued endlessly over each point, or avoided 'taking charge'. This fear of being the one who takes the initiative ends up being an endless 'gentleman's excuse me' – as when two people try to go through the same door

– and a loop of 'after you, no after you' starts. This vacillating becomes infuriating. It gets people nowhere. When we have good leaders, male or female, amazing things can get done – if they have the loyalty of their community, which a good leader attracts by example. Would Britain have defeated the Nazis without a Winston Churchill to rally the troops and the nation? If everyone had fought for themselves, rather than presented a united front, we would have been defeated. Divide and rule has always been an effective way to conquer people.

Growing up in the shadow of the Cold War, the legacy of 'bad kings' it is understandable why so many men and women turned away from any form of patriarchy and how all things masculine were seen as 'bad', yet this has produced a generation of emasculated men, perhaps in touch with the feminine side, sympathetic to Women Mysteries, Goddess Worshipping, (all good things by themselves) but consequently unsure of their role – now that women have claimed their power and can apparently do everything themselves. The modern woman can have a career, children, and as many orgasms as she wants – so the magazines insist. With the closure of much industry in the Eighties, male employment surged. Women became the breadwinners and many earn more than men, except in the top 'fat cat' captains of industry league. Yet there are many examples of successful female entrepreneurs, celebrities and sports stars – breaking records, pushing the envelope of what women can do, which is great. But it has left men floundering. If they aren't even 'bringing home the bacon' anymore then where does that leave them? Films like *The Full Monty* (dir: Cattaneo, 1997) explored this conundrum in a comical way. The irony is that some women still like men to be strong, to be the stereotype of a man in a way – the virile hunter and warrior, defending the hearth, providing shelter – while at the same time as wanting everything. Conflicting signals that don't make it any easier! Modern men have been afraid to claim their power – like Aragorn in *The Lord of the Rings,* seizing the sword of his wyrd – frightened by the blood that flows in him, by his potential to turn into a 'bad king', to be tempted by the Ring. But when opened to the light, when reclaimed, the father archetype can be positive. Key figures in the Men's Movement like poet Robert Bly have done a lot to heal this woundedness and reclaim the 'wild man', as he calls it. Yet this can go beyond growing beards, making fires and male bonding. Men don't have to dwell in their wounds to celebrate their maleness. Not all men were wounded by their fathers, or abused as children. Certainly, such issues need to be brought out into the light, expressed and released – but Male Mysteries can be so much more than this 'licking of wounds'. The Green Man symbolises the enervating force of male creativity. Male power doesn't have to be 'macho' – it can manifest in many ways. Camaraderie, co-operation, brotherhood, fatherhood, grandfatherhood. Leadership. Stepping up to the mark. Shouldering responsibility. Being in command of oneself can lead to being in command of others. People are drawn to it. One earns respect – it is not something you can impose. It is interesting how, in difficult times, people often elect 'strong/wrong leaders', hence we end up with gung-ho Bush jnr for US president and an action film star as governor of California. People feel drawn to the archetype of a 'strong leader' and this is exploited by the spin-doctors and campaign marketing departments, thus in the 2008 US elections there was another 'war hero', John McCain, as the Republican candidate. This is akin to what transpires in the Anglo-Saxon saga of *Beowulf* – a threatened land recruits a veteran with a reputation for victory, Beowulf, to see of the monstrous threat. Later on Beowulf, now king, lives off of his reputation – cashing in on earlier victories – until 'a dragon too far' finally gets him. This was perhaps his karmic debt finally being repaid – he basically had it coming. Even when it is apparent a leader is flawed people still want them to fulfil the role they have projected onto them – they see the legend, not the reality.

Maelgwn had his own spin-doctors – his twenty-four bards, a formidable PR department – but this 'glamour' was finally dispelled by Taliesin and his bardic utterances. Even the mightiest of kings cannot withstand the truth – when things come to light, they are toppled. And so people are rightly suspicious of power – but are unwilling to take charge themselves. And without doing so, they abdicate responsibility to others. Unless we are willing to pull the sword from the stone, this shall always be so. Until then we will always be ruled by others.

When they had all made an end of thus praising the king and his gifts, it befell that Elphin spoke in this wise. "Of a truth none but a king may vie with a king; but were he not a king, I would say that my wife was as virtuous as any lady in the kingdom, and also that I have a bard who is more skilful than all the king's bards." In a short space some of his fellows showed the king all the boastings of Elphin; and the king ordered him to be thrown into a strong prison, until he might know the truth as to the virtues of his wife, and the wisdom of his bard.

The Tyrant's Golden Daughter

Song of Eurgain
I am Maelgwn's real treasure –
Brightgold he named me –
The fairest thing in his life.
Even within the darkest hearts
A gleam may glimmer
Of all they are not.
Any kindness or grace that my father
May possess
He stored in me, his treasure chest.
Kept his heart in a strong box –

And gave me the key.
The mead-horn I bore
In my father's hall.
Summer's tears,
The golden liquid
Did not run dry.
A young maiden no more
Now that Elidyr has wifed me
We have made our home
On the Fort of the Bear,
Round-backed hill,
It presents its broad shadow
To the biting sea,
And licks its paws of rain
Deep in its own wintering.
The yellow plague will take my father,
Now that he is bereft of his
Bright gold darling.
The sun has left his life, he said,
When I departed my father's caer
And what can follow –
Only night.

Eurgain

Life is seldom black and white. Even the worst tyrant can have redeeming qualities (certainly if they are fully-rounded characters, and not just stereotypical baddies). Hitler was a vegetarian and an artist – although that doesn't make what he did okay, of course, it just makes him more complex. We are full of contradictions, of paradoxes. Maelgwn is small fry compared to such megalomaniacs, but in his kingdom, mythic or otherwise, he stands for the same Draconian principles. And yet he too has one good aspect, as embodied by Eurgain, his beautiful daughter.

This motif, of the monstrous father-in-law with the fair

daughter is not uncommon in mythology and legend. In the *Mabinogion* Olwen 'flower-foot' is the daughter of the giant Ysbaddaden, who sets her suitor, Culhwch thirty-nine impossible tasks.

In Irish myth Fionn MacCumhail is out hunting with his friends Diarmuid and Conan when, benighted, they come across a lowly but welcome dwelling. They enter and are greeted by an old, old man who asks them to tether a goat, which they – the greatest heroes in Erin – fail to do. Then a beautiful young maiden enters and haughtily ignores them – saying they once had her, but did not appreciate her and now she is lost to them forever. It is revealed in the chilling conclusion of the story that the young maiden is Youth; the goat is the World, and none can tether it but the old man, who is Death – come to the heroes at the last.

Thus, death walks hand in hand with the maiden. This perennial motif could be the symbiotic connection between the two fundamental forces of Thanatos and Eros, death and love, which influence the great wheel of life. Fear and desire govern the behaviour of virtually all beings. Depending on which one holds dominance we move forward or backward, act or retreat, forever teetering on the tipping point. Hollywood screenwriters call this the Fear/Desire Axis and use it to gauge characters' behaviour: the ultimate push/pull principles.

This relationship, between Death and Desire, could be also symbolic of the peril that is often associated with great treasure – the dragon guarding the golden hoard. In every Fafnir gloating over its blood-stained gold, and every Sigurd who would win it, we see the folly and fatal ambition that often attends wealth. This is one of the key themes of the Anglo-Saxon epic, *Beowulf*, which Robert Zemeckis brought alive through CGI in his 2007 film version, co-scripted by Neil Gaiman: Grendel's mother is improbably but memorably depicted as a stunning femme fatale played by a computerised Angelina Jolie – clothed only in dripping gold. She is the 'genie in the lamp' of the majestic horn – whoever possesses it becomes king, but at a price. In Gaiman's reworking of the story, Grendel's mother becomes the sovereignty of the land – without whose 'blessing' it is impossible to rule. It is a double-edged relationship. All men desire her – what she represents: power, wealth, glory – but her maddening riches proves the catalyst of conflict and ultimately deadly. Much blood is shed in her name, seeking her elusive boon.

The original poem ends on a gloomier note – on the futility of all glory-seeking. Beowulf wins the ultimate hoard, slays its guardian dragon, but dies in the process. Shrouds have no pockets. What use is earthly wealth, the poet seems to be saying. Turn your efforts to spiritual riches – to higher things. Abandon vain ambition. All things must perish.

As the wise Prince of Morocco says in *The Merchant of Venice*: '*All that glisters is not gold*'.

Yet sometimes the gold motif does not symbolise simply mundane riches, but otherworldly wealth. Its appearance in descriptive passages in the *Mabinogion* is a sure sign things are of a rarer coin – the yellow ox-hide that Rhonabwy lies down upon to receive his shamanic dream; and more frequently the uncanny livery of fairy princes and princesses, e.g. in 'The Lady of the Fountain' Owain encounters a yellow man who owns a castle:

And he went forward towards the Castle, and there he saw the chamber, and when he had entered the chamber he beheld the maidens working at satin embroidery, in chairs of gold. And their beauty and their comeliness seemed to Owain far greater than Kynon had represented to him.

Apart from the rarity of yellow in the physiognomy and landscape of the Cymric – thus making it seem otherworldly as it would not be to, say, a desert dweller – in the symbolic language of myth and legend 'gold' symbolises the sun – the solar principle, Higher Consciousness, the Godhead and literally source of all life, where ultimately we must return.

Oisín, the son of Fionn, the greatest hero of Erin meets Niamh of the Golden Hair while out hunting with his father and son on the west coast of Erin. Her heart has been won by his enchanting words (for he is the poet of the Fianna) and she has come to husband him. He is enchanted by her song describing the paradise of Tir nan Og, and off he goes with her, on the back of her fairy steed – never to see his father, son, friends or hounds ever again. When he finally returns, he discovers that three hundred years have passed and all that he has known and loved has long turned to dust. He has 'followed the gleam', as Tennyson phrases it, and paid the price. The pot of gold is not 'somewhere over the rainbow' but right beneath your feet – with your family, friends, at your own hearth, as the Peddlar of Swaffham discovers in the Fenland folk tale. There is indeed 'no place like home', as that other, more fortunate visitor to the Otherworld discovers, Dorothy in *The Wizard of Oz*.

In the fairy story, Goldilocks and the Three Bears, the heroine, a young girl with a golden mane, learns discernment, to take the middle way – out walking in the wood one day she comes across a cottage, its door ajar. She enters and finds three bowls of porridge. The first she tries is too hot, the second too cold. The third just right. The same occurs with three chairs – too big, too little, just right. Then finally, the three beds – too hard, too soft, just right. But the bear family return, discover the intruder, who is frightened away.

Goldilocks learns to take the middle way, as Thomas the Rhymer does in the eponymous Scottish Border Ballad – shown three roads by the Queen of Elfland: a narrow, broad and bonny way, he takes the middle one, between the extremes of right-eousness and wickedness (the road to Heaven or Hell), negoti-ating between Christian dualism, a moral Symplegades – the clashing rocks that Jason and his Argonauts runs the gauntlet of, or the two sea monsters Scylla and Charybdis which Odysseus wins through, returning from the fall of Troy.

True harmony comes from transcending dualism and finding balance, as echoed in WB Yeats' poem 'The Song of Wandering Aengus', which tells of how the god of love is haunted by a vision who appears before him, a *'glimmering girl/with apple blossom in her hair'*, whom he grows old trying to find. Eventually he achieves her love between the *'silver apples of the moon, the golden apples of the sun.'*

Apples are associated in Celtic Tradition with the Otherworld. Emhain appears bearing a silver branch from the apple tree of her fairy homeland, a sign of her otherworldly lineage and of the bounties that await all who follow her.

Goldilock's choice is a late echo of the Judgement of Paris – with less devastating consequences! When the goddess Discord is not invited to the wedding of Menelaus and Helen, she gatecrashes and casts a golden apple amongst the guests: on it reads 'to the fairest'. An argument develops over who deserves it for no less than Hera, Athena and Aphrodite are present. To settle the matter Zeus sends Hermes to Earth to find an unfortunate mortal to choose. Paris, son of Priam of Troy is selected. The goddesses appear before him and make their claim, offering him their various gifts. He chooses Aphrodite and the others are so put out they swear vengeance. Aphrodite honours her 'election promise' and orders her agent, Eros, to shoot a dart into the breast of Helen. The new wife of Menelaus is instantly smitten with love for Paris, who manages to elope with her – thus causing the Ten Years War. Helen, 'the face that launched a thousand ships', is summoned up from Hellenic legend by Mephistopheles for Doctor Faustus – yet he loses his soul to the Devil as the price for this vision of beauty, immortalized by Goethe and Faustus.

Lancelot, the 'best knight in the world' loses his honour by becoming embroiled in a destructive love affair with Guinevere, his queen and wife of his liege, King Arthur. Tristan finds himself in the same eternal triangle with Isolde and her new husband, King Mark. In Irish myth, the same pattern is played out between Diarmuid, Grainne and the old Fionn MacCumhail. These women are embodiments of the sovereignty of the land: sometimes those in power have not 'deserved' her, or have lost her favour through their actions – failing to live up to their earlier commitment, corrupted by their position, become complacent, failing to appreciate the woman who has empowered them. And so she bestows her favours on another – usually a younger, more virile champion – who loves her with all of his heart, and usually his life: caught in the crossfire, a pawn in an old game.

Blodeuwedd, a bride made of flowers by the magicians Gwyddion and Math for Llew Llaw Gyffes, who is cursed to wed no mortal woman by his own mother Arianrhod, proves her fickle fairy heart by bedding a lover, Gronw Pebr in Llew's absence. Together they plan his demise. Through her wiles, Blodeuwedd discovers the complicated circumstances of her husband's weakness. A spear is made on the Sabbath for a year and a day for the assassination – a spear which Gronw himself is forced to receive when the resurrected Llew returns with a vengeance.

Gwythyr and Gwynn ap Nudd must fight every May Day until the end of time for the flower maiden Creiddylad (daughter of Nudd of the silver hand, the Welsh Nuadu). This seems to be a symbolic combat between the lords of the light and dark halves of the year – the Oak and Holly King in Western magical tradition – to be the consort of the goddess. In fact, they take turns – six months each. But, crucially, this is not their choice – a polite gentleman's agreement – but that of the goddess.

In the Welsh version of Tristan and Isolde, Trystan and Ysseult, Arthur decrees that the feuding suitors – Trystan and King March agree to share Ysseult: one in the time of leaf, the other in the time of no leaf. Since March is her husband, Arthur lets him choose. He chooses the time of no leaf (when nights are longer for the loving) but Ysseult triumphantly declares: 'Holly and ivy and yew are never without leaf'. Because of evergreens, there is never a time without leaf, and so the flower maiden wins.

Yet the 'flower maiden' is not always the cause of such conflict, destruction and misery. She is the bearer of life, the renewal of all things. She is as welcome and as comely as the Spring after the hardships of Winter. Her beauty bestows grace upon our lives. Without her, without her 'woman's touch', her softening feminine influence, existence would be too hard – Maelgwn's castle would be dark and bleak. Our lives are enriched by her presence.

Rhun and the Ring

Now when Elphin had been put in a tower of the castle, with a thick chain about his feet (it is said that it was a silver chain, because he was of royal blood); the king, as the story relates, sent his son Rhun to inquire into the demeanour of Elphin's wife. Now Rhun was the most graceless man in the world, and there was neither wife nor maiden with whom he had held converse, but was evil spoken of. While Rhun went in haste towards Elphin's dwelling, being fully minded to bring disgrace upon his wife, Taliesin told his mistress how that the king had placed his master in durance in prison, and how that Rhun was coming in haste to strive to bring disgrace upon her. Wherefore he caused his mistress to array one of the maids of her kitchen in her apparel; which the noble lady gladly did; and she loaded her hands with the best rings that she and her husband possessed.
In this guise Taliesin caused his mistress to put the maiden to sit at the board in her room at supper, and be made her to seem as her mistress, and the mistress to seem as the maid. And when they were in due time seated at their supper in the manner that has been said, Rhun suddenly arrived at Elphin's dwelling, and was received with joy, for all the servants knew him plainly;

and they brought him in haste to the room of their mistress, in the semblance of whom the maid rose up from supper and welcomed him gladly. And afterwards she sat down to supper again the second time, and Rhun with her. Then Rhun began jesting with the maid, who still kept the semblance of her mistress. And verily this story shows that the maiden became so intoxicated, that she fell asleep; and the story relates that it was a powder that Rhun put into the drink, that made her sleep so soundly that she never felt it when he cut from off her hand her little finger, whereupon was the signet ring of Elphin, which he had sent to his wife as a token, a short time before. And Rhun returned to the king with the finger and the ring as a proof, to show that he had cut it from off her hand, without her awaking from her sleep of intemperance.

Song of Rhun

I am the henchman who makes
All tyranny possible.
Without me to do their dirty work
How would they rule the world?
There's always somebody willing
To do worse for less.
They sent me to test
The virtue of Elphin's wife.
He had boasted she was beyond compare –
A moral paragon who outshone
The women of Maelgwn's court.
Rash words. Landed him in the dungeon,
Nephew or no.
Silver chains they say,
But no blue blood will save him
If his boast proves idle.
I take pride in my work.
I'm a professional.

With Maelgwn's horses and Maelgwn's men
I made my way to Gwyddno's hall.
There I met Elphin's wife.
She was easy to seduce.
When drunk asleep,
I cut off her wedding finger,
Ring and all,
And took it back
To Maelgwn's court –
Evidence of Elphin's wife's fickle heart.
Alas, Elphin brought out of his cell,
Refuted this, pointing out
The flour beneath the nail,
The untrimmed horn.
His wife never baked bread,
Never forgot to trim her cuticles.
I had been deceived!
That young whelp with the strange eyes,
The shining brow –
He knew I was coming, could see
The colour of my trade.
A maidservant they surely have used,
And I misused,
And now must face I Maelgwn's wrath.

Rhun is Maelgwn's 'heavy' and he joins the ignominious rank of henchmen – who crop up throughout world culture in oral story, fiction, opera and film: dull thugs destined to be outwitted. Such minions, who are 'only following orders' (the Nuremberg defence) make the tyranny of the world possible. Without their muscle the Maelgwn's of this world would not last long. In the Norse Myth of the slaying of Baldur, the sun god, Loki the Trickster uses Baldur's own brother, Holdur, blind god of darkness, to unwittingly be the instrument of his destruction –

striking him with a spear made from mistletoe – his one weakness. In the story of Math and Mathonwy, Blodeuwedd, Llew Llaw Gyffe's amoral 'wife made out of flowers' uses her lover Gronw Pebr to be the assassin – to cast a spear at her husband made over a year and day on the Sabbath. She arranges for her solar hero spouse to be vulnerable – neither on land nor on foot, inside or out – but it is Gronw who casts the spear and who suffers the consequences when his victim is restored. The modern version in popular culture is the Bond 'heavy' – the Oddjob or Jaws-type – doomed to be dispatched by our hero but powerful enough to provide some excitement, a short shot of plot adrenalin. Pawns of the super villain, whose loss is never mourned, they are seldom given rounded characters – perhaps because they seem to represent certain archetypal fears, the shadows in our psyches, hard-wired into us from inchoate fears felt in the cot, in the child's bedchamber, in the school-playground, in the workplace. The shadow beneath the wardrobe. The universal bully. We demonise them, give them more power and potency than they deserve. Tolkien's epic is full of them: from goblins, orcs, spiders, wargs, to Uruk-hai, trolls, Balrog, Angmar the Witch King, even Saruman – the pawns of Sauron. Dickens' literature is similarly peppered with them – Bill Sykes in *Oliver Twist*; Mr Creakle in *David Copperfield*.

In Philip Pullman's *His Dark Materials* a fanatical priest, Father Gomez, is dispatched to neutralize the threat to the Authority. In modern fiction this malcontent has become the anti-hero, with a strange allure of his own. Steerpike is a particularly fine example, in Mervyn Peake's *Gormenghast* Trilogy – an unpleasant social climber (literally) who wheedles his way up through the hierarchy of the castle until finally meeting his comeuppance, as all bullies – in fiction at least – are destined to do.

For now, let us return to the narrative. Rhun has returned with the ring – still attached to its finger – a sure sign, so he and Maelgwn think, of Elphin's wife's infidelity.

The king rejoiced greatly at these tidings, and he sent for his councillors to whom he told the whole story from the beginning. And he caused Elphin to be brought out of his prison, and he chided him because of his boast. And he spake unto Elphin on this wise. "Elphin, be it known to thee beyond a doubt that it is but folly for a man to trust in the virtues of his wife further than he can see her; and that thou mayest be certain of thy wife's vileness, behold her finger, with thy signet ring upon it, which was cut from her hand last night, while she slept the sleep of intoxication."

But Elphin has a riposte to this slur on his wife's character. He knows her better than any man:

Then thus spake Elphin. "With thy leave, mighty king, I cannot deny my ring, for it is known of many; but verily I assert strongly that the finger around which it is, was never attached to the hand of my wife, for in truth and certainty there are three notable things pertaining to it, none of which ever belonged to any of my wife's fingers. The first of the three is, that it is certain, by your grace's leave, that wheresoever my wife is at this present hour, whether sitting, or standing, or lying down, this ring would never remain upon her thumb, whereas you can plainly see that it was hard to draw it over the joint of the little finger of the hand whence this was cut; the second thing is, that my wife has never let pass one Saturday since I have known her without paring her nails before going to bed, and you can see fully that the nail of this little finger has not been pared for a month. The third is, truly, that the hand whence this finger came was kneading rye dough within three days before the finger was out therefrom, and I can assure your goodness that my wife has never kneaded rye dough since my wife she has been."

Thus, the 'bully' is stood up to – and defeated in this 'round'. First point to Elphin. But he still has his other claim to be vindicated and Maelgwn is not giving up the game yet:

Then the king was mightily wroth with Elphin for so stoutly withstanding him, respecting the goodness of his wife, wherefore he ordered him to his prison a second time, saying that he should not be loosed thence until he had proved the truth of his boast, as well concerning the wisdom of his bard as the virtues of his wife.

And so all now depends upon the thirteen-year old boy whom Elphin fished out of his father's weir. He has raised him as his own and now he is relying upon him to set him free. Yet Taliesin has to compete against Maelgwn's twenty-four bards. The odds are stacked against him. It is a classic 'gunslinger' scenario. The young hero must make his way to his appointment with destiny. Its high noon at Deganwy and it is time for Taliesin to show the world what he is made of. It is time for his bardic debut. He has experienced the cycle of life – as hare, salmon, wren, grain of wheat, a helpless babe cast on the sea – and for twelve years has been honing his skills, like the Anruth who has to spend as long studying to earn the title of Bard. This is Taliesin's testing – his 'finals'. Will he pass this exam, or fail? The modern equivalent is participating in an eisteddfod. The prize is: the Chair of Deganwy, the emancipation of Elphin and the establishing of his reputation as a bard.

All these thoughts must be swimming around the young Taliesin's mind as he sets out on his journey to Deganwy: where we started this story and where it ends.

Chapter 13

Taliesin

In the meantime his wife and Taliesin remained joyful at Elphin's dwelling. And Taliesin showed his mistress how that Elphin was in prison because of them, but he bade her be glad for that he would go to Maelgwn's court to free his master

The time of reckoning has come for the young Taliesin. For nigh on twelve years he has served his apprenticeship, under the patronage of Elphin and now he must vindicate the trust his master has placed in his ability. He is now thirteen years of age and has, in this society, come of age. He can no longer hide in his youth, hidden away from the world and his destiny, somewhat like Parsifal. Destiny has come a-knocking. There's no escaping it anymore. The onset of puberty is a common time for shamans to be 'tested' – often by life-threatening sicknesses. If they survive, they are 'twice-born' stronger than before and ready to fulfil their potential – to inhabit the role allotted them.

Interestingly, Taliesin 'showed his mistress how that Elphin was in prison because of them.' Does he use a form of 'remote viewing', or do we take this more prosaically, i.e. a simple explanation? Even Eliade says that poetry is a form of telepathy.

By whatever means, Taliesin seems somehow aware of his master's fate – and his part in it – and acting with honour, he declares his attention to meet this 'call to adventure'. When Elphin's wife asks him by what manner he hopes to achieve this, the young bard responds with a poem:

A journey will I perform,
And to the gate I will come;
The hall I will enter,
And my song I will sing;
My speech I will pronounce
To silence royal bards.
In presence of their chief,
I will greet to deride,
Upon them I will break
And Elphin I will free.
Should contention arise,
In presence of the prince,
With summons to the bards
For the sweet flowing song,
And wizards' posing lore
And wisdom of Druids.
In the court of the sons of the distributor
Some are who did appear
Intent on wily schemes,
By craft and tricking means,
In pangs of affliction
To wrong the innocent,
Let the fools be silent,
As erst in Badon's fight, —
With Arthur of liberal ones
The head, with long red blades;
Through feats of testy men,
And a chief with his foes.
Woe be to them, the fools,
When revenge comes on them.
I Taliesin, chief of bards,
With a sapient Druid's words,
Will set kind Elphin free
From haughty tyrant's bonds.

To their fell and chilling cry,
By the act of a surprising steed,
From the far distant North,
There soon shall be an end.
Let neither grace nor health
Be to Maelgwn Gwynedd,
For this force and this wrong;
And be extremes of ills
And an avenged end
To Rhun and all his race:
Short be his course of life,
Be all his lands laid waste;
And long exile be assigned
To Maelgwn Gwynned!

In some ways, this is merely the boasting of the prize fighter before entering the ring. Mohammed Ali was adept at this, often bursting into verse – protective cantrips ('*I float like a butterfly and sting like a bee, I am the greatest and my name's Ali*'). Ali is not unique in uttering pugilistic loricas – indeed 'lorica' means breastplate, and were often a prayer for protection placed upon the actual armour of the knight going into the fray. Here, Taliesin explains exactly by what means he will vanquish his foe, at the same time as making it clear what role he is claiming, his eyes firmly on the prize:

I Taliesin, chief of bards,
With a sapient Druid's words,
Will set kind Elphin free
From haughty tyrant's bonds.

By drawing upon his tradition – the wisdom of Druids – he can access wisdom and allies beyond his brief span of years. He does not go to Deganwy alone. He walks with his ancestors. And with the Awen, a bard is never unprepared – by being in the moment, aligned with the Source, he can respond to any situation. Thus equipped, he sets out:

After this he took leave of his mistress, and came at last to the Court of Maelgwn, who was going to sit in his hall and dine in his royal state, as it was the custom in those days for kings and princes to do at every chief feast. And as soon as Taliesin entered the hall, he placed himself in a quiet corner, near the place where the bards and the minstrels were wont to come in doing their service and duty to the king, as is the custom at the high festivals when the bounty is proclaimed.

Having arrived, the young bard loiters at the threshold – perhaps in the gatehouse, the ruin of which can still be seen on Deganwy's heights. Like the young Irish hero Setanta, the embryonic Cuchullain, Taliesin must overcome the 'threshold guardians' of the royal bards – Maelgwn's 'guard-dogs' of verse, his spin-doctors who help maintain his aura of power. He disarms his foes with his first display of enchantment, 'acting the fool':

And so, when the bards and the heralds came to cry largess, and to proclaim the power of the king and his strength, at the moment that they passed by the corner wherein he was crouching, Taliesin pouted out his lips after them, and played "Blerwm, blerwm," with his finger upon his lips. Neither took they much notice of him as they went by, but proceeded forward till they came before the king, unto whom they made their obeisance with their bodies, as they were wont, without speaking a single word, but pouting out their lips, and making mouths at the king, playing "Blerwm, blerwm," upon their lips with their fingers, as they had seen the boy do elsewhere. This sight caused the king to wonder and to deem within himself

that they were drunk with many liquors. Wherefore he commanded one of his lords, who served at the board, to go to them and desire them to collect their wits, and to consider where they stood, and what it was fitting for them to do. And this lord did so gladly. But they ceased not from their folly any more than before. Whereupon he sent to them a second time, and a third, desiring them to go forth from the hall. At the last the king ordered one of his squires to give a blow to the chief of them named Heinin Vardd; and the squire took a broom and struck him on the head, so that he fell back in his seat. Then he arose and went on his knees, and besought leave of the king's grace to show that this their fault was not through want of knowledge, neither through drunkenness, but by the influence of some spirit that was in the hall.

Taliesin, at a tender thirteen years of age, has managed to defeat Maelgwn's twenty-four royal bards, including Heinin Vardd, the chief bard of the court, who is disgraced before all. Heinin, gathering his wits a little, is able to explain that it is not through any lack of ability or dereliction of duty that he is not able to perform – his 'bardic droop' has been caused by another kind of spirit. He names his demon:

And after this Heinin spoke on this wise. "Oh, honourable king, be it known to your grace, that not from the strength of drink, or of too much liquor, are we dumb, without power of speech like drunken men, but through the influence of a spirit that sits in the corner yonder in the form of a child."

Maelgwn realises what is afoot - suspecting sorcery, he summons the boy bard:

'Forthwith the king commanded the squire to fetch him; and he went to the nook where Taliesin sat, and brought him before

the king, who asked him what he was, and whence he came. And he answered the king in verse.

Now begins Taliesin's famous sequence of poems, which prove, if there was any doubt, he is the greatest bard there – a virtuoso performance. The poems are covered in detail in other texts (e.g. *The White Goddess*, Robert Graves; *Taliesin – the Last Celtic Shaman*, John Matthews) although it is difficult for there to be any definitive exegesis – each poem is packed with obscure references combining a beguiling mixture of invention and lost knowledge. The collection contained within this section may not all 'belong' to Taliesin directly – but be the result of several poets working over time in the Taliesin tradition. I have taken this route, finding the actual composition of a Taliesin style poem the most effective way to decode them – to 'understand' them as much as poems need to be 'understood' (they often work in the same way as music, in a subtler, more lateral way); and to get 'under the skin' of Taliesin. I have not been unique in finding this to be the case. John Cowper Powys, in his Dark Age epic, *Porius*, (1951; 2007) includes invented verses to Taliesin Penbeirdd. In a footnote he explains:

The exact period when Taliesin lived is not known, nor has it been possible to determine which of the many poems attributed to him are authentic. His verse had, however, a weirdly original character unlike that of any known poet except, perhaps, Walt Whitman. Its entirely individual character makes it easy for a writer who is no poet to imitate it, as has been done in this book. JCP

Nikolai Tolstoy adopted a similar approach in his unfinished Merlin trilogy, *The Coming of the King*, although in it he attributes them to the famous magician who seems to follow an almost indistinguishable Bildungsroman as Taliesin.

Perhaps more faithfully than anyone poet, Vernon Watkins,

who lived on the Gower Peninsula, South Wales – where the historical Taliesin was said to have been based – has maintained the Taliesin Tradition in poems such as 'Taliesin in Gower', and 'Taliesin and the Spring of Vision'. In 'Taliesin and his Mockers', a riposte to: *'Those hired musicians,/They at Court/Who command the schools'*, Watkins adopts the sardonic stance of the Penbeirdd who has seen the creation of the world:

> *Who has discerned*
> *The voice of lightning,*
> *Or traced the music*
> *Behind the eyes?*

It is the poet's job to trace the music behind the eyes, to discern and translate the 'voice of lightning' – to transform the flash of inspiration into gramarye. And so here is my very own Hanes Taliesin, created soon after Taliesin 'took over my life', during my year as Bard of Bath:

The Song of Taliesin

I hail from the realm of the summer stars –
I am the living memory of Merlin.
My lord, Elphin, caught me in a weir –
His bard I became: behold, Taliesin.

Yet this is but one branch of my ancestry –
Before I was a boy as old as history...

I have been a mountain hare, crazy-eyed, tail high,
I have been a silver salmon swimming up stream,
I have been the king of the birds, catching sky,
I have been a wheaten seed of golden gleam –
Swallowed into the belly of the Black Hen.
By White Sow reborn,

A helpless babe on a boundless sea –
Deep waters where I was also the wind's shadow,
The wrathful wave upon promontory.

My eyes are the fiery tears of the sun,
My Muse from the Moon Queen's Cauldron.

Poetry is my spear,
I am a warrior of words!
I know the lays of this land
And the language of birds,
The tongue of stone
And the song of trees
And the forest of your families.

I know the first name of constellations,
The blessed ancestors
And the Undying Ones.

I was born when the world was still in womb,
I shall be with humanity 'til the crack of doom.
Proud kingdoms I have seen ebb and flow,
Their glory I have sung and echoed their woe.

My curriculum vitae is universal and timeless,
I am the quicksilver serpent of the caduceus.
By fire and fur and feather and scale,
I, Taliesin, bid thee hail!

Songs of Freedom

And while he was thus singing his verse near the door, there arose a mighty storm of wind, so that the king and all his nobles thought that the castle would fall on their heads. And

the king caused them to fetch Elphin in haste from his dungeon, and placed him before Taliesin. And it is said, that immediately he sang a verse, so that the chains opened from about his feet.

Art can set us free. It can make our souls soar. Anthropologist, Mircea Eliade, in the epilogue to his seminal *Shamanism: techniques of ecstasy* writes: '*Poetic creation still remains an act of perfect spiritual freedom*', (p510). He connects the ecstatic states of the shaman with those of poetic composition:

> *The purest poetic act seems to re-create language from an inner experience that, like the ecstasy or the religious inspiration of "primitives," reveals the essence of things.*
> (ibid, p510)

It is this essence of things which all true poets seek to express, to unlock. William Blake, in his poem 'The Crystal Cabinet' included in the Pickering Manuscript, describes how he is taken into the Otherworld by a Muse-figure, placed into a crystal cabinet, not dissimilar to the crystal cave of Merlin, the tower of seventy-seven windows his sister Ganeida builds for the magician, or the place of poetic initiation – Caer Arianrhod – with its revolving silver wheel. From here he beholds 'another London' and tries to 'seize the inmost form' – the essence of things – perhaps to take back to manifest in this world through his art, but this breaks the spell, the crystal cabinet bursts, and he is ejected from paradisal intimacy with his Muse. Blake is cast out, like the knight 'alone and palely loitering' in Keats' losing-the-Muse poem La Belle Dame Sans Merci.

The very word 'ecstatic' derives from the Greek ec' stasis – out of body. The shamanic trance enables the shaman to leave the confines of his mortal coil and journey to other worlds, as Taliesin's 'song' enables him to shapeshift. Art can provide a window to others worlds, even doorways. It can provide a means for us to escape a mundane existence, like Gwion Bach – who leaves his village to become a bard – and to live a creative life. By finding your song, you are finding your soul path – your road to personal happiness – fulfilment on a deep soul level, by honouring your creativity. Expressing your essence. Your soul-song. So many do not, and sicken. Families, communities, and society become diseased because of its lack. We fail to connect with ourselves – our true Selves. And the soul of the land. The spirit of place in us and around us. We are mostly self-imprisoned. Blake called these shackles of social conditioning 'the mind forg'd manacles'. We made them and we can shatter them – with bold acts of the imagination, with leaps of compassion and logic, pushing the envelope of what is possible, like Wilberforce did, like Obama. We can all sing our songs of freedom.

The Song of Awen

I am the awen,
Mysterious inspiration
That moves Shakespeare's quill –
Waterfall of spirit
Flowing through all.
I spark the fire in the head.
The poet I make tremble and quake,
The lesser pathways to take.
I am the lightning in the brain,
The quickening in the blood,
flickering tongues of flame.

I feed on warmth and light.
In merriment and good company
I manifest best at night.
Faces aglow in friendship and love

Around the hearth and pyre.
The loom of conversation woven
From the thread of voice,
The warp and weft of gaze and touch,
The whorl of love.

I quicken men's minds to eloquence and wit,
Through me the musician's hands move faster,
The instrument becomes invisible,
The apprentice becomes the dancer.
I make brows glisten and shine,
The spark divine flash within bodies.
I have been present since the first fire
Was stolen from the skies.

When men touched mystery
And gave it song.

When the secret names of Creation
Were found on the tip of the tongue.
When the world was sung into being
And the story paths were first walked,
The labyrinth of myth explored,
Monsters slain on glittering hoard.

Elusive muse, men have chased my
Evanescent gleam through
The glimmering of their own soul forests
Since desire first met with dream.
They have rendered me
With their unattainable perfection,
Dressed me in a thousand names.
Given me qualities they possess
And made me play their Eros games.

Women see me as their shadow lover,
The tall, dark stranger,
Their daemon, their anima.
From the dripping foliage I step,
Into the red bed chamber I slip,
Through the window of moonlight,
Ready to whisper and caress,
With strong hands secrets undress.

I gave mankind languages,
Helped them to express
Their needs and fears.
Unlock memory's palace,
Where the treasures of wisdom can be stored.
Hieroglyphs and alphabets
Set in stone. Wood-words, clay-words,
Rosettas and runes. Codex and tablets,
Bibles and folios. The word forged the world.
Through me civilisations were built.
Laws enshrined, a nation's pride –
Its philosophy and poetry,
Plays and prayers.
It has raised men to greatness,
Summoned symphonies and cathedrals,
Treaties and accords,
All that is noblest the awen has born –

I am the awen,
My river flows on.
On my quicksilver web,
We are all one.

Finding the Treasure

Taliesin's release of Elphin – vindicating his claims in Maelgwn's court that he had the best of wives and the best of bards – has a surprising 'third act'. Elphin has been cleared of all charges. Taliesin has sung him free from his chains. Maelgwn had been forced to eat humble pie. They would have been wise, one would think, to make good their escape there – to 'cut their losses'. Instead Taliesin risks all they have gained – the good name of Elphin, Elphin's wife and himself – for one final gambit. He challenges Maelgwn to a horse race:

Then he bade Elphin wager the king, that he had a horse both better and swifter than the king's horses. And this Elphin did, and the day, and the time, and the place were fixed, and the place was that which at this day is called Morva Rhiannedd: and thither the king went with all his people, and four-and-twenty of the swiftest horses he possessed. And after a long process the course was marked, and the horses were placed for running. Then came Taliesin with four-and-twenty twigs of holly, which he had burnt black, and he caused the youth who was to ride his master's horse to place them in his belt, and he gave him orders to let all the king's horses get before him, and as he should overtake one horse after the other, to take one of the twigs and strike the horse with it over the crupper, and then let that twig fall; and after that to take another twig, and do in like manner to every one of the horses, as he should overtake them, enjoining the horseman strictly to watch when his own horse should stumble, and to throw down his cap on the spot. All these things did the youth fulfil, giving a blow to every one of the king's horses, and throwing down his cap on the spot where his horse stumbled. And to this spot Taliesin brought his master after his horse had won the race. And he caused Elphin to put workmen to dig a hole there; and when they had dug the ground deep enough, they found a large cauldron full of gold.

And then said Taliesin, 'Elphin, behold a payment and reward unto thee, for having taken me out of the weir, and for having reared me from that time until now.' And on this spot stands a pool of water, which is to this time called Pwllbair.

This, it soon becomes apparent, is no ordinary horse race. Maelgwn is going to pitch his two dozen horses against Taliesin's one. Once again, the number twenty-four appears – the same number as Maelgwn's bards. It is number which appears in other stories from the *Mabinogion* – usually in an otherworldly context, e.g. four and twenty maidens of rare beauty. Of course, the famous nursery rhyme mentions four and twenty blackbirds baked in a pie – in itself a disturbing image! But what significance does it have here? It seems too much of a coincidence that it matches exactly the hours in a day. When this collection was first written down the 'Book of Hours' was a popular Medieval form. Yet perhaps it signifies something more literal – that treasure can be found in any hour of the day. What Fiona Macleod called *The Immortal Hour* in his famous play performed in Glastonbury in the Twenties, Kathleen Raine echoed this by saying *'the immortal hour is always now'*. Every moment is precious and filled with potential. Blake was very eloquent about this, not only in his famous lines: *'To see a world in a grain of sand and heaven in a wild flower, to hold infinity in the palm of your hand and eternity in an hour'*, but also in his poem 'The Building of Time':

Every Time less than a pulsation of the artery
Is equal in its period and value to Six Thousand Years;
For in this Period the Poet's Work is done; and all the great
Events of Time start forth and are conceiv'd in such a Period,
Within a Moment, a Pulsation of the Artery.

The twenty-four horses could be actual letters of the alphabet (bearing in mind the Welsh language does not have an 'x' or 'z') – which the bard commands in his craft. The twenty-four burnt holly sticks sound very particular – as though a divination system, or alphabet. Could this be referring to the prognostications of runes or the Ogham alphabet, which for a master bard like Taliesin would have been his 'secret language', in the same way Latin has been for doctors for centuries. The apparent problem with this theory is there are twenty-five Ogham – but Taliesin would make it up to the correct number. Certainly it seems like an odd horse racing practising – hitting the rival steeds with blackened holly sticks. This echoes a part of the British ballad, 'Sir John Barleycorn': 'They sent men with holly clubs, to beat the flesh from bones'.

The youth who is charged to ride 'his master's horse' (the identity of the rider is not revealed) is told to throw down his cap when his horse stumbles. This seems to symbolise 'losing one's head', but also could signify the 'head of a river' – this is the source of the wealth. Here, hidden treasure lies, waiting to be discovered. This could be the gold of wisdom within all of us, or within each moment.

What is most telling about this episode is that the treasure is contained within a cauldron – echoing Ceridwen's own (indeed it could be said to be the Crooked One's broken cauldron restored. In Celtic myth there is the legend of the four-sided cup. If four untruths were said over it, it would break. If four truths were spoken, it would mend. Perhaps Taliesin's noble actions have restored that which he shattered in his earlier incarnation as the inept 'sorcerer's apprentice'). We have come full circle in the story – and the rounded cauldron represents that wholeness. Buried beneath the earth, it is a chthonic mandala. It could be seen as the Earth itself, now healed. For we have travelled from the poisoning of horses to a spectacular horse race, as though Gwyddno's horses have been resurrected. Even though there is no direct connection made here, the symbolism speaks volumes. That what was broken has now been mended. Harmony with the Earth has been restored. The cosmic order is once more in place, the hours of the day race once more and the world can continue. All karmic debts are repaid in full (if we see Afagddu as a stage of Taliesin's development, along with Creirwy and Gwion Bach, rather than aggrieved half-brother – the alchemical 'slag' that has resulted in achieving the Philosopher's Stone). The lead of the uninitiated soul has become the gold of the Shining Brow.

Taliesin is now free to follow his destiny – as head-bard of Albion, Penbeirdd, to Arthur no less. Legend meets legend and the game begins in earnest.

Now I shall turn to my own experience of walking the Way of Awen – because, ultimately, this is what matters: how we walk our talk; how we manifest the wisdom and eloquence of the Taliesinic Force in all of our lives.

All that can be learnt from these tales of transformation needs to be applied to one's life for it to have an especial validity. For me, such myths and legends are always relevant – for beneath their shifting patterns and paradigms, they say something universal about the human condition. What does it mean to be alive in this life? How should one act? How is it possible to stay on the path – and how it is necessary to sometimes stray from it? To journey in one's story, while seeing outside of it. To be both the teller and the told. And what happens when bard meets world.

Taliesin's Apprentice:
Journal of a Bard

Here are extracts from my journals, notebooks and, more recently my blog, kept over twenty years, relating to my journey as a bard. They are transcribed verbatim to preserve the archival integrity of them as the 'tree rings' of my growth [the only modern additions being my comments/clarifications in square brackets]. At times my younger self writes things that seem cringeworthy in hindsight, but I wish to remain true to the experience -- and my learning curve, from foolish 'Gwion Bach' onwards. To begin with, an edited selection from my embryonic Year One, 1991, when I turned twenty one and came of age in unexpected ways. This was a pivotal year for me – my Gap Year when I finally stepped off the treadmill of formal education through which I had been channelled since the age of five. Although it had been building since at least 1989, with inklings of 'something more', something beyond the mundane surface of things, 1991 was the year when the 'lights switched on' – when my inner world started to manifest in my outer world; when I started to walk my talk (co-running a 'find your path' series of talks; organising a Greenpeace benefit). It was the first year that I decided to celebrate the full turning of the wheel, marking each festival of the pagan calendar with ceremony, poetry and pilgrimage. The year I began the Way of Awen.

My Pen is a Traveller
1st March 1991

...As my pen is a traveller upon these pages, so this journal begins with a journey... [of creativity – to work on a short film with an old school friend and fellow art student Garrie Fletcher]. I was glad to get away from the old town – things were getting on top of me a bit: last night's disappointment; the lack of any female company; the lack of direction, enthusiasm or amicability in the group; and financial hassles at home [the latter mirroring Elphin's domestic misfortune – his father had lost all of his horses due to the cauldron-spill]. Thus, this weekend provided a convenient escape route.

The journey there was horrendous (an interminable train journey – delays caused by a bomb-scare in London, which affected even my journey north to Bradford). ...Later on I had an inspiring conversation with this charismatic bloke met when packed in by the toilets. We talked of ambition and how he had achieved his, through sheer discipline and dedication. 'If you want it, here it is, come and get it.'

There's nothing really stopping one from achieving one's goals apart from oneself – the greatest hurdle that must be overcome. You must become the taskmaster – if something is really worth it then it warrants hard work...it's not enough to want to do something, one has to say 'I will do it!' and then do it, and *see it through to completion*. [I was reading Carlos Castaneda's classic, *The Teachings of Don Juan* on the way up]. Don Juan said it all:

'for me there is only travelling on the paths that have heart, on any path that may have heart. There I travel, and the only worthwhile challenge is to traverse its full length. And there I travel looking, looking, breathlessly.'

The Search Inside
3rd March 1991

It's interesting to note that Garrie's film ('She Said' – after the Beatles' track 'She Said She Said') has several themes that are pertinent to me and what Zeitgeist [an arts initiative I set up with my friend Justin Porter] has been doing.

[Esoteric knowledge being one of them: 'She said "I know what it's like to be dead..."' Lennon/McCartney]

One of the universal ideas in his work is 'a man in search of

himself' and going on a journey to do so, i.e. finding oneself –
something I considered before, realising that exploration has to
be internal.

Healing the Wasteland
5th March 1991
…Gazing from my window, I witness the poisoned surroundings
– the train runs along the gashes that scar the countryside. Stirred
by this grey unpleasant land, I write about the wasteland – and
makes me realises how much needs healing, and how little we
do.

A Glorious Day
13th March 1991
A glorious day – the skies cleared and the Sun's warmth was felt
upon the Earth. Nature excelled Herself. She danced in joy and
the world danced with Her. The Spring Maiden was in the air,
intoxicating everyone with Her heady perfume.

The Spinning Wheel
14th March 1991
Meditation: first I saw a white horse galloping along riderless –
was it Epona (the great white horse forever running the dragon
paths of the land)? Then, a labourer quenching his thirst in the
stream before resting in the shade of the oak after his morning's
toil. It was mid-day, midsummer. The heat pressed down upon
everything, like an iron. The stifling stillness was split by a
scream – he run up the dusty track to an isolated dwelling in the
copse. He found a spinning wheel and a dead woman –
murdered by the men in black that were scuttling away over the
horizon. I felt this scene actually happened – witch-hunters
executing a local wise woman.

Finding the Celtic Muse

[I had become increasingly obsessed by all things Celtic and read anything I could get my hands on. There seemed to be some real glimmers of magic here, something within reach. I was inspired to go on a pilgrimage to Croagh-Patrick after watching Frank Delaney's TV series on *The Celts*, which showed footage of pilgrims ascending the mountain in the West of Ireland on the Sunday nearest Lughnasadh – a tantalising vestige of pre-Christian tradition, blended with the Catholic against a stunning backdrop. There was also a family connection I wished to explore. So, 'young, gifted and broke' I decided to hitchhike across Ireland – making pilgrimage to the sacred mountain – and in doing so, I found my Celtic Muse.]

Hitching to Ireland
31st July 1991

This is it! I awoke early and packed my kit, leaving the flat at eleven o'clock without looking back. I headed through town to the old house, getting a flavour of walking with a pack on my back. It was good to get moving.

I reached Eastfield Road – Dad was in. He had bad news about my railcard but I knew I would hitch if I had to anyway. I cashed my giro and Dad drove me up to my grandparents to pick up my tent. He drove me out to my first destination, Weedon, where we stopped for a drink. The Guinness gave me a taste of things to come – one for the road! Father was pleased to see me off, he even made me some sandwiches – peanut butter and jam, yum! I think he was glad to see me make the most of my freedom, doing something that he would like to do, and in all likelihood, will, if I connected with his old pal, whose address he thrust into my hands just before we parted company. The moment was charged with significance – we had a drink in the Globe and now the whole world was at my feet, and we left each other at the crossroads. A father was seeing his son off, his presence was an approval I for once appreciated.

I hit the road and walking out 'into the wilderness', not knowing what fate may befall me. It was an exhilarating feeling, the freedom mixed with uncertainty. I was in the hands of destiny now.

[I stuck out my thumb, and got my first lift ten minutes later – I was on my way! I connected with my fellow traveller further down the road – Jason Lineham – we had set out independently hoping to improve our chances, planning to rendezvous at Holyhead. We ended up getting a lift from a boy-racer who took us all the way to the terminal at break-neck speed. He boasted about how he had recently crashed his own car. He claimed he was driving his mother's car back from his girlfirend's but we weren't entirely convinced – had he stolen the car or not? He talked about accompanying us to Ireland, but we were glad when he left us at a service station outside Bangor!]

...Our next lift took us the short way to the coast. It was a good feeling seeing the ocean. The sun was low in the west, the water was ablaze with golden flames. It was satisfying to have come this far, yet we were so close to Holyhead – it would've been agonizing to have been stuck, and we very nearly were. We walked for ages, the beauty of the vista losing it's novelty as we lugged our packs along the long and winding coastal road.

[We eventually got a couple more lifts, made it to the terminal in time for last orders and crossed over that night, bumming a lift with a kind woman, a teacher – toasting the dawn in from the prow of the boat with a pint of Guinness, hailing Lughnasadh as we arrived on Erin's shores! We made our way to Dublin where we booked into a hostel. Exploring the city, we befriended some locals, who gave us a taste of city's mighty nightlife. We were offered a place to crash – which was a stroke of luck, having lost our bunks at the hostel. The next day our host, Colum, offered to take us on 'an authentic tour of Dublin': Bram Stoker's house; Parliament building – where I sat in the PM's chair; and Trinity College, where I beheld the Book of Kells]

The Work of Angels
2nd August 1991

...The library [Trinity College] is like a church, full of awe and knowledge – something that deserves reverence. There was an exhibition on astrology 'Vox Stellarum', which was a bit of a coincidence. I was awestruck by all the old books, none more so than the sacred text itself. Seeing it was a religious experience, I was spellbound. There were two of the gospels out – Luke and Mark, the latter being the equivalent of Leo [lion the traditional symbol of this Saint/Archangel]. Their power and beauty was truly amazing – the detail was beyond belief, definitely divinely inspired. I had seen the face of God in those infinitesimally small spirals. Wow!

[Jason wasn't feeling too good and suddenly decided to head back home – somewhat dampening our pilgrimage together. I was determined to continue, realising this was something I had to do for and by myself.]

Divine Intervention
3rd August 1991

[Left Dublin at 4pm, after a farewell drink with Colum. He and his friend seemed sceptical about my chances of reaching Croagh-Patrick by thumb – and that was all the spur I needed]. I had faith in myself. I knew I would make it. When you are on the holy road of pilgrimage, you are a holy fool and everything seems to conspire to help you reach your destination – because you are doing it with the right intent, a ley-line of love and spirit. After waiting for ages I got the lift with my name on – taking me 222 miles across Ireland from a charming old archaeologist interested in Celtic myth and word origins – my angel!

...We stopped off at an ancient Hill of Inauguration no more than a grassy hillock now guarded by frisky cattle.

I got dropped off at Foxford about 11 pm. I got something to eat at the Cosmo Restaurant, a friendly chippy. I was determined to keep going so I walked out into the darkness, fifty miles from my destination. I was in the middle of nowhere, in the middle of the night and I didn't seem to mind, it was quite fun.

I came upon an unusual sight – a glowing shrine to Mary, lit-up neon pink in the night. I took this as a sign in my hour of need, although not too seriously. I prayed for a lift and voila – one turned up! A car full of young people, off clubbing! They took me to Castlebarr, where I kept on walking, the momentum of my will carrying me along.

The chances of a lift were minimal, but by God I got one! My pilgrimage was blessed, it seemed. I got to Westport and couldn't believe it – I'd almost made it. Delirious with success and exhaustion, I stumbled into the night, resolving to get as close as possible to this Holy Mountain. I came to the sea; it was a beautiful still midsummer's night. I found a couple of trees to shelter me and fell asleep, resting in the arms of the Goddess.

Top of the World
4th August 1991

I awoke at dawn, sleeping between two trees, overlooking the sea. I could have been anywhere or when; I was a child of nature, resting in Her garden. It was the first time I had slept in the open [without a tent] it was a special feeling. I had a simple breakfast, packed up and hit the road. The mountain was further away than I had thought – it was a substantial trek to get there – but so is anything worth getting to. I put my nose to the grindstone and trod tarmac – sometimes you know you're not going to get a lift.

I reached the local watering hole where I had a much needed drink and dumped my pack before beginning my ascent. I started my climb at 13:00 hrs. I learnt a lot on the way up – it took a lifetime to climb...

It was a dream come true just to have made it there, the journey in itself was an initiation. I felt privileged to walk upon those slopes; it was an ancient, sacred place. I may have been there at the 'wrong time' for the [official] pilgrimage but it was the right time for me. I wasn't doing it in honour of Saint Patrick, I was doing it for Lugh, for myself and because it's there!

No great enlightened thoughts entered my head while I was climbing it (in fact most of them were blasphemous) only a feeling – it was an extreme experience, one to savour for ever.

The first half of the journey was tough going – mainly because of doubt, I think – because the second half wasn't any less easy. I felt unfit, I almost felt unworthy, as if the mountain was rejecting me. I could have turned back so easily, but it was only faith that kept me going and [that] can move any mountain.

The climb was an exercise in will and endurance. It was a test of strength and faith (in oneself) and humbleness, as one had to accept the dominance of nature and man's insignificance in comparison. One developed a respect for the mountain in climbing it – a bond was forged through a mutual experience. It was exhilarating and life-affirming.

As I reached the half-way point, the crest of the hill, I was blasted by an awesome gust which quite literally took one's breath away. One couldn't ignore nature here.

There followed a plateau of peace, which allowed one to recover and resolve oneself to the final half. I was overcome by a sense of well-being; the magic of the place had taken over. I chatted to an old man making the climb; we are all making that mountain climb – it's up to the individual if they want to go higher.

The second half of the ascent was ridiculous – all loose rocks, one just had to scramble up, rather like in the Stairway to Heaven picture. The miracle was I got blown up this part – the wind was behind me.

Beyond the point of giving up, one just kept going – it was as simple as that. In one of those legendary moments, I stumbled onto the summit, 2530 ft above sea level – I had made it! I kissed the cross in respect and thanks, then just sat and contemplated my achievement – I was on top of the world, ma!

I couldn't believe the sight I was seeing – the view over Clew Bay with its '365 islands' was truly magnificent, almost unreal. It was the kind of beauty one only sees second-hand, in film or photograph – one becomes desensitised to it. I had to almost keep pinching myself.

Sitting on top of Croagh-Patrick I was overwhelmed by a sense of total fulfilment – I had achieved this goal, but I knew it was only one of many. Like the multiple 'Heavens' in *Jonathan Livingstone Seagull,* paradise is only the next step up from this plane – there is always room for improvement. When one plateau is reached it can be used as a platform for the next initiative.

I had achieved what I had come to Ireland to do; Croagh-Patrick… I could have left at that point totally satisfied, however, when a goal has been attained it dawns on one that it was only a rung up the ladder and not an end unto itself. The mountain's peak wasn't my journey's end; it was where it truly began. A launch pad to higher things. Pilgrim's progress, they don't stand still. I left the mountain thirsty for more. The road was open to me now, my journey was a book yet unwritten.

I stuck my thumb out once again, letting the wheels of fortune take me where they will…

[I got a lift with two down-to-earth Irish guys who plied me with Guinness and took me to a wake; spent at a night camping at Aasleagh Falls – location for the Jim Sheridan film, *The Field*; then onto Galway, where I pitched by Spanish Arch and met a lovely local lass in Eyre Square]

A Golden Day in Gort
7th August 1991

[I hitched to Gort, where an old friend of my Dad's lived – Greg Lundon – whom he befriended when they worked together as young men. Greg became my Dad's best man. He hadn't seen him for over twenty years, but had kept in touch with the odd

Christmas or birthday card. I had never met the man, but I thought it would be interesting to call in on one of my father's old buddies, and so, with the confidence of youth, I rocked up on Greg's doorstep and knocked. A woman answered it. I wasn't sure how to introduce myself: 'the son of an old friend of Greg's'. I said is 'your father there?', expecting an older man, in fact it turned out to be her husband, so I think she was flattered! Greg, when he made the connection, invited me in and was extremely hospitable considering he'd never met me before and I hadn't contacted him in advance. He let me put my tent up in the garden, his wife made me a snack and then we sat at the kitchen table, sharing our stories. Later he took me on a tour of the area.

I had arrived like the unnamed Taliesin in the leather bag – and had been received most warmly by a kind hearted 'stranger'. In some ways Greg inadvertently played Elphin or Gwyddno to my embryonic bard!]

I know now the reason why I came to Ireland was to find my roots [my father's backstory] and that's exactly what I've done. I've come to terms with my past before dealing with the future – the time here has been spent as a period of self-clarification, initiation and dedication; a rites of passage from one phase of my life to the next; I returned a new man, I had come of age.

Later I wrote to an old friend saying I had got lost in Ireland to find myself and that is what happened. I realised what I was capable of, how far I could push myself. When I arrived in Ireland it felt like I was coming home, which is perplexing initially because of my absence of relatives or apparent connection with the place. However, coming here I found out about my father's past through his old friend, Greg Lundon who I met today when I reached Gort. It's funny how I had to come all this way to find out about one of the closest people to me.

My connection with the Emerald Isle is multi-faceted, if tenuous, I was never happy with my name until I found out about its Celtic/Irish origins – here, at least, it is an acceptable name. A strange thought entered my head – that perhaps my parents chose my (Irish) name because of their meeting with Greg (my father's best man). It could possibly go back further than that, with my mother's early interest in Ireland show by a school project she did. She desperately wanted to go there and perhaps I finally satiated that subliminal urge for her.

Hypothesising even further – my interest in the Celtic Tradition maybe the legacy of a past life – who knows?

...Thank you mother and father, for everything.

The Tower of Poetry

The actual place itself [Gort] is packed full of little historical idiosyncrasies, but the main treasures lie just a few miles out of town. The first one I was shown to [by my kind host, Greg] was this amazing monastery with a twisted tower straight out of a fairytale [Kilmacduagh Monastery, 7th Century 'church of Duagh's son']. This place was magical alright. We then headed down to Coole Park, which was the location of WB Yeats' famous poem, 'The Wild Swans at Coole'. We walked through gloom of the forest as night drew in until we came to the lake view, which was magnificent. The sun was just going down behind the trees in the west, silhouetting them with a deep golden glow. The rest of the sky was cool blue burning purple. The water was still and soothing. The effect was totally enchanting. It was one of the most breath-taking sights I had ever seen. I had found my Celtic twilight.

I find a real attraction to the poet Yeats, his special mixture of the poetic and Hermetic. Earlier we had visited his old residence, the wonderful Thoor Ballyleee – an isolated tower with its own river and woodland – no wonder he was so damned inspired. There is certainly something about Ireland that makes one want to put pen to paper, as you can see!

[Hitched back across Ireland. Visited Newgrange. Spent a night at Janet and Stewart Farrar's place – though, alas, the host's themselves were out; met up with Colum in Dublin; then caught the ferry and train back home, with my head and heart brimming with Celtic magic and golden memories.]

A Blaze of Creativity
16th December 1991

[Throughout this year I worked on what was to become my first poetry collection]

I will break the ice even further with an explosion of eloquence in the form of 'Remembrance Days' – my anthology of writing for 1991. I will send it to my friends, valuing their opinion and wanting to share my thoughts and feelings with them. My life shifts between extremes – silence followed by pages of poetry, stillness shattered by delirious dancing. I will end the year in a blaze of creativity.

Remembrance Days
17th December 1991

Today I completed my [hand-written] manuscript ready to be printed by Ted [the Qabalist – a spitting image of Alec Guinness and as grumpy], or so I thought. It was an outlandish demand to make unexpectedly; he couldn't possibly (have) done it in time – so the responsibility lay with me. If you want something doing…

It resolved me to get the manuscript printed myself, by hook or by crook.

I stayed in all day and wrote the final poem of my yearly sojourn – Epiphany the last turn of the wheel. It was an achievement to be proud of – my first year as a 'poet' commemorated by the publication of an anthology of my writing – the year in the life of… It encapsulated so many things for me. It was a statement signifying many things – in some ways it is an attempt to reach out and touch – to share with people my thoughts and feelings – to communicate. I hope the work provides an insight, at least – into themselves, if not into me. Into Nature. I want it to be a mirror, used to reflect on. Look back in wisdom. The best I can hope for is that they (the poems) transcend their personal idiosyncracies and develop a universal appeal. Let people get of out of them what they will. The poems will live and die in other people's minds and hearts. At least if I died tomorrow there is something for people to remember me by. [I printed 20 and gave them to my friends for Yule gifts – hardly a guarantee of literary immortality! At the time though it felt like I had finally done something of value and 'permanence' – and indeed I have found the Wheel of the Year a priceless discovery and I still perform a couple of poems from that first, flawed collection.]

Burning the Midnight Oil
18th December 1991

[I've never mastered touch-typing, but my typing was even slower when I typed up my first poetry collection... Home PCs were rare back then in my neck of the woods. I had to go to Coventry Poly where I was studying Fine Art. Even then I only got to use an electronic typewriter!]

I set off for Coventry, armed only with my manuscript. I was determined to get it all typed up, come hell or high water... The typewriter was there, thankfully, and I set to it. I was rather shaky at first, not having typed before [I managed to type the whole thing in capitals for some reason...] but after a couple of pages I was getting the hang of it and was picking up speed. I had twenty-four pages to type [like Maelgwn's bards and horses – a number that keeps cropping up]. I stuck at it all day, overwhelmed by my desire to complete the task, denying myself food or rest. This was the last 'mountain' I had to climb, and it demanded just as much stamina. I was lost in my work; it was travelling through the year again and was emotionally demanding. I was purging it all from my system with the stab of the keys. The typewriter is a wonderfully aggressive object – I took my angst out on it.

It was a monumental task [to tackle with my lack of skill] but I finished it, although somewhat later than planned… I packed up and went to leave the building only to find it was all locked up. It had gone twelve o'clock; everybody had gone home a long long time ago. I was trapped in a large building all on my own – it was the nightmare I had when I was a child, but then it was a shopping centre and all the dummies came alive. Here, the figures in the sculpture studio took on an eerie new aspect (as I searched for a way out). It was a hysterical situation, in both ways. I couldn't believe it was happening to me – I had just been plunged into a dark, disorientating world, a la Adrian Lyne's disturbing film *Jacob's Ladder*. It doesn't take much to transport oneself there. I eventually broke out and rushed to the station, but I was too late! I had missed the last train back. There was no way out!

I had considered my options and decided that the best thing to do would be to return to the art block and spend a night in my work space – at least it would be warm and dry and I would be undisturbed. Or so I thought. I bought some greasy food and sadly scoffed it as I 'broke' back into the building. I got a cup of tea and was just going to go up to my room when someone else came in after me! I managed to get out of the way in time to avoid my unseen assailant. I heard footsteps above me – it took me straight back to my childhood and the first book I bought: *Challenge in the Dark*. It could have been a security guard, the police, or another prowler. I thought I was rumbled. I heard whoever it was approach directly above me – if he had come down the stairs I would have been caught and would've had quite some explaining to do. Fortune smiled as he just got himself a drink from the vending machine and walked away. The biggest risk was yet to come – I had to get to my room, the chances of my discovery there would be lessened anyway. I had to get the lift, which would go by him. If he saw or heard the lift I would be caught. It was a shot in the dark, a spin of the wheel…and it worked! I made it to my room and finishing my food, made the semblance of a bed, out of sight, under my desk, and fell asleep, eventually.

My night in room 6.4 was restless and uncomfortable to say the least. I kept hearing noises and didn't know if, at any minute, I was to be discovered. I had to say 'come what may' and hit the hay.

In the morning I was woken by cleaners entering the room – they vacuumed around the table, but they didn't seem to see me. I felt like a vampire. The lurker in the shadows. How many times have we barely avoided discovery or being discovered? We live on a razor's edge.

I emerged from my cocoon and tried to make myself look presentable. It had been a night on the tiles alright. I felt rough indeed – not as bad as those who sleep on the streets, although I did get a flavour of what it felt like to be homeless.

Mortality and Nativity
23rd December 1991
Remembrance Days is a year in my life, albeit selected and coded, however it is still a powerful talisman that could be used to invoke me. It was kind of like giving birth – there's a lot of me in there. It may be my ticket to immortality, but it seems to have been draining me mortally. C'est la vie!

A Transformative Year
30th December 1991
This year has been the most incredible of my life – encompassing extremes of dizzying excellence and dismal depths.

…This was the year when I did things: moved out of home [for good – having previously left for college], started the [Zeitgeist] forum, hitched to Ireland, organised a festival, printed my poetry. I think I surprised a lot of people with my resolve and resourcefulness, including myself. In terms of achievement, it has been a tremendous year – I finally came into my own.

...This is the year I lost a meaning to life and found it again. I visited the underworld and came up laughing. I want to live more than anything. I have so much to do. The future looks bright. I hope I can rise to the challenge I've presented myself with. I can't let myself down now. I know I can do it.

***

[Throughout this period I was deeply interested in the shamanic path, especially the Beuysian notion of artist-as-shaman, inspired by the shamanic psychædelia of Jim Morrison and The Doors. Here's a quote from my notebook of the period, from Rogan P. Taylor's *The Death and Resurrection Show*:

Change causes terror. It can also create joy. It is feared and worshipped, pursued and shunned. Inevitable. Unavoidable. It is the very basis of our human nature.

We cannot escape this fact; to move or change from one state into another, we must pass through a third condition, which is neither one thing nor another. We humans are this third condition. We can no longer remember what it was that we were, nor yet know what we might become. All we can make out is Change itself.

Religion is a tool for both surviving and accomplishing transformation.]

Turning Point
31st December 1991

Today is the turning point of the year – it is like the summit of a mountain high as we can look back over the days gone and the days to come. Our memory recedes into the distance like foreign lands covered by clouds. We seem to have such power from our vantage point, selecting what we want from the year's events and obliterating those we want to forget. We can wipe people and places out with the minimum of effort – like dots of humans seen from the big wheel in *The Third Man*. As the Gods are we at this turning point, like Janus looking backwards and forwards. We stand astride two years, seemingly master of both. We savour the fruits of successful projects and plan future triumphs, planting seeds in the orchards of our minds. It's an exhilarating feeling, akin to the momentary defiance of gravity when a car dips over a bridge, or a lift plummets away. We seem to levitate when in fact it is just a deceptive suspension. The momentum of the year has whirled us around, creating g-forces that lift us temporarily out of our seats. It is a time when the Law Wheel appears briefly stilled – we can do what we want for one night. The air is charged with expectation. Folk are intoxicated with uncertainty. They mark this day like the wall of a prison. We've 'done' another year of our life sentence, and tonight we're on parole. Let's party!

***

[Echoing Eliade's notion that shamans are technicians of ecstasy is this quote, from the same journal (Henry Miller, *Tropic of Cancer*, 1934): *'Do anything but let it yield ecstasy'*. I became very interested in the creative process, especially 'inspiration' itself – this became the subject of my Fine Art dissertation. In my notebook of the time is a quote from Louis Pasteur, cited by Arthur Koestler in *The Act of Creation*:

> *The grandeur of human action is measured by the inspiration from which they spring. Happy is he who bears a god within – an ideal of beauty and who obeys it, an ideal of art, of science. All are lighted by the reflection from the infinite.*]

The Wheel Turns

[The following year I completed my Fine Art Dissertation: 'Illumination: the divine experience of art', the writing of which taught something of the discipline of writing. Having grown disillusioned with the Fine Art world, which seemed overly concerned with the mundane, with commercialism and the cult of the personality, I turned my back on it and started to channel my creativity into writing instead. I found inspiration for my first novel, *The Ghost Tree*, which took two years to write. I started to attend poetry readings at the Royal Mail Club and joined the Northampton Poets, having my first poems officially published in their 'Stealing Ivy' collections. With this new company I participated in the John Clare Bicentenary Celebrations, reciting his work around the town and appear in the paper. I made pilgrimage to Helpstone to honour the so-called Peasant Poet. In 1993 I began performing poetry publically around my hometown and published my second poetry collection, 'A Pennyworth of Elevation'. I started to run open mic nights at a wine bar called Slurps. This was a popular venue because you got a free drink if you performed! In 1994 I completed my first collection of fairy stories, 'The Book of Make Believe'; and another poetry collection, 'Gramarye', which included 'The Bard's Prayer' (around this time I must have seen Robin Williamson perform at the Sunnyside Inn, Northampton – to behold and be entertained by a living breathing bard enthralled me: a formative experience). Perhaps inspired by this living legend – whom years later I was to meet and work with professionally – I decided to connect with another Celtic legendary bard. Over the last couple of years I had taken to visiting 'mythic sites' and writing about them, but it was time for another bardic pilgrimage inspired by a certain Scottish Border Ballad...]

On the Eildon Hills
14th June 1994

Here indeed is the entrance to fairyland! I am bedazzled by its beauty so that I find it difficult to leave. Each path I take doesn't take me further away but deeper into it. There is a labyrinth of pathways which it is easy to lose oneself in – and I do willingly, for this is as close as paradise gets.

I am sitting amid the dark green cushion of furze which upholsters the hills, upon the eastern side with the sun warming my face, the breeze refreshing my wings and the contours of the earth energising my legs.

I have never felt so alive. This is life. The real stuff – everything else is distraction. I feel at the centre of things here – the heartwood. Though the winds rage above me (1385ft – the tallest hill) it is so still here. I can hear birdsong; they call to each other as they fly below me. I am even above the birds. Higher than the birds. Now there's a phrase to play with.

I sit on the more sheltered side of Eildon, looking towards Earlston, where True Thomas was born and apparently buried. Further out, past the horizon – I can see a very long way, is the sea and Berwick-upon-Tweed, where first I alighted.

As I sit under a hawthorn tree (the Eildon Tree itself?) I feel so peaceful and content. Nothing else matters at this moment. I am resting on the bosom of the Goddess. It occurred to me just before I sat down that the three hills could represent the Triple aspect of the Lady of the Land. One seems quite rounded and resilient – the mother. The Tall one was harsh and haggard – the crone. Whilst this hill is the greenest and most pleasant, surrounded by a patchwork skirt of forest and field; her fertile flanks – the maiden. I'm glamoured by her summery aspect. Take me away, O fair queen!

Our Lady of the Eildons

Cloud shadows
Slide across her flanks,
Revealing a glimpse of furzey thigh,
A meadow sweet stream.
She sings to me,
In the teasing breeze of day,
Or the passionate soughing of night.
When she is adorned
With her most velvet gown, embroidered with golden flowers,
Bejewelled by the starry silver bells,
Brought out and dusted, until
They shine brighter than the sun.
You can see her smile in the nimbus of dusk,
As her pale teeth gleam through
Reflecting solar light.
Finally she is crowned with a lunar tiara –
but she is not the celestial majesty.
Oh no, her home is far nearer.
Close enough to touch.
Place your ear against her breast
And you may hear the thumping of her heart.
For you lie in the bosom of the Lady.
Safe in her soft sanctuary,
Though lost in another Laird's realm.
She will guide and goad,
When you slack from your pace.
Teacher and teaser,
Loving and loathing
In equal measure, but always for your own good.
Mistress of mischief and magic,
Carry me across your threshold,
Beyond the Borderlands into a bonnier scape.
Eildon Hills, 14th June 1994

[I didn't meet the Queen of Elfland, alas, but I was inspired by this numinous place, and by further Highland 'jaunts'. I had the bardic bug.]

The Foliate Mouth – Early Performances

[I had started to read my poems from early 1992, just as a means of getting them 'out there' and to share these magical places and energies that had inspired me. One May Day the green man burst into my life and has stayed there ever since. My green man poem – One With the Land – was one of the very first I wrote and is still one of my favourites. His energy took over me as I chanted it. It is a kind of shamanic invocation – yet at the same time cheeky and down-to-earth. I started to work with the different archetypes or god-forms in my poetry and performance. Come Lughnasadh 1994, three years on from my pilgrimage to Croagh-Patrick I was ready to attempt something ambitious. It would be the first time I was to attempt something truly bardic – a piece of ritual performance poetry based upon the green man in his summer guise, Sir John Barleycorn.]

Blood and Grain
1st August 1994

Phew! I have had a languid Lughnasadh after a hectic Lammas Eve yesterday. I was heavily involved with the Courtyard Fayre at Lowdown – the first summer Sunday 'Salad Daze' [my title] and hopefully not the last. The centre is threatened with closure and this was a fundraiser to help it stay open...

...I was 'entertainments manager', sorting out the performances.

Highlight of the first half was seeing my brother come down – after calling in to see him yesterday. And he came back later to catch some of my act – and he liked it! It was the first time he had seen me perform – see me as I really am. I was showing my true colours: the pagan flag was flying. I didn't pull any punches in my performance – I virtually relived my experience last year at West Kennet, blow by blow – Caroline thought I was tripping. The adrenalin certainly surged through me, or something like it. I shook like, well, a shaker, delivering my provocative discourse (or load of drivel). Triptych [myself, Andy Clayson, Dominic Reid-Jones] had spent less than a month getting the twenty minute mind-blowing epic poem of 'Vision Quest' [later retitled 'Last Rites for John Barleycorn'] together – an ambitious piece at the best of times. We have been rehearsing solidly for the last couple of weeks around here, at Hood St, or Justin's or Dom's. I am touched by the amount of dedication Dom and Andy put into it. Rob [Farmer] helped out, knocking up a backing track for us in a couple of days. It is so wonderful when one's vision becomes manifest – aided by talented people of similar inclination. As with Salad Daze, so with Triptych, a part of the whole – for me, its raison d'etre. In Vision Quest I pay homage to the spirit of the corn and the Goddess – John Barleycorn and the Mothersun. After much debate (in my own head) I decided to perform a communion of sorts, with ale and fresh bread. I had doubts as to its efficacy – how the audience would react, etc... but I did it, and, as the whole event proved – some thing done in the right spirit will pay off. The communion was a success as far as I could tell (I was chanting 'John Barleycorn is dead' throughout) thanks to Justin and Caroline passing around the beer and bread. Bless 'em!

Then, as the piece peaked, Sarah and Ian joined in the dancing, then others, until we got a circle dance going, singing 'hail to the mothersun' and 'let the sun shine'. It was magical. Although the performance was overtly pagan, the crowd seemed to take it in the spirit it was meant – one of celebration, sacrifice, seasonal synchronisation. Basically, a sacred drama to mark a special occasion. It helped that most of the audience were sympathetic to such things. The event was in fact more a kind of elaborate party, a fair for friends. [It was at this event I met Emily, a beautiful Italian-Iranian graduate who later became my girlfriend – thanks to her I moved to Bath. I had stepped into my power and my goddess of sovereignty had appeared...]

First Commissioned Poem
5th December 1994

A fine start to the festive month – I've been helping out at the NADACI [Northampton AIDS Day Arts Community Initiative] event at the Roadmender, helping to make gigantic red ribbons and lanterns, preparing the venue for the big launch on World AIDS Day – at which I was asked to read out a poem specially written for the occasion, in front of a room full of so-called VIPs (including – gosh – Countess Spencer!) I was just going to read out 'To Those Who Will Die In Vein' from the manuscript, but at the last moment, I decided to learn it off by heart (as befitting the performance). This I did with relative ease, but the actual stress of the anticipation and worry – In case I forgot or fluffed my lines – nearly creased me! Still, it was worth all the angst: I was having palpitations but at least appeared in control. People remarked how 'cool' I looked and how powerful my poem was – several came up to me afterwards to tell me so. I was rather light-headed with relief as much as my success – it is still sinking in. How can I bemoan my lack of recognition when I am asked to perform at such an event, get interviewed by local radio and receive an audience's acclaim? The honour and burden of having to encapsulate and summarise the spirit of the day meant more to me, and had more effect on me and created more response than anything I've done before. Far more important than getting printed in some dusty old journal!

It was an emotional evening and I felt almost out of depth – being a complete layman...

...I thought I may as well look the part – it helps people to suspend their disbelief, and helps me to get into character. A shaman's regalia is an intrinsic part of the act, not that you'd catch any medicine man worth his potions poncing around in my Romantic threads, but for that night I was the Byronic man.

[at this event I purchased my first 'bardic hat' – a velvet medieval-style hat onto which I attached a golden chain: behold the shining brow!]

My First Storytelling Performance
Mid-March 1995

The following evening I had far more fun – at Roz's Arthurian theme party. I went as a minstrel and told a couple of tales from *The Mabinogion* (Taliesin; and The Countess of the Fountain). I had been learning them all week and considering they were the first stories I've told in public without a script, they were successful. The first was more enjoyable for both parties I feel – the second one, only done after repeated request was too long for that time of the evening. A couple of people even nodded off! But I am only just started to learn this skill and art – one which I want to channel my energies into from now on. It is my destiny! An ideal way to travel, socialise, impart and receive wisdom, perform and play a role that appeals to my Romantic sensibilities. That night saw the birth of Taliesin's apprentice. It is a craft I have longed to learn, and I've finally begun in earnest.

[After a long trip around South-East Asia '95-'96 I moved to Bath, Somerset with my partner at the time, Emily Tavakoly – and that was when things really took off! I met a druid, a king, a faerie queen, a pixie, and a gentleman of the Sidhe – and became involved in the Bardic scene in the city. See *The Book of the Bardic Chair*, RJ Stewart Books, 2008]

Awakening into a World Asleep
22nd Dec 1998

Still enshrouded in dreams, the land is dimly remembered with half-forgotten features. A passenger, I journey along dark lanes to the sun stones to witness its rebirth. Gathering with other pilgrims, extras in a prehistoric epic, waiting in the wings while the stars make their dramatic entrance – King Arthur emerging out of the mists of myth to a horn blast. Mystified we are led by a woman's intuition straight to the Great Circle – first a mere mass of shadow, then slowly manifesting in their magnificence – the legendary Stonehenge! Magnetically we are drawn towards them, only to be repulsed by the shadow-wraiths. Escorted off the premises we join the other pilgrims. Waiting for the word. Painted and robed, they patiently and peacefully queue – English through and through. Albion's children, a tribe with no name. A family of the familiar kith and spirits kindred. Good natured we heed the law of the Lady. Then we begin, the procession moves, accompanied by mandolins and gongs, bodhrans and bells, through the tunnel to the other side. To the Giant's Dance…We circle the Great Wheel before forming a circle within. The ceremony begins. We sing the stones to life, tuning forks of infinity. They resonate until human and stone are in harmony. The chorus of the Dawn. We celebrate the return of the sun; its winter solstice rebirth. The salvation of the Earth! And the death of winter. A natural symbol of solar life, an acorn child is named by the oak priests and priestesses. A couple are handfasted for a year and a day, taking a leap into the future of a golden bouquet of mistletoe. The wheel of life turns once again… The sun rises within us all, the star fire is rekindled. After the longest night is the brightest dawn. The Children of Albion are reborn! The Ancestors descend in us inside these millennium stones.

Midwinter over Aquae Sulis
Above the dreaming valley
standing on an island in the air
I watch with widening eyes
the stars go to sleep
and the Earth's star awake.

The grey becomes green.
Frozen dew thaws from
holly bush and ivy tangle.
Robin jigs to dawn's tune.
Below, a black bird glides
across a world of white.

Winning a Chair
23rd December 1998

It is accomplished! The first festival of the Bardic Chair of Caer Badon is over and it was a success! Nearly a month of profound festivities we pulled off. New friends were made, old ones confirmed, people brought together, the song of life sung. From Samhain to the Winter Solstice – what an intense, exciting, exhausting time. From the moment we entered the gateway between the worlds things have not been normal. We have been in the lap of the Gods. Servants of the Great Festival. Our lives have not been our own. The last three months have been full on. It has tested all who have been involved but more than anyone, considering my total input, I feel I have been tested in the Green Chapel and *I have been found worthy*. Being awarded the Bardic Chair is my just rewards, surely, for all the effort I put into not only the festival but my submission – Spring Fall, which was the result of a good few months' work in the first half of the year. This certainly has been the Year of Bladud for me – I've become obsessed by him and Sulis to the exclusion of any other subject matter. Now it's time to look for fresh inspiration…

Luck in the Head
27th December 1998

With the Wales trip on the horizon I am turning my mind to the stories of that land – the *Mabinogion* is the Welsh Dreamtime cycle, mythologizing the landscape. Staying there for a few days will really help it to come alive. I want to shape some tales for the

Bladud Society – as 'Bard of Bath' now I feel it is my duty. I've been working on Bran and Branwen for some time but it hasn't materialised properly – now is its time. The Cult of the Severed Head has subconsciously welled up this year with my obsession for the 'solar pediment' – Bladud, Hermes, Sol or all three. The head has it! I think '99 could be the Year of the Head for me, starting with Bran and ending with Janus. As we 'head' towards the Twenty First century, what better symbol. In these hedonistic times one must be careful not to lose one's head! The head must be always in touch with the heart to stop it flying off into the emotionless abstract.

My mind is bursting with colour. I must paint! For too long have I been fallow with my own art – although I see the BC Festival [my name for the pre-millennium Bardic Chair Festival] as a work of art, community art. Having just seen Vincent Ward's visionary film, *What Dreams May Come*, I am inspired to explore and portray the Otherworlds myself. If I am truly to be an artist then I must cleanse the doors of my perception. I have to paint what I see (in my mind's eye). In these darkest nights it is time to light the candle of vision. God is light!

Recalling the dawn at Stonehenge, there was no visible sunrise but the sun shone within us (except the guards and police).

'He whose face gives no light shall never become a star.' William Blake

I started on a painting of the stones at sunrise but after this experience there I have reimagined it. *The light came from within.* When we chanted we took on a similar frequency to the stones. They acted as tuning forks. We become one. Strange and powerful energy was raised. We connected with our ancestors and descendants, beyond time. In the mists the shadowy forms of pilgrims could have been stones. The pilgrim stones…

Imbolc 1999

I love this festival. Peaceful. Purifying. Inspiring. Introvert – yet soon the 'vert' will emerge again. You can feel the Earth holding its breath, bracing itself for the creativity and activity to come – as I am. I am glad to say today I got the go ahead for 'Lost Forest' [an eco-arts festival at Rocks East Woodland]. The hard work starts here! This year is going to be busy in many ways. So much happening, so much to do…

I've been working on my 'Taliesin' and it's finally come alive, after a month of effort (at least – I've worked on the story before). I've penned my own version of his arcane creation song and I feel that I know the rest of the story off by heart too. Time to tell it – at the right time. The tale has gained real significance for me now, as I realised on Sunday morning at the Cross Baths. I can relate to Taliesin, who spends a year stirring the cauldron as Gwion (as I did working with Sulis and Bladud and the hot springs). He escapes with three drops of inspiration, the cauldron cracks in two (me and Emily). Without the wisdom the potion is poisonous (without love a relationship is bitter). It kills horses (freedom). Yet our hero escapes using his new powers (to shape-change, to adapt). The Goddess gives chase – she doesn't want to let him go. She outwits his metamorphoses and eventually captures him/is impregnated by him. Her lover, he is reborn her son – a child, the Divine Child. He has the gift of prophecy, for he has been blessed with the Muse from the Moon Queen's cauldron. He becomes Chief Bard…

Thus, Taliesin has become for me a personal icon, as Bladud was last year. Then I awakened the King archetype within, as this year it is the magician. Shaman come… Master of transformations, word magic, power animals, and otherworldly journeys. This is my path. Time to walk my truth.

A Radiant Day
2nd February 1999

I have finally finished my [written] version of the Creation of Taliesin and I feel I have invoked his spirit within me. He has become my psychopomp, my initiator, my inspiration!

Taliesin Lives!
4th February 1999

The Quickening has begun. The full moon at Imbolc has really kick-started the season. After our Imbolc Eve gathering on Sunday, which was more elemental than anything (fire and water), came (for me) the spiritual acknowledgment of it on Monday night with oblations and meditation, then the social celebration of it last night at the [newly-formed] Bladud Society. It was the best night yet – people had prepared stuff, new faces turned up and everyone got a chance to speak (thanks to my idea of a talking stick. I thought of it when picking up the rod 'spine' of the Bardic Chair – uncanny, since both are based on the caduceus. And, by Hermes, it did the trick!) Everyone introduced themselves, some talked about Imbolc, others offered a poem, or talked about local issues. And Ceridwen manifested! A wise woman from Wales graced us with her presence and she was delightful. She went through the wheel of the year explaining the significance of the eight festivals. And then got us to sing a beautiful Imbolc song... this was the best Imbolc Celebration I could have wished for – a triumph! It was especially for me as the version of Taliesin I'd been working on for the last month was finally finished and performed – to a rapt audience. His story has really come alive for me, as the legend of Bladud and Sulis did last year. It has become my guiding myth. So much that I felt compelled to shave my hair off to play the part. I was planning to do this anyway – my hair has been bothering me for ages. I've just had too many bad hair days, it had just become dead weight. I was going to wait until summer but I felt in the wake of recent dramatic changes in my life that I had mark to them. [I revealed my new haircut in the middle of the performance – pulling off my hat that I'd been wearing all night at the point that Elphin declaims: 'Behold the radiant brow!' It provoked a suitable gasp from the audience. It shows I am committed – or should be!].

Taliesin's Blessing
8th December 1999
Tonight I asked for Taliesin's blessing. I work under his name to acknowledge the Bardic Tradition I am working in. I am a remebrancer. I strive to keep the wisdom alive.

Avalon Calling
9th December 1999
I journeyed to Glastonbury and performed at the White Spring café benefit. My first as 'Tallyessin' and in such a setting it was ideal. I fitted in well to the Avalonians, meeting Merlin et al. Performed my millennial tale to children for the first time – difficult! My poetry worked better, although people were entertained by my story – the adults probably more so. Still, an auspicious start. It seems people are willing to accept my stage persona – it brings a little bit more magic into their lives. And when I perform I am taken over by the spirit of Taliesin. He gives me the weight of his authority and the light of his wisdom. I become more than Kevan, with his peccadilloes and neuroses. I gain confidence and eloquence. Thus I consciously invoke the Pen Beirdd, but I don't confuse myself with him. When I'm not performing I am simply myself. Is this my inner shaman I call upon? This deserves clarification. My next magical exercise will be exploring this. I have much work to do. Having the master's tome I can begin my studies in earnest.

Behold the Radiant Brow
1st June 2000

[Today was the official start of my business – Tallyessin – thanks to a Prince's Trust Loan – the day that I went professional]

Tallyessin is shining! Exhausting but exciting time – making a living from my creativity at last! Living my truth: this is the moral of the week. Telling my tale 'The Green Queen' on Monday at the Bath Storytelling Circle to an audience that included four former love interests was gruelling. It presented a mirror of my story. Was I speaking the truth or being a hypocrite? Really brought the truth of my tale home to me – afterwards I was overwhelmed with the reality of it. I was completely washed away by it, and the effort of a day of bardism (Victorian Centenary Celebration at Art Galley, then Stories@the Edge in the evening). Somehow I summoned the energy in the evening and managed to successfully perform my tales. The Awen was with not only me but all of us – it was a bonding experience. Even though the audience hasn't been as big as at the weekend (3 instead of 300) it's still been worth it. I'm finally living my dream. I am so fortunate. Yet I have made my luck. All my efforts have paid off. Months of planning have culminated in this success. I hope I can sustain it. But one thing I must surely learn is to decide and stick to my choices. I must avoid over-committing myself and then being forced to let people down.

Awakening to Life
5th June 2000

I am awake to life once more. I want to experience the rich tapestry of creativity manifesting now. 2000 promises to be a golden year, especially this summer. At last I have a role to play – to be able to participate. To belong. To dance my song. After a successful fortnight I have evidence that I can do it. I am not a charlatan. I am a BARD! Tallyessin lives!!

The Wheel Turns

[2000 – Began attending Bath Storytelling Circle regularly. First professional gigs. Launched 'Tallyessin' – became self-employed 'bard', offering workshops and performances. Invited to perform at Sacred Arts Festival, Rhode Island, USA, September. Formed Fire Springs with fellow storytellers from Bath Storytelling Circle.

2001: Performing professionally as a storyteller. Co-created and performed in 'Arthur's Dream' with Fire Springs at Rondo Theatre, Bath.

2002-2003: MA Teaching and Practice of Creative Writing, Cardiff. Began work on *The Long Woman* and *The Sun Miners*. Began teaching evening classes at the University of Bath. Ran Creative Writing and the Environment course, leading to the publication of *Writing the Land: an anthology of natural words*.

2004: Finished *The Sun Miners*. Published *The Long Woman*. Literary Tour funded by Arts Council. Started tutoring for the Open University in creative writing. Ran 8 bardic development weekends. Hosted Lammas Games Eisteddfod. Performed live on BBC TV. *Speak Like Rain, Fire in The Head & Green Fire* published.

2005: worked on *Windsmith* (follow up to *The Long Woman*).

2006: *The Bardic Handbook* & *Windsmith* published.

2007: Performed storytelling in Malta. *The Sun Miners* published. Limited edition of *The Book of the Bardic Chair* published for Tim Sebastion Woodman's 60th. Held first Handfasting Ceremony.]

Modern Journal 2008-9

I will share some of my journal written over the period of this book (June 2008- March 2009 – 9 months, analogous to Gwion's time in Ceridwen's womb) in the hope that it illustrates the journey of at least one bard in the present day. It is traditional to record the diurnal journey in a journal – as the very root/route of the word implies:

> *One journey meant one journée, a full day's march, perhaps thirty miles.*

(Marc de Villiers, Sahara)

A New Awe

The Way of Awen is about seeing the nascent wonder of the world, the miracle of every moment. It is Blake's opened doors of perception – when everything is shown as it truly is, infinite. Truly, awe is at the heart of awen.

Wessex Gathering, Isle of Purbeck
31st May 2008

My slot was moved to Saturday night, after the ceremony – which was probably a good thing, because I was weary from the road when I arrived on Friday, and I would've had to have gone on almost immediately. Instead I performed after the main ritual, which Phil led in his inimitable green man way. I didn't feel like joining in fully – my head was too full of my material. Instead I drummed from outside the circle, as 200-300 pagans circle danced. Then I gathered folk in, sat them down and performed, 'warming them' up with my fool tale of 'the Gurt Wurm of Shervage Wood', before embarking on my main piece, the 'premiere' of my epic poem Dragon Dance, which had never been performed lived before. I had spent the last week committing it to memory, all fourteen pages of it. It is good to set oneself challenges, even if it's terrifying! I still get nervous, which is healthy – it stops one getting complacent. And you can channel the nervous energy into the performance. It gives you adrenalin. I didn't feel it went too well. I stumbled on a couple of bits, although like a 'true pro' I soldiered on, managing to reclaim the rhythm, by skipping a line. Unless you draw attention to your goofs, no one normally notices – especially if it's a brand new piece. Yet I wasn't happy – I had been doing it word perfect all day. I knew it back to front. Afterwards I felt drained – it didn't seem to go done too well. How wrong I was. Nearly two month later I received an email from someone who had seen it at Wessex:

Hi Kevan,

I loved your jawdropping rendition of Dragon Dance at the Wessex Gathering this year – not just for the startling feat of memory required to recite it, and not just for the way that you'd skillfully maintained a dynamic structure and undiminishing passion throughout writing what is certainly an epic piece in length and scope, but that simply the words themselves, with each line and stanza taken on its own merit, are beautifully conceived, intricate and deeply moving. Thank you for your performance, and for your poetry.

You have a rare talent, and it is truly wonderful to see it being used. The world needs more Bards, I think :o)

With warm regards,
Amy

These kinds of comments make it possible to keep going (I've performed the piece several times successfully since). Just shows you can never know what effect you might have on someone!

Afterwards, I must have looked wiped out and miserable – because Tammy came up to me out of the blue and gave me a lovely hug. 'I just thought you looked like you needed one', she said. Perceptive girl, and a darling! Her and her partner, Michael, bought a copy of *Lost Islands* as well, bless them. I gave a talk the earlier that day and although I had a fair crowd, I didn't have any sales! Sold a couple at Jerry & Diane's Green Man bookstall, but the reaction was a little disappointing.

Sunday was my 'free day', so I took advantage of it, to head for the coast.

Brownsea Island
1st June 2008

Here on Brownsea Island – on the south coast of England – in the second largest natural harbour in the world I begin [in earnest] my book on the Way of Awen. It feels like a good place to start: Baden-Powell sowed the seeds of his international youth movement here, and there's perhaps something of the 'bad boy made good' through rites-of-passage in Gwion Bach, the originally hoody! One could imagine him as a hoody these days – a 'menace to society' to a master bard, via his journey to Deganwy. He has a long way to go before he can call himself a bard [doing the equivalent of 'community service']. He may have spent a year stirring the cauldron but the hard work that makes a boy into a bard is about to begin. He has scalded his fingers in the three drops splashed on his hand (like the three rays of awen) and imbibed the potion of inspiration meant for Afagddu – he's had the 'overdose' of awen, which has released his potential, but now he has to fulfil it. First, he has to escape the wrath of Ceridwen: he has split her cauldron in two! (a kind of Caesarean; the waters have broken – but he is not yet 'twice-born'). Realising he's in hot water he hightails it out of there in the form of a hare, thanks to the power of shape-changing he has gained from the potion: the druidic gift of fith-fath. The chase is on! [shortly after arriving on Brownsea, I spotted a red squirrel but it got cornered by visitors with cameras and dashed away]

The Changing Man

The Way of Awen is about the ability to change. All real journeys change you. If you are no different from when you set out then no real journey has been undertaken. For Gwion to become

Taliesin he must undergo the journey of the bard or he remains simply Gwion. The process began for him with the seemingly monotonous hard work of cauldron stirring (symbolic of the sexual act – Gwion's spoon a wooden phallus; Ceridwen's cauldron her labia/womb – leading, eventually, to the ec-stasis of orgasm?). He had to put in the graft, in the hours and elbow grease. Such rhythmic activity can be trance-inducing. Watching the spoon turn and turn, hypnotic (love spoons are a traditional gift in Wales to a sweetheart). A spoon is not dissimilar to the shaman's beater, as well. It would alter Gwion's hyperactive adolescent brainwaves from alpha to theta – to a state of mind conducive to making lateral leaps, from hare to salmon, salmon to tiny bird, to grain of wheat: meta-state metamorphoses. Gwion must become the changing man.

While I wrote this, one of the wandering peacocks which had been eyeing my vegetarian Sunday roast leapt up onto the table and took a greedy stab at my pie with its beak – plunging it right in! This impertinent bird could be seen as a kind of Gwion – who gobbles up the drops of awen meant for disadvantaged Afaggdu – but the truth was the bird wasn't a peacock; it was a pea-hen! It seems the filching of a man's 'chips' is endemic to the female, whatever the species!

Burnbake
2nd June 2008

Here at Burnbake [the name of this woodland campsite on the 'Isle of Purbeck' seems to echo Gwion Bach's cooking disaster with Ceridwen's cauldron. John Cowper Powys called Taliesin: 'the runaway 'Stir-the-Pot' from Caer Einion'. In *Porius* (Overlook 2007) JCP describes him as chef-bard: 'The young man's genius seemed to brim over at times, and the inspiration that was fulfilling itself in his poem flowed outwards naturally and spontaneously into the preparation of the meal,' p373] on the morning after the Wessex Gathering I prepare to take to the road. Last night I ran the bardic cabaret around the campfire, which went well. It's always a popular night – everyone's chance to shine. I summoned some bonhomie from somewhere and played the congenial host, but in truth after my day out on Brownsea Island I was in a better mood than when I had left the camp – wearied out by being around people. I started the cabaret by invoking both the awen and Taliesin, with my 'Song of Taliesin' – to inspire the performers and audience. It all begins with Penbeirdd. It is his shining example, quite literally, which inspires all on the Bardic Path. He walks by our side – all the way to Deganwy.

(From here, on the south coast of England, to North Wales, it's a winding 255 miles – but it's the spiritual and transformational distance which is the most significant).

First we need the alacrity of the hare – to flee 'Ceridwen's wrath'. As I sped off on my bike yesterday I felt like Gwion the hare. It was an exhilarating feeling. Sometimes it's the best thing to do: if a situation doesn't agree with you, just leave. No point enduring it, for the sake of it. (Or exhaust ourselves trying to confront it, change it, etc). We often put up with too much – feeling it's our lot to grin and bear it – our masochistic culture. As Brits we don't like to complain. Make a fuss. Cause a scene. So we suffer in silence. Stew. Stagnate.

So with Gwion the Hare's speediness, it is time for me to strike camp and hit the road – hightail it out of here, jinking to confuse my 'pursuers', non-literal, right-brained leaps of logic. Hare-brained.

Stopped off at Badbury Rings on way home – a fairy place, full of deep peace, the consoling green of trees, everything fecund, heavy with summer... After the hustle and bustle of a public event it is essential to ground yourself and recharge the bardic batteries. Replenish the cauldron. Before speech, silence. After speech, silence. Return to the sacred silence. Let the buzz of voices, of personalities and opinions, fade away, until you can hear yourself think again.

Heron-priested Shores
9th June 2008
I catch the silhouette of a heron flapping its way across the fading glory of sunset.

Awen as Grace
12th June 2008
Awen is universal – which is not surprising since it is 'flowing spirit'. One thing it is similar to is Grace – possibly not the first definition of the noun ('unmerited divine assistance given to human beings for their regeneration or sanctification'), although there's elements of that – but certainly the second ('a state of being pleasing to God'); and also 'a charming trait or accomplishment.' When one performs and the awen is with you, it feels like a state of grace – it comes through when we act gracefully and at the same time makes us act so. John O'Donohue, in his book *Divine Beauty* said 'real presence is natural'. When we shine we are fully ourselves – the soul-light pours out of every pore. And yet, however desirable, its ways and appearances are mysterious: 'No one set the limits on the flow of grace. Its presence and force remain immeasurable and unpredictable.' It comes and it goes. Sometimes it is indisputably with us – when we are 'on fire'. Sometimes, it is not. We 'die on our feet'. All we can do is make ourselves willing channels. As Shakespeare said: 'the readiness is all.' I call this state 'creative preparedness'. We create the frame for it to manifest – we become the field of potential.

Flag Fen Eisteddfod
14th June 2008
I sit by the Mere at Flag Fen. It is a sunny afternoon. I hear the

conversation of birds, the fen winds soughing through the reeds in the lake, the willows on the shore. Clouds move with stately grace across the sky like ocean liners leaving port. Ripples undulate across the surface, giving the illusion it is going somewhere – busy about its business – when in fact it is staying put, protecting the remains of the ritual island and causeway beneath it. Stillness. Peace. Bliss. It is good to have arrived.

I'm here at this Bronze Age ritual centre to host the inaugural eisteddfod to find the Chief Bard of the Fens, organised by Jody Copestake and the Ancient Muse team. It was an honour to have been asked. Previously I have hosted the Lammas Games Eisteddfod and been involved in the Bardic Chair of Caer Badon in my home city of Bath. Bardic Chairs are springing up all over Britain. Next month there's one scheduled in my old home town of Northampton, just down the road from here – in my old haunt of Delapre Abbey. The area around Flag Fen was the stomping ground of so-called peasant poet, John Clare, one of my literary heroes. I made a pilgrimage to his grave in nearby Helpstone in 1992, the year of his bicentenary, and took part in poetry readings around Northampton in his honour (Clare was to spend the last quarter of a century of his life there, incarcerated in Northampton County Hospital and Lunatic Asylum. On day-release he would wander the town and hand out poems to passers-by, written on the hoof and lost forever). In Helpstone graveyard Clare's modest memorial stone bears the inscription: 'Poets are born and not made', but the last letter is worn away by the centuries and so it seems to read, 'Poets are born and not mad...' It seems to come with the territory: to want to be a poet is perhaps a sign of madness. There's at least a couple of places in Wales, where, if you hazard to spend a night you could end up 'dead, mad or poet'. Well, having climbed Cader Idris and made pilgrimage to Bedd Taliesin half a dozen times by now, I must have come down a 'dead mad poet'!

In my introduction to the contest I suggested Clare should be made Honorary Chief Bard of the Fens. This would be a respectful gesture, for Clare was the Fens poet-of-place *par excellence*. He witnessed the Enclosures Act first-hand and was able to sing its subtle beauty with far more authenticity and intimate knowledge than many of the Romantic poets on their high horses – for he worked on the land as a labourer; his hands and feet knew it. Psycho-geographer Iain Sinclair and East Anglian storyteller Hugh Lupton (with Chris Wood) have honoured the poet in their own distinctive ways, and I featured Clare in my first (and still unpublished novel), *The Ghost Tree*, written 1992-1994. One of my first published poems was about Clare in a local anthology of Northampton Poets. Knowing this bard of quiet beauty on my doorstep inspired me as a young poet, setting out on my own journey.

Knowing the Flow

I believe the Way of Awen is about living in the flow all of the time. When we're not – that's when it goes wrong. This current book came about because I was 'in the flow'. It all fell into place – though not without a little nudging. The Way of Awen is not about just 'going with the flow' – it is about *knowing the flow*. Being proactive, rather than reactive. About hooking into the current of life and responding to its vibrations, its variations. A spider on the web of life!

Lucid Living

A moor-hen just flapped madly through my legs and shot out onto the Mere in a flurry of wings and white water: Awen!

The Way of Awen is about finding inspiration in unexpected places! It is the craft of inspiration – not waiting for it, but seeking it in every moment, fully present. Living life as though one is a character in a tale from the *Mabinogion* – journeying through a landscape of vivid symbolism. It could be called lucid living, akin to when we know we are dreaming – being fully conscious of being alive. In the moment. In the Awen.

Later, by the Fire in the Roundhouse

It begins in fire and shadow... Afaggdu and Creirwy... Utter darkness and fair face... The primal darkness and the primal spark... I write these words by firelight in a Bronze Age-style round house at Flag Fen. I enjoy the fruits of my efforts: a bed earnt by my bardic efforts, a fire built by my own hands. The grey matter of thought placed, twig upon twig, stick upon stick, branch upon branch, until the vital spark occurs. The spark at the kindling is akin to the Divine Spark.

The fire around which the people gathered to keep the night at bay, the day's work done. The storyteller's fire. Ancient and timeless.

In the Taliesin story fire is fundamental. First there is the cauldron in the iron house – heated and escaped from by the chthonic deity, Tegid Foel and his giantess wife.

Strange and awkward – the embarrassing relatives. They stick out in the Taliesin tale – not quite fitting in with the rest of the narrative, Tom Bombadils. What does it mean? We'll return to those later... [see sections on **The Crooked One**, and **The Man of Gentle Lineage** in **Chapter One**]

And then there's the fire that cooks the potion of inspiration. Stoked by Morda the ancient of days, and stirred by Gwion the little boy. For a year and a day. Imagine the dedication. The tedium. The trance-inducing monotony that leads to a flash of inspiration. It's like any long-term project that you have to keep chipping away at, any reward a long way off. You need staying power. The journey, not the destination. Process, not goal. Attention to detail along the way. Of course, fire is the element of transformation, of quickening. We all get a chance to shine.

After a tough contest, Robin Herne won the Chair, becoming Chief Bard of the Fens for a year and day. This is the vindication of the bard – now Robin has the remit to serve the Chair, which will be based at Flag Fen. Without a community's mandate it is almost impossible for a bard to operate. They cannot function without a community serve. The winning of a Chair is the culmination of the 'journey to Deganwy' that all bards must undertake. It is the proof of the pudding. Then, and only then, can you call yourself a bard with any humility. After your community has named you one. This is the bard's moment of glory, and they should enjoy it. They have earnt this. All the hard work has paid off. This, their defining moment. They stepped up to the mark and proved themselves worthy – like Taliesin in Deganwy. He hadn't gone there for self-glorification. He had gone there to free his master. His first act was one of emancipation. And it was then he was freed to follow his destiny. This was when his bardic career began in earnest. Winning the Chair is not a time to sit on your laurels. It is when the hard work begins. With the Chair comes responsibility. It is the path of service – the 'green ray' along the Qabalistic Tree of Life. Not a path to riches, but for its own sake.

The journey is the destination.

I went to say hello to my neighbours in the other Bronze Age roundhouse – a small group of family and friends – and one of them turned out to be Robin Herne, whom I didn't know but had heard of. We had a pleasant evening, chatting by their fire and they were most hospitable, offering me a welcome vegetarian alternative to the BBQ organised for those on site. I returned the favour later with some Guinness after the session in the large, less smokier Iron Age roundhouse. I thought there was something special about the man, a spark in his eye, for the next day Robin was to win the Eisteddfod, as judged by Bobcat, Ben Haggarty, Albion Conclave's Stefan Allen and a Flag Fen representative – the Awen was with him! It needed to have been – for it was a tough contest, the standard was high, and the day went well. Yet I had a long ride home, and the heavens opened as I left.

Fortunately, after a pitstop in Northampton at my Mum's, the skies cleared and the rest of the ride home, over the Cotswolds, was pleasant as I raced the sun into the West.

Solstice Madness in the West Country
18th-22nd June 2008

Very full-on solstice few days, typical of the season. Midsummer madness! Everything intensifies around these festivals, and the full moon didn't help.

19th Book launch in Glastonbury at the Cat & Cauldron (kept waiting, but only because it was a pleasant atmosphere – Trevor wanted to give folk plenty of time to mingle...but it didn't help me to relax. I found it difficult to enjoy until afterwards). A meal afterwards in The Hawthorn, courtesy of Trevor and Liz, which was nice of them.

20th A couple of stories at Tim & Jade's BBQ (including a special request for a man whose daughter was called Niamh) I was asked to do a story, then was kept waiting for half an hour as people fidgeted about. Most frustrating.

[Still, I am glad I got to perform for this lovely couple, because tragically Jade was to die suddenly seven and a half months later].

21st-22nd: Alice in Wonderland show at Tyntesfield, National Trust – Sat & Sun. 4x 20 min sets: White Rabbits, Red Queens, Mad Hatters, Terrible Twins. Fearsome Beasts. All the way to Bristol and back, then back to Bristol in the evening. Cosmic Acoustica gig, Bristol – Oisín and Niamh, and Dragon Dance, which went very well. It was worth the effort of getting there – a magical, awen-filled evening of beautiful music and poetry. An excellent kora player, a good singer-songwriter and a spectacular performance poet called Analiese, whom I connected with, although we didn't seem to get off to a good start. When I arrived there in my bike leathers, she was by the door – turned, and exclaimed rather scornfully 'Oh god!' The heavens opened in the middle of the evening, and the sky flashed with lightning. It was indeed, a dark and stormy night... Atmospheric, but I had to ride back in the storm. Not fun. Could hardly see. Had to ride almost by intuition. If I had gone with the flow it would've been easier to stay over in Bristol. Exhausted the next morning but had to go in – it was touch and go whether it was going to happen or not, because of the dodgy weather. Was praying for a call to say it was cancelled, but no such luck. Had to drag my sorry bones out of bed (so wanted/needed a lie-in that morning) and get to Tyntesfield. It was actually a pleasant day. Breezy, but sunny. And had punters! Not loads, but enough to make it seem worthwhile. Did six slots in the end (to make up for the two missed yesterday due to lack of audience). Felt like the white rabbit racing back and forth: 'Oh dear! Oh dear! I shall be too late!'

23rd: We said farewell, and I returned to Bath and finished my OU marking. It was a day to tie up loose ends before I headed for the mountains.

24th: Freedom! I spent the morning packing, and was off by around 1pm. I was prepared for the long haul. The weather stayed kind and got to Corwen by just before 7pm, after a couple of stops on the way. It was a nice ride up. Traffic flowed okay and bike ran sweet.

Had a lovely evening catching up with Kirsten Manley, living in a truck on some land above Maerdy (see below).

Midsummer Night at Maerdy
25th June 2008

I have embarked upon my journey to Deganwy – and I'm nearly there! I set off from Bath yesterday – relieved at finishing my duties and commitments – and had a good run in the sun up to Corwen, right in the Welsh heartland with its magnificent statue of Owain Glyndwr seeing off the English. This charming place was the adopted home of my literary hero, John Cowper Powys, who rendered his own vast version of the historical legend.

Stopped to pick up some supplies and called Kirsten to let her know I was nearly there. Didn't reckon on the obscurity of the location and the really steep lane to get there! Eventually found Kirsten's place – Hafotty Gelynen – a smallholding she's staying at near Maerdy, after one wrong turn and several steep tracks. It was great to see a friendly face at the end of the track, waving as she opened the farm gate. Last time I saw Kirsten was in London, I think. She'd organised a bardic workshop for me at Treadwell's, Covent Garden. And now I'm working on a new bardic book. Finally I can stop. It's been relentless until now. Last night was lovely sharing stories, songs and poems over a bottle of organic mead from Glastonbury. Kirsten cooked the food over a campfire, despite the intermittent rain (using vegetables picked fresh from their poly-tunnel) and we sat outside, enjoying the view until the rain had other ideas. Then she brought the fire inside, using a shovel to transport the logs, practical woman! And we got cosy by the burner. So satisfying, having a real fire. It's so conducive to camaraderie, conversation and contentment. The fire of awen crackled and glowed. Kirsten sang a spine-tingling version of 'La Belle Dame Sans Merci'. I recited my version of 'Thomas the Rhymer' and my own poem 'Heartwood'. Midnight came, eyelids drooped and I retired to my caravan, armed with fleeces and blankets. It's great to wake up in Wales. To open the double caravan door and be greeted by a vista of vale and mountain, rain-washed colours subdued, subtle and soothing.

As we had watched the snakes of flame we talked about serpents: Kirsten was going to have a Celtic snake tattoo to mark her move to Wales. I mentioned Lydney, the healing temple dedicated to the apparently unique Celtic God Nodens – dramatically situated on a wooded headland overlooking the Severn (several hound icons were found there – an interesting Ceridwen overlap). We agreed it would be good to spend a night there, sacred dreaming [if it wasn't on private land]. Lydney is akin to Epiduaros in usage, Asklepios the Greek Nodens – associated with snakes: his caduceus still a symbol of medicine to this day. Interestingly it is also associated with Hermes, who held a rod – sometimes depicted with snakes and wings. Thoth: Hermes: Mercury – all brothers of Taliesin, I think. The Penbeirdd is part of the same lineage, if not the identical archetype/deity/energy. The spirit of inspiration, of eloquence and communication, that 'enters' people so their words flow – like the waters of Llyn Geironydd, Lake Silvertongue, which I plan to visit.

Dames said the ancient Welsh believed if a white snake was eaten all the tongues of animals would be understood. There is a Taliesin-type story about a boy who has a dream about a 'green-garlanded god' and receives the 'hawk tongue', the bardic gift – and perhaps a double-edged one, like the Tongue that Cannot Lie which Thomas the Rhymer received from the Queen of Elfland.

Lake Silvertongue
25th June 2008

I sit on the base of the stone erected for the Chief Bard of the West, by the glittering shores of Lake Language. Can't believe I'm here – it was quite a journey! The roads here from Trefiw were very narrow, steep and slippery. Gravel and rain – the biker's nightmare! And it's not the easiest of places to find. There's a dearth of signage, as though the locals want to keep it for themselves. I initially ended up at Trafnant, but I was going in the right direction. Always trust your instincts! If yesterday was like being a hare, hightailing it to the hills, then today has been like being a salmon – riding in the rain, winding my way along the serpentine roads, which shadow the water courses, returning upstream, higher and higher, against all odds, back to the source – to Taliesin's birthplace. I'm home!

In Michael Dames' *Taliesin's Travels* (Heart of Albion Press 2006 – coming out after I had conceived of *this* book – one of those 'in the aether' things), which is superb for following the

'Taliesin trail' he writes: 'He arrived at Llyn Geironydd entirely drained and literally speechless.' This is how I feel after a very demanding first half of the year: book launches, gigs, eisteddfod, courses, making a living and dealing with death. I am ready to have some time off the wheel, some time away from the crowd, sometime for myself. Time to replenish the cauldron.

Llyn Geironydd is said to be the birthplace of the 6th Century Welsh bard, Taliesin. At one end stands an austere monument erected by Lord Willoughby in 17850 to the 'Chief of the Bards. The remote lake was also the site of the poet Gwilym Cowlyd's annual 'Arwest' – a cultural festival, 'less Anglicised' and formal than the eisteddfod. Held annually until 1927. The Taliesin Festival has been held more recently. I was invited last year to perform in the ritual drama of Taliesin and Ceridwen by the poet Gwdihw ('little owl') but was prevented due to the floods of Summer 2007.

Lake Silence

...A lake filled with silence. From this silence everything comes. This is where the Awen is born. First comes not the Word but the Silence. The Taw. It is wonderful to listen to the gentle sounds of the lake, the trees, the wind. Peace is sacred. There is much too much noise in the world. White noise. Stopping us thinking straight. Unlike pink noise – calming and conducive to lucid thoughts, to deep wisdom. O, to spend a season here – to have a house here, on the shores of Llyn Geironydd (*gay-ree-on-ith*). To be plugged into this source. Hydro-powered Awen! Listening to the sacred silence.

Deganwy Castle, later

I arrived in Conwy in glorious sunshine and so decided to 'make hay' and headed for the castle of King Maelgwn. It concluded my journey to Deganwy rather prematurely! But it was worth it (and in hindsight, a wise decision, as the weather turned for the worst for the rest of the week). It was absolutely stunning on top – spectacular views over the Conwy estuary and the sea towards Anglesey. I wasn't expecting it to be so beautiful. Maelgwn's fortress always looked so forbidding in the photos, and maybe it's just the associations: a stern ruler. Taliesin arriving in winter, a frosty reception. The scariest eisteddfod. Apparently, Maelgwn would force bards (poets and harpers) to swim across the Conwy, presumably to cut the wheat from the chaff or to prove his power (an Alan Sugar of his day, making his wannabe apprentices jump through hoops) – only the poets could perform because it would be in their heads, whileas the harpers' instruments would be ruined! Professional sabotage!

The only way to the castle now was via a housing estate that crowds its flanks (what would Maelgwn have made of this suburbia?). Maybe there's a more direct route but it eludes me (another non-signed ancient monument). Place names like Castell Close give me clues. I parked my bike somewhat incongruously in amid the bungalows and took the footpath between them into the field. And there it was! I instinctively sat on rounded stone protruding from the nearest hillock rather than head straight there. I needed a moment to prepare myself, like Taliesin waiting to enter Maelgwn's court – it felt right to wait. On the other side the two hills (one rounded, one rocky – feminine and masculine?) I found the ruins of the gatehouse, at least the remains of one from the 13th century according to an inscribed sign: proof! This is from later than the Taliesin tale's setting if not composition – contemporary with Edward Ironshanks' ring of iron – but the site was probably in use for centuries (Conwy Castle was in military use until the 1700s). It holds such a strategic position, overlooking the Conwy and surrounding landscape. Standing upon top of this 'Amon Hen' one certainly feels like the King of the Castle – lord of all one surveys. It has a resonance of temporal power, of saturnine male energy – the dark father archetype. Taliesin as Luke Skywalker,

Maelgwn as Darth Vader here in this 'Cloud City': 'Yes, (heavy breathing), I am your step-uncle!' On the summit of the 'male' hill there's a kind of dungeon – an open air, steep sided pit on the top. I spotted a rotting sheep carcase down there. One could easily imagine Elphin incarcerated there – in silver chains because he was the royal nephew after all. Maelgwn is the stone king, *par excellence* – he rules 'the world' from his stern fortress crag, a fastness of Cambrian rock.

Taliesin's famous journey – undertaken at the age of thirteen – was with one prime purpose: the vindication and emancipation of Elphin, which could be seen as a metaphor for the freeing of spirit (Elphin/Elffin/Elf/Fairy/Fey – otherworldly energy). Liberty from the bonds of Maelgwn – from matter. It is also his defining moment – his Gorsedd of Efficiency, as Morgannwg would put it. This is when he proves himself as a bard, against Maelgwn's best – and wins the Chair of Deganwy. Interestingly, in the eponymous poem, it mentions the bloodshed of Arthur's battle – at Badon (possibly Caer Badon: Bath). Taliesin has fled from here, from the wanton slaughter, like Merlin, into the hills. I have 'fled' from Bath too! From the pell-mell of life. Weary, bardic batteries worn low. I would love to live up here, in the mountains, where you can feel the dragon in the land, and see it!

Blake wrote of the 'mind forg'd manacles' and railed against any form of enslavement. His work celebrates the emancipation of the imagination. We all need to find freedom from the bonds of matter, from the treadmill of work. Only Spirit can set us free, can completely fulfil us – for with matter, we always want more. There's never 'enough'. We have to find our Source, like Blake, from 'Another Sun'.

Orme's Head to Capel Currig
26th-27th June 2008

'I seek what is lost,'
Taliesin, The Chair of Deganwy

Made it to Capel Curig – finally out of the rain. Everything is soaked. Even this journal got damp! And all my clothes inside the tail-bag! Thank goodness for the drying room! Now I have a cup of tea, some Welsh cakes and a lounge. Guess rain is to be expected in Wales, especially Snowdonia – but this monsoon has come suddenly. After waking up to rain pattering on my tent it cleared up, but I decided to go, thank goodness! Conwy Touring Park wasn't that atmospheric (an old quarry?). The rules stipulated 'no groups of bikers; only couples and families', so I don't know why they let me in then!

This morning I went to Orme's Head – rode around some of it on the Marine Drive, then visited the summit. Almost immediately the weather turned for the worse. So I had some lunch at the 'Captain's Table' with the pensioners – the summit-restaurant had the ambience of a kind of Valhalla for OAPs. Awful muzak and kitsch Fifties décor. Aborted my full loop of the Orme and scarpered down the hill in the lashing rain to a town, where I took shelter in a pleasant coffee shop. Served by a nice local lass with blonde hair who made me think of Eurgain – Maelgwn's daughter – whose name means 'bright', 'gold,' 'gloriously radiant' (Taliesin's female equivalent, says Dames). I decided to visit Bryn Euryn ('little gold coin, gold jewel, darling') which seems etymologically connected to Eurgain. This was a revelation – showing a different aspect of Maelgwn (like Olwen – the flower-maiden daughter of the giant Ysbaddaden, the father-in-law from Annwn). On one level Maelgwn's bright, golden daughter is literally that: his monetary wealth. This is the prize the bard who convinces Maelgwn of his merit – Maelgwn a kind of Dark Age Simon Cowell to Taliesin's 'contestant'. But although shining-browed Taliesin has undoubtedly the 'X Factor' it is he who rejects the judges. He wins the contest but does not seek the enticing hand of Eurgain (your-gain?). Elidyr wins it instead. If Eurgain is symbolic of fortune (the Goddess Fortuna, Lady Luck), then Taliesin's choice shows he knows what true wealth is to the authentic bard – not Maelgwn's bright-gold, but the Way of Awen. He turns his back on worldly riches. Only to the Muse-Goddess does he belong.

Of Eurgain it is said she: 'set the candle to the wild birds to show her lover the way to Wales'. An amazing, arresting image – echoing the enchanted birds of Rhiannon, and perhaps seen in the flame-coloured red kites that have come back to the valleys of Wales.

It seems Maelgwn's prophesised death is connected to that which he hoards and lusts after:

> *'A most strange creature will come from the sea marsh of Rhianedd.*
> *As a punishment of iniquity on Maelgwn Gwynedd;*
> *His hair, his teeth, and his eyes being as gold,*
> *And this will bring destruction upon Maelgwn Gwynedd.'*

As in the Anglo-Saxon epic Beowulf, gold is eventually the downfall of all men who crave power and immortality. This prophecy might be referring to Y Fad Felen, the yellow plague (Cholera?) which broke out in 547 AD across Wales.

Visited Caer Eurgain in the pouring rain – meant to be connected to Taliesin, but this seems spurious fancy. Locals refer to it as Derthin, the Bear Fort... Certainly felt surly, brooding, massive shoulders hunched against the rain. If the bear-bard was here, he was hibernating.

Village of the Harpmakers, Capel Currig Hostel

Pennies from Heaven...The relentless rain has made me stop and take stock – as I hung my clothes and biker accoutrements to dry. Warmth, shelter, peace, a warm drink, hot food, a soft bed – these are true wealth. I succeeded in my quest – I made it Deganwy – and, so far, I have lived to tell the tale…

Earlier I had a potentially nasty confrontation with a van as I tried to make my way up the ridiculously steep roads to the obscure YHA. The van appeared suddenly around a blind bend. I was only going about 20 miles an hour and I'm always careful on country roads, slowing right down if I can't see what's around the corner. A combination of gravel, rain, narrow road and fatigue made me take a spill – the bike nearly went under the front wheel of a white van that came hammering around the corner. It stopped … just in time. I was undamaged – thanks to my protective gear – and the bike seemed okay. It started up again. The guys helped me back on and were apologetic. Relieved, I rode off. Later I discovered the front headlamp was cracked but I mended it with some wire and black tape – adequate to get me home.

I discovered to my annoyance it wasn't even the right road (the YHA had an absence of signage). When I eventually found the right road, the way got steeper and steeper until, beaten, I had to stop the bike and walked up the hill, to scout ahead. Nothing in sight. I asked a local woman, who pointed ahead…up and up. The YHA was a white speck on the mountain side. No chance, not on my weak-hearted Jinny, loaded with gear. I gave up and headed for Conwy YHA. It was full up! I had a couple of cups of tea until 5pm, when I rang to Capel Curig, the next nearest hostel, to check there was a bed. And then, I set off, through the driving rain…

I had wanted to visit the 'Bard's Stone' the next morning, but nature and circumstance had other ideas.

The Way of Awen can be hard… But H Rider Haggard said: *'There is no journey upon this earth a man may not make if he sets his heart to it.'*

There's some serendipity here though – Capel Curig was renowned for its harp-making up until the 17th Century. The village of the bards, hail!

After I had dried out, eaten, rested, settled in I went to the local pub to enjoy their open fire, real ales and Welsh whiskey – reading my enchanting De Lint novel, *The Little Country*, while gazing out at the flood waters...(from the heavy rains earlier – water always finds the quickest path).

Medicine Farm
28th June 2008

I'm sitting in the caravan at Keith and Annie's place, a small farm cottage in the rugged backcountry above Porthmadog, slowly waking up after a lovely night of food, fire and conversation. The awen manifests in such moments – in lively discussions between friends. Points of view expressed like synapses firing. In the love felt between old friends, kindly tolerant of each other's foibles and quirks. It was great to get here and get warm and dry again after another near drubbing. The rain came again yesterday – instead of going up the mountain (toyed with climbing Snowdon) instead I went with the flow, revisiting Llyn Geironydd (to walk around it) and then Swallow Falls – this is the way of awen too. Rather than resisting the water – going with it. Make your enemy your friend. Attune to its element. Learn from it. Well, I think I have learned the lesson of rain now!

Bikes and Bards in Bala

Had a good run from Porthmadog to Bala via Dolgellau road and Trawsfynydd, which turns out to be a favourite blat-track for bikers, as I discovered upon arriving in the town: there were dozens of bikers there congregating outside a couple of the cafes on the high street. I had stumbled into a weekly bike-meet. I parked my humble steed amidst the ranks of big boys' bikes, and went to get myself a baguette and a tea. I didn't get chatting to any of the bikers. Sure some of them were fine, but I dislike the snobbish machismo and clan mentality in the biking fraternity – the size of your penis seems to depend on the cc and make of your machine. Most of them seem middle-aged bluecollar types, and the odd wannabe rebel executive. Not much edginess or bohemia really. Just everyone in their biker bling, their uniform of rebellion. Pretty harmless. The 'wild ones' grew old, had families, settled down. Now they have family estates or people carriers and bring their bikes out at weekends. To counter that, you have a nice camaraderie on the road – most nod or wave (can you imagine every driver doing that?). Some pull over, if they see you by the ride side apparently struggling (especially if you have L plates). A guy on a blue Yamaha Fazer pulled up by me on the windy Trawsfynydd road as we waited for some roadwork lights to change. We got chatting briefly – instantly friendly. I asked him where he was heading and he said: 'Just following my wheels', and roared off. Cool.

Anyway, it made an interesting atmosphere for it was Eisteddfod Proclamation day in Bala. Families were lining the High Street in expectation of the procession. I asked an old lady who explained it all, pleased to see my interest. A newspaper stand said: 'New Bala UFO spotted'. Bikers, druids and aliens. It was the silly season alright! It was great to watch the procession when it finally passed – local VIPs, community groups, arch-druids in gold regalia, banner-carriers, a sword-bearer, a woman carrying the Hirlas Horn, another the Blodeuged, and the battalions of bards, ovates and druids in their blue, green and white. It was a real community affair, with the spectators people-spotting as much as anything, the locals enjoying it with a mixture of pride and good humour. This wasn't a fringe thing – but the heartblood of the community, of the nation.

The ceremony was all in Welsh, of course, which was lovely to hear – especially the singing (there was also some beautiful harp-playing as the procession spiralled inwards to the gorsedd circle, taking their places). I spoke to Keith this morning about how singing spontaneously is a way of giving praise. I felt it at Tyn Llwyn (when I instinctively began chanting the awen, confronted with the stunning view – realising this is possibly how the famous singing in Wales must have originated, as a natural response to the landscape) and I saw it at Bala green today, as the ranks of blue, green and white gorsedd members sang around the gorsedd stones. It seemed familiar from over a decade of attending such ceremonies in England – obviously very inspired by the Eisteddfod, itself largely the invention of a fertile mind – Iolo Morgannwg's.

I sit looking towards Bala and its lake now – in a lovely little wooden seat, which I've had to 'contest' with a couple of local 'fairies/pixies' kids belonging to a large family gathering nearby (who have a marquee set up, a couple of BBQs and mean business!) interesting that I got them talking about fairies (because they were acting like a couple of cheeky ones) because the lake is said to be frequented by various kinds: including Plant Annwn (Children of the Deep) and the eponymous Y Twlywth Teg (possibly connected to Bala/Llyn Tegid's own Tegid Foel). Tegid Foel is said to be the father of Taliesin and he has his own story-thread – Chieftain of Penllyn (where Gronw comes from, rival of Llew Llaw Gyffes for the love of Blodeuwedd) the five parishes around the shore of the eponymous lake. Apparently Tegid continues to dwell with his supernatural bride in the submerged 'temple city' below Bala's glittering surface. It too has a legend about a well that was negligently forgotten to be covered: 'one evening the task was overlooked'. Thus, the spring, Ffynnon Gawr, still is believed to flow below the lake like the Well of Segais of Irish legend. Another tale says how a minstrel was told to play at a festival there, but a 'bird lured him to the hill, where he fell asleep. In the morning he awoke to find Llyn Tegid covering the city'; and, most memorably of all: 'on the lake's surface floated his harp', a haunting image reminiscent of the Bard of Thessaly, Orpheus' head, floating with his lyre down the Hebron. Fishermen are said to see chimney pots and hear church bells on calm days, or after a thaw. Bala is also said to be the home of a monster, and a lost city! It seems its deep waters provide a dark mirror to people's fantasies and fears. And yet its pure waters perhaps feed the racial consciousness here – the purest form of Welsh is said to be spoken in Bala. So today's eisteddfod proclamation could not have been more appropriate. Bala's deep streams inspire many to this day.

Last year I visited Bala for the first time, staying with Rowenna Williams, whose father owns the land through which flows the Stream of the Poisoned Horses, Aber Gwenwen Y Meirch – it was, in fact, a beautiful burn flowing through a wooded vale. I was honoured to be taken to it, and up to its source. I also walked down to where it flowed into the lake. Such places bring the legends alive.

Llyn Tegid
28 June 2008

By the shores of Lake Bala, listening to its endless stories – a bottomless cauldron of myth and legend. Awen is like this deep and broad lake – an endless source of inspiration. It is always there, waiting to be tapped into. One just has to sensitize to it, sit, listen, wait…like a fisherman of words, wait for a line to catch. The Muse to bite. Lady of the Lake, lake maiden, goddess of the subconscious, mistress of dreams. Swifts dart like the shuttle of a loom, creating the warp and weft of lake life. Soothing song of the lake – let it work on your weary body, ease your soul. Hwyll to Taliesin's father, Tegid Foel, and his 'sunken city' (the treasures of the subconscious).

I think I see a stone head below the water – ancient and mute. Raise it from the deep. Let it speak. What would it say? Would it talk of Tegid's lost city, of monsters and lake maidens? How do we discern real dreams from false? Have they arrived to us from between the gates of horn, or of ivory?

The lake must be replenished, otherwise it runs dry. It gives freely of itself to the river, while fed by many streams.

Over the last couple of years, while researching my book *Lost Islands*, I collected tales of 'lost lands' around the British Isles, of which there are a plethora. I particularly like the one associated with Cardigan Bay (Seithennin, the drunken steward and Cantre'r Gwaelod). Here is one I stumbled upon at Penmaenmawr: The Tale of the drowned palace

> *'When the tide is low take a look over Trwyn-yr-Wylfa and towards the sea. It's possible to see rocks in the sand. It is believed that these rocks were the foundations of a palace belonging to a wicked prince named Helyg. One day his wickedness was punished and the sea came in drowning his land and palace. Helyg and his family ran for safety to nearby Trwyn-yr-Wylfa.'*

From Conwy walk guide pamphlet

Bedd Taliesin and Beyond
29th June 2008

The Way of Awen is, among other things, about going with the flow and I certainly have done that today. Making a slow start at Pen y Bont campsite because of the rain and feeling slightly groggy – a good night's sleep but one filled with dreams of lake maidens! I wended my way from Bala along the lake, stopping briefly at Llangower at midday, but the rain drove me on and I ploughed on to Machynlleth – over stunning scenery, no doubt, but in the driving rain I could see or appreciate it little. I had to completely focus on the road, although a tune did come to me as I rode, whether original or remembered I could not say. I passed by Cader Idris and made it to Mach, thawing out in a local café over some leek and potato soup. My fave place, The Quarry Café (run by the CAT people) was closed, so I had to go in a real local place – in my dripping bike gear. It was busy and the only space was sharing with a couple of folk. I asked if I could and they nodded. I got chatting with a fellow 'biker' – an Israeli girl who was cycling around Britain, which put my own jaunt into perspective. I wouldn't want to tackle these hills on pedal power! Refuelled, I made my way to Tre Taliesin – stopping off at the 'Half way House', with its hobbity waterwheel, and surely one of the most beautiful waterfalls in Wales – not large, but lovely, right at the divide of the Dyfi. It was easy to imagine a water nymph frolicking in the clear water – moon-pale skin, long white hair flowing over a svelte figure in green velvet. I certainly could as I sat there, eating my cheese baguette and apple! I went on to Bedd Taliesin, paying my respects to the Penbeirdd, reciting Dragon Dance in the mist on the mountain-side. A hareglow grew from the grave. I felt a sense of stillness and completion. Then I blatted down to Borth, to the realm of Gwyddno Garanihr. The waves rolled in – refreshing – but the place has a desultory air, the desolate feel of a seaside resort out of season, even though it's late June and summer, apparently! Feels like winter! The endless rain is depressing and draining. It would've been a sad note to end my trip on – a feeling of flatness, rather than euphoria – so I followed a whim and rode along the winding, hilly coast road to Aberystwyth, which was a pleasant surprise, bathed as it was in sunlight under – finally – clear blue skies! I parked the bike and walked up to the castle, and stood upon the gorsedd stone. Full circle! I've decided to stay the night – rather than slog it back. Must visit the National Library tomorrow, and check out a couple of bookshops I've spotted. This is awen-town!

Wyrd Epiphany in Aberystwyth

Stood on the end of the pier gazing along the sun road, thinking about the second half of the year and all the things I have to do… and about the Way of Awen – and it dawned on me what it actually is. Arriving in Aberystwyth and changing my 'wyrd' illustrated it brilliantly. Not just going with the flow, for that shows lack of will, a lack of ambition. It is about living by inspiration. Being spontaneous, in the moment, fully present, fully conscious – not just being blown by the winds of fate, but living consciously. It is just like a performance – rather than worrying what is going to happen next, trusting in the tale and your craft. Let the Awen come through you. If you worry, then you forget, then you stumble. It is about attaining a certain level of grace, of equipoise and equanimity. Living with dignity and wisdom.

Watched the sunset from a promenade bar with a sense of completion. So glad I stayed – a gentle, satisfying end to the holiday, rather than a long slog home in the evening. I still have to do that tomorrow, but then I have a Monday mindset – a 'back to work' attitude. This is the first day I really felt like I had stopped and relaxed fully. I was overcome with tiredness earlier – it finally hit me, after pushing myself all week. I was too tired to head back yesterday. Besides, it's not everyday I get to see the sun slide into the sea. This has probably been the first day that's been possible for a week in Wales. Rainland! Still, I feel I've got what I came for. I've kickstarted my book. I've definitely embarked upon the Way – and gained insights along the way.

Now it's time to bring them home.

[A quick visit to the National Library of Wales, to view – on screen at least – the fragile original texts of Llyr & Hanes Taliesin. Plus sourcing some elusive Charles Williams. Then it was time to hit the road home. Total mileage of my journey to Deganwy: 698 miles – hardly 'Long Way Down', but enough for me this week].

Back in Bath
1st July 2008

I am back home after a long ride yesterday. Had a good night's sleep and a hot bath and feel better – although I'm still stiff and it'll take at least a day to recover. Mind is still 'groggy'. Shows how tired I was – yesterday wrote 'Shrewsbury' on my bike directions instead of 'Hereford' and ended doing an 80 mile detour! And so the journey back took two hours longer – 7 hours in total since leaving Aberystwyth, although about an hour of that was taken up with pitstops. Guess I didn't want to come home, for I was heading back to north Wales!

Now I have to assimilate what I learnt last week, and channel it into the book. I began this journal exactly a month ago, and have had some good experiences to get the Awen flowing. I could use extracts of this in my book, or use it to jumpstart the Awen (as in the Morning Pages exercise). The main thing is to let the Awen flow every day as I'm writing it – would be lovely to be based in a cottage by Geironydd – rather than use loads of quotes. I want the text to flow, to come from embodied wisdom.

From the heart, not the head.

Bookbarn, Hallatrow
6th July 2008

Sitting in the vast *Raiders of the Lost Ark* Bookbarn warehouse – Britain's 'largest second-hand book warehouse' apparently – as the rain lashes down outside. The wild elements rage and all we have to counter them, to placate these ferocious gods, are these countless words. An elephants' graveyard of books. Pile after pile. Aisle after gloomy aisle. A labyrinth of words. What minotaurs lurk here? Anyone brave enough to enter its endless maze is a possible Theseus. It's the kind of place you could lose your sanity if you took a wrong turning. Were there gibbering bibliophiles wandering these corridors, lost in their search? The odd skeleton of a bookworm? I could imagine doorways to other worlds here – each book a portal. It would make a great setting for a story, as I've noted in another notebook last year. How could such an inconsequential thing as a book hope to encompass the world? How can the frailest, most insubstantial of things counter such wild vastness, the unpredictability of creation? A bookshop is a good example of a practical manifestation of the Way of Awen. If one attempted to run through the shelves methodically (difficult when there's only the vaguest attempt at cataloguing here) it would take forever and a day. Instead, it is best to trust to intuition. Often the first book you lay your hands on is the right one. I came here with the intention of finding a copy of *Voss* by Patrick White – and I found one, a lovely old '58 hardback for £3. I used the computer catalogue to see if they had any Charles Williams, for I wouldn't know where to start – where is their poetry section? It revealed they had a copy of *Taliessin Through Logres* at a snip for £90! I ordered his Selected Writings instead for a more reasonable £12. A lad, possibly the boyfriend of one of the 'book-muses' behind the counter had to run the gauntlet to fetch it from the other barn. I waited in the café, enjoying a coffee while writing this. I wonder what other treasures lay undiscovered here? I carefully wrapped my finds and sealed myself into my biker gear. The 'typhoon' had eased, but it was still raining. Time to get home with my spoils from this book-Annwn.

Later, looking through Charles Williams' rich bardic verse, I came across this quote:

> *But I was Druid-sprung;*
> *I cast my heart in the way;*
> *All the Mercy I called*
> *To give courage to my tongue,*
> (Charles Williams, *'Taliessin's Return to Logres'*)

This is all the committed bard can do – 'cast your heart in the way' and hope for the best. We must trust our hearts to the Way, and hope it will guide us through the vicissitudes of life. Ship of Awen, carry me through the storm!

Hawk Songs
30th July 2008

The fierce shriek of a hawk caught our attention. We looked up and, yes, there, through the branches of the pine trees, we caught a glimpse of a hawk. We had just finished planted a commemorative acer tree for Tim Sebastion Woodman, Arch-druid of Wiltshire, at Rocks East Woodland – on the borders of Somerset, Wiltshire and Gloucester. I knelt by the tree, talking with Angela Long, old friend of Tim's and first Ovate of Caer Badon. The others had already left, heading back up to the centre for a cuppa and I must admit I was keen to join them – planting a tree for a lost friend along with some of his (unground) ashes is thirsty work. Tim would've wanted a drink too – but of a stronger variety! Yet something made me stay a little while longer, to 'stand and stare' and savour the moment. There had been a flurry of activity as a small group of us applied ourselves to the task (Miranda, Rob, Steve, Angie, myself, plus Marylyn and Philip from the centre). It was all over rather quickly. Some words were said – I read out Tim's song, from his Gryphon days, which we've quoted on the plaque, Steve read out a new poem and Angela lead the Druid's Oath. We chanted the awen three times as well. And then time seemed to slow – pausing between each awen.

I had often seen a pair of buzzards up there, but not a hawk – if that's what it was. I'm no twitcher, but it made a sound very similar to the one I heard when a hawk had nested in the spire of St John's – the tallest spire in Bath, right in the city centre – to nurse a couple of its chicks. They became local celebrities, with film crews and tourists recording them. I was going to the station early one morning when I heard the shriek – an incredible primal sound, as though a pterodactyl flew above the city! I looked up to see an extraordinary sight: a body of a pigeon being cast out of the nest. Followed swiftly by the mother, who plunged down and caught it in mid-air (like some fancy stunt out of a

Hollywood movie) before flying around the spire with it, terrifying any other bird in the area with her defiant cry. It seems she was trying to coax the fledgling hawks out of the nest, using the bird-carcase as bait. But they were still too timid – and I must admit it even made my spine tingle. Mother's around their young can be the fiercest of creatures – as I experienced with my mum's cat last week. She's just had a litter – now a couple of months old – but still she hisses when I come into the room.

I love seeing kestrels, or windhovers, by the roadside. You can see clearly where they got their nickname from. Their control, sometimes in strong winds, is impressive. I've often spotted them on the flanks of hill forts on a blustery day – hovering, seemingly effortlessly, when it no doubt involves great skill and will to 'hold your centre' when buffeted by forces around you. This for me is one of the things the hawk represents – absolute focus. Their eyes are amazing – they rivet you to the spot.

Apparently a hawk got killed, mobbed by fifty seagulls, at a bird of prey display in Glasgow this week. Hoody birds! Glaswegian ones at that. Obviously not taking kindly to this fellow predator on their turf. They ganged up on it, when one-to-one they wouldn't stand much chance.

One of the very first films I saw at the cinema (the second in fact) was Ken Loach's *Kes* – a slice of social realism, telling the story of an estate kid who rescues and rears a kestrel.

The bird symbolising freedom, nobility and the unattainable lifestyle deprived to one of his class. Such birds traditionally were the province of Norman royalty and falconry still is a royal past-time in Arabia. Tomorrow I'm off to the Forest of Dean and I hope to have a chance to go off into the forest on some trips, perhaps to Symonds Yat – where I saw a mating pair of hawks a few years ago, along with lots of excited twitchers.

The hawk waits, watches, and plunges down to strike with no indecision. It teaches us to act with accuracy and alacrity. To be decisive. It can come across as fierce, but in fact it is just focused.

No time for dilly-dallying. For foolery. When an opportunity presents itself – grab it. Don't make apologies, don't justify, just act.

A merlin has been my companion for the last three years as I've worked upon my bardic series of novels, *The Windsmith Elegy*. In my story Merlin the magician, has been trapped in the form of a small hawk, his namesake – in his legendary esplumoir, a 'moulting cage'. We all must reside in our own esplumoir at some point in our lives; when we must wait for nature to transform us into what we need to move into for the next phase of our existence. Often, this time can feel frustrating, as we wait to move on. For a new opportunity to present itself. It feels like we are stuck. That things are out of our hands. But we must use this time to incubate, then, when the window of opportunity arises – to act. As Mr Morrison once said, 'No eternal reward will forgive us now for wasting the dawn'. The early bird, does indeed, catch the worm.

Buckstone, Forest of Dean
2nd August 2008

The Buckstone is believed to be a 'Clacha Brath', a druidic judgement stone. Its rocking would decide matters of great importance. They were apparently used in divination – their oscillations interpreted by the oracle. And they could produce a great sound heard for miles around – so could be used for relaying messages. A couple of miles away there stand two sets of 'listening stones' known as Near Hearkening and Far Hearkening Rocks. So this high place feels like the stone viewing chair out of *The Lord of the Rings*. I can imagine Tolkien here, being fired up by the place as he gazed out over the woods into the darkly wild west of Wales (later I was discover two Tolkien connections – his notes on the Lydney temple, and his time with Sir Mortimer Wheeler, archaeologist). Here I must hearken to my heart and make a judgement that will rock my world. Which way will the stone tip? I must be true to myself and act with honour and honesty. That is my only benchmark.

Above the Buckstone is a flatter stone with a hollow indentation and a neck-shaped notch – and it has inspired several writers to speculate whether it was used for human sacrifice. In one poem it is a woman; in another it is the bard himself. Will I lose my head? Or my maiden?

I sit on the beautiful precipice at Near Hearkening Rocks, overlooking the rolling wooded fastness of the Forest of Dean, listening to the wind in the leaves, sending me their whispered messages, the message of the heart. It is a joy to be alive here in this numinous place, the sun upon my face. Freedom. Space. Room to think. To hear the quiet murmurings of the heart. I cried out my Lady's name and it was snatched away by the wind. Did she hear? Are our prayers received? Will the secret wishes of our heart find their shore?

Later I made my way to Symonds Yat and spotted a female peregrine falcon through the RSPB's telescope – bigger than the male, because they have to defend their nest... on the way back along the Wye I found a place to sit and stare. I bathed my hot feet in its lovely waters, actually warm – not freezing as I expected. I plucked a hazel leaf and cast it into the waters, and with it the vow: 'let love be my river'.

Bardic Camp
3rd August 2008

It is the festival of Lughnasadh and I reach Wheat in my journey of the bard, aka Cian, 'wheat of song'. I write to the strains of the heavenly harp of Sian James, appropriately enough. I watched her with friends last night in the café – her songs echoing the secret music of our hearts.

Later, Lydney

Just visited the amazing dream temple of Lydney in the banks of the Severn and I'm now sitting in Taurus Crafts, a lovely arty centre next door, for a reviving coffee before I hit the road. After thwarted attempts to find a public road in, I had to 'trespass' – driving up the drive into Lydney Park itself, a bold move but it paid off. I parked behind the manor itself and walked through the deer park to it. The land there was so rich, so numinous with devas with spirits. Massive trees. Hidden valleys, I don't agree with private ownership as large pieces of the country by individuals but there is something to be said for such arcadias – it felt sensitively managed, virtually nature's own. Deer gambolled across the wooded vale and verdant sward. Incongruously my bike leathers, I hiked up to the hill top temple, the adrenalin giving me the energy my sleep-deprived body lacked. I felt protected – I entered this sacred place with deep respect – and perhaps that's why it paid off. The ruins were enclosed or obscured by high swathes of bracken. It felt a 'hidden' place. Finally, I could stop.

My departure from the bardic camp was emotional. I hate goodbyes. I never do them well. I just wanted to up sticks and go, and I did this with as much alacrity as possible, honouring the friends I had made or spent time with over the weekend. Yet it was a slo-mo start to the day, after little sleep, and I gave myself all morning to pack, as I was running low. I said my farewells and left just as the Closing Ritual was starting. Guess I was 'tired and emotional' and I was quite choked up on my ride to Lydney. I was close to giving up, hitting dead-ends, but persisted.

Relieved to make it to the temple I asked its resident deity, Nodens, for healing of the heart. I was feeling bruised and battered. Blodeuwedd had struck! Nodens' temple is deeply peaceful and one can imagine it being conducive to sleep/dream therapy, if that is what took place (it seems similar in purpose to the temple to Asklepios at Epiduaros. Certainly to visit it is deeply healing in itself. I would love to spend time here – even write a book set here, exploring its story (Celtic-Roman interface). Instead, it was but a flying visit. I ate a peach and offered its seed, burying it in the soil, a gift to Persephone. It was interesting to discover the temple so close to salmon-runs on the Severn and dog-effigies, making two Taliesin/Ceridwen connections. Bronze greyhound figures have been found here, and the interpretation board postulated that temple-dogs were kept here, to lick the wounds of those who visited for healing (saliva is an effective antiseptic).

Nodens could be connected to Nuada from Irish mythology, famed for his silver hand – and in Welsh mythology with Ludd? The wounded fisherman – evoked locally to aid with the catch on the Severn. The wounded hero makes his affliction his gift. I felt like my fingers had been burnt and I needed healing – need to heal the rift that has developed, the wound of my heart. Rather than be rocked like the Buckstone perhaps I should hold my centre – stay strong. Not be pulled hither and thither. And yet had I not vowed, on the banks of the Wye to 'let love be my river'?

On the way down a mouse or vole crossed my path, telling me to tread cautiously in my iron boots, left-footed in fairyland. Walking the green maze of the temple I spotted the nuclear power station through the trees, on the far bank of the Severn, a modern temple of power, an obscene blot in the landscape. Returning to the bike, heart-pounding as I hoped to avoid detection, what looked like a white hound or even hart darted across the hill below the house directly opposite. I froze, expecting it to be the landowner walking his dog, but when I reached a clear view I saw no sign of man or beast. Was it one of the fairy hounds of Nodens, or was it a white hart? Was it the sign of lovers or was it Ceridwen on my tail?

In Taurus Crafts (outside of which stood a massive wooden boar, ready for their annual fire festival, the end of August) I connected with the manager of the new bookshop, Cliff. His shop consisted mainly of titles connected to their governing 'deity',

Steiner. The other Teutonic savants completed the triumvirate: Goethe and the artist Joseph Beuys. It is the latter I could relate most closely to. Got chatting with Cliff and he agreed to take a couple of my books, and provisionally booked me for a Beuys event. Having made this nice connection, I hit the road, girding my loins for the running the gauntlet of the motorway back home. The gods were with me and I gratefully pulled into the back of my place in beloved Aquae Sulis. I had survived these intense few days, but was exhausted, and collapsed on the sofa, falling asleep.

The Barge Inn, Honeystreet
13th August 2008
Sitting at one of my favourite pubs, The Barge, on the Kennet and Avon canal in deepest Wiltshire – the verdant Vale of Pewsey. Live-aboards and trippers are moored up along the towpath. The beer garden is busy with visitors: cyclists in spandex, campers, lunchers and crop-circle hunters, like my partner and I – who had gone traipsing along the tractor-tracks earlier to visit one below Knap Hill. I don't believe extra-terrestrials make them but I find the whole phenomenon fascinating, i.e. *why* humans feel compelled to make them and why others believe aliens made are responsible. We laid in the flattened circle, soaking up 'the vibes'. Thirsty work in the heat of the day. It was, for once, a sunny day (a rarity this July with its relentless rain). We had gone on a lovely ramble around the hilltops, enjoying the view from Knap Hill and Adam's Grave, and the somewhat tatty white horse. And now we sat by the canal and I was happy with my mug of light summer ale, my partner with her Solero! A boy was throwing stones at the ducks, and some hit me, although his parents looked on in benign obliviousness! Despite the idyllic situation, there was a querulous atmosphere: maybe we were all hot and bothered. Something was building. A storm needed to break and clear the air.

Late, we tried to find a couple near the Sanctuary end of the

Ridgeway, to no avail, searching like mourning Demeter through the golden grief-dewed fields.

A Blood-tainted Bird's Nest
August 8th 2008

Today sees the start of the Olympics in Beijing, for better or worse – with an expensive and spectacular opening ceremony at the multi-billion 'bird's nest' stadium. It seemed China didn't have the same problems at finishing it as Athens four years ago – I remember being there, seeing all the paraphernalia in the shops. There was a lot of excitement then, but none of the political controversy like now. All the fireworks cannot cover up China's shameful human rights record. Some say sport should be kept separate from politics, but it's impossible. The truth is all the nations taking part are condoning China's regime by being there. In terms of PR it is priceless. China opens its arms to the world, yet incarcerates, tortures and kills its own people…

A bard should be aware of the connections. See as many perspectives as possible.

Earlier in the Spring, I was in London in a hotel overlooking Hyde Park running a workshop (Awaken the Bard Within) for Alternatives when there was an uproar outside. We were in the middle of the intensive workshop, but it turns out the Olympic torch had just gone by, with its ensuing chaos: Chinese State Security running shotgun – ninjas in tracksuits – a phalanx of London bobbies in fluorescent jackets jogging alongside and a 'mob' of protesters with placades, justifiably protesting against China's presence in Tibet. We watched the rolling footage in the hotel lobby – the game of flatten the protester played against the backdrop of London landmarks. Whenever one tried to make a lunge for the torch they were rubgy-tackled onto the tarmac by a scrum of coppers. Seemed like a new Olympic sport. It was a 'difficult' situation – especially since those who were selected to carry the torch were clearly delighted to have the 'honour' – it was their moment of glory, but it was sullied by the 'nasty politics' going on, and yet...we can't bury our head in the sand.

The image of the torch against the snowy backdrop of Hyde Park was a surreal one... (At least that's how I picture it) And the fact that history had just passed us by, and we had failed to see it! How much of history happens like this – with those nearby oblivious of the momentous events transpiring around the corner?

Earlier, on the train up – I watched, bleary-eyed after an early start, the world turned Narnia after a rare snowfall. It was austere and soothing – in contrast the hectiness of the City, which I always find draining. I always seem to turn my head at the moment when the White Horse of Uffington comes into view. This time, its white contours were filled with snow, and surrounded by snow – white on white. Ancient, timeless... The Long Man of Wilmington – no longer turf cut, used to be visible as the snow melted. Some would remain in the indentations, revealing its outline.

That icy day in Winter seems a long way away now, here on a muggy Summer's evening.

Love & Awen
14th August 2008

Love is a direction which excludes all other directions
DH Lawrence, 'Women in Love'

The Way of Awen is very akin to the path of love. Once you are in love, there is no being out of it. There is no separation. It cannot be just 'something for the weekends' if it is true love. And the same with the Way of Awen – it cannot be reserved just for performances, for workshops, for bardic gatherings and showcases. It has to be a way of life. And it needs to transform everything – what I call the Awen Effect. Every aspect of one's life should be scrutinised in the light of awen – work, play, home, family, friends and other relationships (family, partner, professional). It would perhaps be close to the truth to say love is awen, awen is love. Love should flow like awen – never static, stagnant, conditional. And awen should have the empathy, the compassion, the awareness and consideration of love. It should be a benign light – those three beams – not a harsh light. The awen's three rays should be shone into every corner of one's life – as with true love. Nothing should be left untransformed, or 'unprocessed' in counselling speak. It is this utter immersion which perhaps terrifies us in love – the feeling of being consumed, being lost – a loss of self. And yet love, like any intense, challenging experience can make us feel more fully ourselves – it brings out the best (and possibly the worst) sides. We can rise to it, or turn away, terrified – never to fully grow, never to fully know the complete experience of being alive ('too laugh but not all of your laughter, to weep, but not all of your tears' as Gibran said). Love is not to judge, to control, to condemn, it is simply to share. And the same with awen – it is not to be hoarded or portioned out 'to be doled out' as Patrick White said in his novel, *Voss*:

> *Inspiration descends only in flashes, to clothe circumstances; it is not stored up in a barrel, like salt herring, to be doled out.*

It should simply be allowed to flow – like a waterfall. Water must be allowed to find its own channels in its urgent desire to reach the ocean. To block it, to control it (like the environmental disaster of the 'Iron Gates' dam) is an insult to nature. All we can do is aspire to be the best channels we can – conduits, nothing more. This removes any egoism. The clearer we are, the purer the awen will flow through us – but as every actor and singer knows – the voice often sounds better when rich in character, rough-edged not anodyne. Think Tom Waits – a voice like bourbon poured over jagged chunks of ice; Bob Dylan's voice of 'sand and glue'; Janis Joplin's heart-rending flamesongs – a voice burnt like a moth. By control of the lungs, larynx, tongue and teeth, we imbue it with personality. Thus we can give awen our own unique 'spin' or flavour – deliver it in our own distinctive style. So the artist shines through his or her art – it provides a channel. And often is the best of us. But it is the 'art in you, not you in the art', which is primary to all true artists. We are martyrs to our art. Our life's work is a labour of love.

Dylan Thomas' 'common wages' of the 'most secret heart' are what motivates us – and so with love, for the countless little tendernesses – not some ultimate reward. Love in the common-place, not in the front parlour or the chapel. Not saved for Sunday best. Not tomorrow, but today – always today, in every moment, in the most mundane instants.

Great art, as with true love is about transcending the ego – looking beyond the personal, the entropy of the solipsistic. Come from a place of authenticity, but looking outwards, not solely inwards. Love/awen is giving – but it is also the knowing how to receive.

Often we believe we 'do not deserve love' – the love another showers on us; that we are not 'worthy' of their attention, their affection, when in fact we are – otherwise, we wouldn't be receiving it. Receiving – letting someone in – is often harder for us, than giving. When you give, you are in control. When you receive, you are not.

It is 'giving' in the sense of opening up – give a little, compromise, yield. It is knowing how to be nakedly alive in the raw, unfinished, imperfect moment. Never perfect, never complete. As in an orchestra, in love, in awen – let others complete you.

Reflections on a Birthday
19th August 2008

A birthday is a time to reflect, to take stock and to look ahead. It is the day you entered the world. No great shakes to anyone else, but to you – everything. Today is my thirty-ninth birthday. I had a small celebration the weekend immediately before, and tonight my partner is taking me out for a meal, but for now I am alone. As an individual soul we enter the world, and as an individual soul we leave it. If we are lucky we'll have loved ones around us. Certainly our mothers were present at our births – and perhaps our fathers too. And when it is time to shuffle off this mortal coil, then we'll be received into the embrace of Mother Death. But for now, it is time to celebrate being alive, being who you are, where you are, when you are. It is time to reap what we have sown, in terms of the relationships in our lives – not that we should act in expectation of 'reward', give in order to receive, but the web of community works on reciprocation, of a fluid exchange of energy. If someone needs a hand, help them. A shoulder to cry on, someone to talk to. Perhaps a disability or illness prevents them from managing a certain task. We all have our fortes, our skills – these can be exchanged for those we lack. Everyone is needed; everyone has a role to play, a niche to fill, a purpose.

A birthday is a good time to look with awen at the relationships in one's life – which are functional, which dysfunctional? Is there love there – openness, trust, respect, warmth? Is there 'bad blood', bitter feelings, unexpressed anger, unresolved issues? Blake in his poem 'A Poison Tree' wrote:

> *I was angry with my friend:*
> *I told my wrath, my wrath did end.*
> *I was angry with my foe,*
> *I told it not, my wrath did grow.*

If there's 'poison places' in your heart, in your relationships –

places of pain, of sorrow, of fear, of hate even – then shine the light of awen upon them. Bring them out into the light. Express them – using sound, dance, paint, clay, fire, whatever acts as a catalyst for catharsis. Talk about them – ideally with the person/people concerned but if not, then with a good friend or neutral 'third party', counsellor, agony aunt or uncle, etc. In the Celtic Tradition there was said to be a four-sided cup: if three untruths were spoken over it, it would shatter – but if three truths were uttered over its fragments, it would mend.

The Shattered Mirror of God

Are we the shattered mirror of God? Each of us has a divine spark, a splinter of Divinity, our sacred self. Whenever we connect, collaborate, forge friendships or fall in love, it seems a little section of it slots into place and heals. Life is full of chaos and conflict, but if humanity ever manages to live in harmony with itself and Nature for long enough, then perhaps all of the fragments will join back together once more and the mirror will be mended: at which point the face of the Divine will be reflected in the perfection of Creation, an equilibrium will be achieved, and maybe the universe will reach its 'conclusion', or attain another level of evolution.

So, on a microcosmic scale, whenever people come together in harmony, in creativity, in love, then the fragments of God mend and, for a while, there's a little mirror of Heaven on Earth.

The Blessing of Friendship

Side by side with this essential 'soul-work' is the joyousness that should attend all birthdays: celebrate the healthy connections you have, the friends and family you are blessed with. A good friend is priceless. Honour them. Employ your bardic skill. Birthdays are good times to write a 'praise-song' for a loved one – dedicate a poem to them, compose a poetic portrait. Perform for them at their birthday gathering, or, if this would embarrass them – write out in calligraphy and give them a copy on parchment, tied with ribbon, or framed.

Looking Back, Looking Forward

Janus was the Roman god of thresholds – with two faces, one looking forward, one looking back. His festival was celebrated in the month named after him: January – on New Year's Day. He is the god of endings and beginnings, and he is a good deity to work with on what is your own 'new year's day' – your birthday. Look back at your last year: what have you achieved? What have you learnt? What have you lost? What have you gained? Do you have tangible things to show for it: a series of paintings, a book, an album, or maybe just a photo album, a bundle of letters, mementoes and souvenirs from places visited or gifts received? Maybe there's a new love in your life: a new partner, friend or even child. Maybe you have lost loved ones. Had a serious illness. Crisis. Trauma. Perhaps it has been a difficult, challenging year – your *annus horribilis* – or it could have been bittersweet, the 'best of times, the worst of times'. Life is seldom one thing or the other for long. Embrace it all. Rejoice in it all, even the pain – for it teaches us many things. From it, we grow.

And turn over a new leaf. The journal of your coming year is unwritten. What do you want to manifest? Make a dream list: write down all things you wish to happen. Some things will be firmed up, others may be only fantasies: a new job, a new house, a new partner, children, travel, winning a prize, writing the 'book inside you'. But unless you give yourself permission for these things to manifest, they never will. Dream them into your life. Visualise yourself enjoying whatever it is you not just desire, but need at a deep soul level. Materialism will not make you happy – ultimately. This isn't a New Age greed-apologist philosophy – one that tells you it's okay to be a capitalist, to be part of the system which is destroying the planet, exploiting people, manufacturing misery. This is about dreaming your soul-medicine.

Know Thyself

Spend time on your birthday completing a 'soul-inventory'. Are you happy in your life? Where are you 'at' right now? Do you feel fulfilled? Frustrated? Sad? Over the moon? Are you following your life path? Are you postponing your happiness? Think about how you act around others. How you carry yourself in this world? With grace and dignity? Or like a clown? Do you tread on people's toes? Put your foot in your mouth all the time? Get the wrong end of the stick? Do you flow through life, or find your life filled with obstacles? These stumbling blocks are part of life – it is how you react to them that matters. What are you finer qualities? Your worst qualities? Good and bad habits? What needs work? Physical: more exercise? Emotional: more openness? Mentally: more studying? Accepting that we can never be 'perfect', that we have faults and foibles that need to be embraced – we can still strive to 'better' ourselves. We are responsible for our own development. Living is a 'boot-strap operation' – no one else will do it for you.

Most people would rather improve, than worsen. We should never stop learning. Growing. Changing. Be happy with who you are, but accept that 'personality' is a construct that can alter. It doesn't have to stay the same way. When things become fixed, they stagnate and die. Life is flux. Dance with the change. Be the change.

Party!

Finally, remember to be in the here and now. Take the day off – this is your 'sacred time'. Do the things which nourish you. Things that you love, or have always fancied doing. Climb a mountain. Dive into the sea. Take a flying lesson, or book a balloon flight. Have a gathering. Celebrate!

Play

An act of awen is one of brave foolery. To pick up a pen, to begin writing upon a blank sheet of paper – not knowing where the line is going, where the ink of your imagination will take you, is an audacious gesture – in defiance of all forces of decay, cynicism, and negativity. The evil voices who whisper – you can't do it! Who are you fooling? Who do you think you are? It's all been done before! Give up! Don't bother! Who tell you that 'you're not good enough', or to 'get a proper job' – to be sensible, be serious, behave. They are threshold guardians of the status quo, who don't want you to use your imagination – to think, to act, for yourself. It's no conspiracy, just piracy – of your precious time upon this planet. They are the time-vampires. Others want you to kill time for them, rather than live time for yourself. It takes courage to overcome these negative messages. To tap into your own well – perhaps long blocked – of creative abundance. Perhaps there's stuff in there you'd rather not show the light of day. Stuff that's long been buried – and perhaps with good reason. But it's time for a spring clean! Shake out the bugs and cobwebs, the dust and shadows from your subconscious. Dust, before you become dusty! Dance with the skeletons in the closet. And, hey, your inner child may sneak out as well. Let the kid have some fun. It's creative playtime!

Spending time with a blank sheet of paper – drawing, writing, making musical notation, brainstorming – is giving your creative self-quality time. It provides a window of opportunity – a doorway, a bridge, a cavemouth or mountain peak – choose your metaphor. The equivalent of sacred time. Time to listen to the universe, to your inner-verse. Who knows what might come through? But have no expectations, no goals, no targets, no demands or parameters. Just wait – in a state of creative preparedness – and see.

And apply this attitude to all aspects of your life – work, love, home, hobbies, diet, wardrobe – start from scratch. How would you want your life to be? Think outside the box, outside old habits, stale patterns, limited expectations, the negative messages given us by family, friends, teachers, bosses, the media or our self. Dream big!

If you don't dream hard enough you end up living in other people's dreams.

Use art to play 'imaginative alternatives'. Like playing dressing up, have fun trying on different 'hats', walking in other 'shoes', just to see what it feels like. Just for fun. No expectation, no pressure. Such goal-less activity acknowledges the permeable nature of reality. It only solidifies when we stop applying our imagination – when we let it ossify into stagnant forms. Sometimes we strike upon the 'perfect form' and quite rightly cease in our experimentation – but more often than not we accept a certain way due to constraints of time and budget. We accept shoddily designed goods because of economics. We mostly live in box-like houses, cheek by jowl, because that's the accepted norm. Windows don't have to be rectangular. The world doesn't have to be the shape it is. Countries. Governments. Religions. Traditions. All patterns created by humankind. All artificial constructs. *Nothing has to be set in stone unless we choose it to be.* The Way of Awen is a personal creative revolution, the ultimate in blue-sky thinking. How radical the change depends on how far you are willing to strip things back. How far down the rabbit hole are you willing to go? The sky in fact is not the limit. The glass ceiling was never there. We've been fooled into leading bonsai lives. Every aspect of your life can be re-invigorated by applying it. Grow to your full potential, and empower others to do the same. Play, of course, is only possible through co-operation between the participating elements – people or things. It needs to be a reciprocal affair. We need to play with awareness and consideration of others space and feelings. It is not an excuse to impose your will on others. It is just a chance to 'lighten up', to dance in joy, to give yourself permission to be free.

Awen and Money

Money can be perceived as an obstacle, an albatross around our necks, a necessary evil or simply evil – the Devil's shilling – or it can be perceived as awen. It is designed to flow. What are your attitudes towards money? Do you always have problems with money? Are you 'always broke'; do you have what Capitalist New Agers like to call 'poverty consciousness'? Trace it back – were you always strapped for cash as a child? Did you grow up in a family who had to count the pennies? Perhaps you did live on the poverty line, even below it – possible, even in Britain. Were you born with a 'silver spoon in your mouth', and feel you don't deserve your wealth? Do you have feelings of guilt around money? Do you see it as 'filthy lucre', dirty money? Or did you grow up in a hard working family, a decent standing of living earnt by graft, not 'sponged off the state'? Or middle class snobs, social climbers, keeping-up-with-the-Joneses types? Or simply in a family that somehow had enough and were happy – not rich, but not broke either. Able to afford the odd holiday. Perhaps you had a car, a VCR, a computer when growing up. Or more – a horse, a boat – more to do with lifestyle or where you lived rather than income bracket – you had other kinds of wealth. Indeed the only true kind: quality of life. Maybe you grew up surrounded by stunning countryside or coastal scenery. Perhaps you travelled a lot – a mixed blessing. Maybe your parents had 'interesting friends' or were themselves cultured, talented, successful – and perhaps you enjoyed some of the fruits of that. Or maybe you arrived as refugees, with only the clothes on your back.

The scenarios are endless.

However the odds are stacked you can make or break yourself depending on your attitude to money and acumen with it. Some people are born in poverty and become self-made millionaires. Others are born with a large inheritance and squander it until they are bankrupt. Millions, indeed billions know otherwise, but there are plenty of examples from both extremes to show that we 'make our fate' with money as with most things in our lives.

Awen is a good financial lubricant. Imagine the cash-flowing like that white light of awen, pouring down into your coffers, and as they overflow they fill other receptacles below them – the good fortune is shared. Money in a box or under the mattress is not bringing anyone happiness. It is prudent to save some for a rainy day, but if you see money as a static thing – to be hoarded – you'll be like one of the people you hear about on the news who dies sitting on a small fortune, perhaps having lived a 'one bar electric fire, dry cracker' existence, with no one to pass it onto except perhaps a cats home. Money is there to be enjoyed whilst alive. As the popular saying goes: 'you can't take it with you'. Shrouds have no pockets.

See money not as the 'root of all evil' (those who have more than enough, or a vested interest, tend to perpetuate such false-hoods, e.g. religious institutions who want you to forsake all worldly goods – by giving them over to them) but as energy. It provides you with the freedom to choose. Without money one's choices are limited – to what others are willing to dole out, often with strings attached. Money doesn't buy happiness. Mindless materialism will not bring fulfilment – the prevalence of cancer, heart attacks, divorce, violence, suicide, etc, among the 'well-off' bears testimony to that. But if you see money as a means to an end – it could buy you time to finish that creative project you've postponed for so long, to go on that pilgrimage, to set up that charity, that centre, that community resource. It doesn't have to be used for selfish purposes.

Let it flow into, and out of your life. Cash flow is more important than accruing vast stacks of wealth. As long as it keeps flowing you have energy to work with, possibilities. Money is a matrix of potential. It allows us to acquire things we don't have the time and skill to do ourselves. If we do, why pay others for them? Bake that bread, make that dress. We can share our skills, informally through our social network, or more formally through a scheme like LETS. Or if you don't have the skills to share, you still have that most precious of commodities – time – and a system like Timebank allows us to exchange time 'currency' instead: two alternative currency systems outside the mainstream. People-centred, rather than centred around financial institutions. Don't let the banks, building societies and credit card companies rule your life. They are only useful if they serve people. Often they are designed only to serve the interests of a few at the expense of the many. But consume less, shop around, shop ethically, use your consumer power and you take the power back into your hands. So often we work to fund a lifestyle that acts as compensation for our work. A ridiculous Catch 22. Change your lifestyle and you won't need to work so hard. Downsize. Ask how little you actually need, not how much. Food, shelter, warmth, company ('fodder, flax, fire and frigg!' as the Norse used to say) is all you really need. True wealth is health and happiness, peace and community, creative fulfilment. Quality of life is what matters. Work to live, don't live to work. Don't make work your god – to make up for the lack of control or fulfilment in the rest of your life. Leave room for others, for time out, for fun. Always have time to stand and stare. A stunning sunset, a walk in an autumnal wood, a glittering river, a glowing moon, a merry bonfire, a rainbow – these things are free. The shining eyes of your pet when you arrive home. An infant's tiny hand curled around your finger. The wise kiss of an elderly relative. Laughter amongst friends. An insight gleaned from great art. Priceless.

Apples on the Underground
22nd August 2008

For once the sun is shining, the sky is showing some blue and it feels like summer. I sit in my hammock between two fruit trees – one gives the Bath Beauty, the other dark red plums. On the newly-mown lawn, exuding its rich sweet of fresh cut grass there's a scattering of early apples, dropped before there time.

Sometimes it seems our bardic efforts fall on barren soil. A performance may fall on deaf ears. Earlier, I had gone up to London and was stuck on the underground in a sweaty carriage packed with people. A busker got on, bearing a ukulele, introduced himself and started playing 'sunny songs', doing his best to cheer people up. Most people seemed to ignore him, perhaps nervous to show signs of appreciation in case it encouraged him or made him elicit a token of such afterwards – or perhaps just plain embarrassed. I enjoyed it – and the busker thanked me for my smile ('you don't see many of them around here', he said). He made a joke of the paucity of audience participation, but the fact was it seemed his efforts were falling on deaf ears. Or so it seemed – and yet I enjoyed it, and perhaps others did. He got some coins in his little net on the end of his instrument. He did a couple of tunes and then, thanking his audience, he went on his way – presumably to raid another carriage: like Arthur in 'Preiddu Annwn', voyaging to the underworld to win the fabled cauldron of plenty. In this instance, the stations of the tube acted as the 'caers', and I imagine some yield greater fortune than others. I wouldn't fancy it myself – it is hard, working to a cold crowd, real hard – but I admire his pluck. He didn't lose his joyousness. And even provided a public service, announcing stations or explaining delays – working with the interruptions of the tannoy, rather than letting them derail him.

So, although the busker's efforts seemed like the fallen apples, rotting on the grass, who knows? Perhaps the odd one will bear fruit. He might get a booking off the back of it, meet the love of his life, get a record deal… A scattershot approach I wouldn't recommend, but at least he's getting out there, being heard. The apples that fall early in my garden seem wasted, but then I realised where they fall a swathe of spring flowers comes every year: snowdrops, then daffodils, then bluebells – from the gift of apples cast onto the earth.

White Horse Words
22nd August 2008

Words provide a map for understanding the universe. Not the only map, but one that works for me. Some see everything in terms of colour, or numbers, or shape, or usefulness, or scent. I'm sure some must see the world in terms of monetary value. But for me, words are my coin.

I was once bored at a dinner party – the hosts were nice people, the food was lovely, my companion was lovely – but my mind was elsewhere. I was observing it all happen, including myself looking bored at the table when an extra-ordinary thing occurred. Perhaps it was the wine, or the intense writing I had been doing lately. I had been working so hard and so long on the computer that I was starting to go 'word-blind' – the words swim meaninglessly in front of me, as I understand dyslexics' experience. I call it not being able to see the words for the trees. That's when you need to step back, take a break, get some critical distance, a fresh pair of eyes. But in this instance, I hadn't been able to switch off that 'editing mind'.

And that's when, at the dinner table, I found everything suddenly turning into words.

Everything the diners said turned instantly into words, emerging from their mouths in a stream. The cutlery, the plates, the food, the wine, the table, the walls, the furniture – everything was suddenly rendered in words. Including the people. Instead of a face I saw the literary description of a face: 'hair, eyes, nose, mouth, chin, ears' – the world had turned to words! The only equivalent I can think of is in *The Matrix* when Neo suddenly sees the world he lives in as it truly is – a construct of endless streams of binary numbers. Bits of information.

I probably just needed to take some time out.

I was turning into the writer Jack Nicholson memorably plays in *The Shining*, writing ream after ream of the same sentence: 'all work and no play makes Jack a dull boy'. Red Rum indeed.

But for me it was a positive revelation.

I've always intimated that there was a 'secret name of things', its *is*ness – what Blake called the inmost form. Even if our language is always culturally specific – another culture would have a completely different set of vocabulary for describing the same things – I believe words, the right words, can express something fundamental about a thing: a place, a person, an emotion, an event, a memory. This isn't an arbitrary layering over of a linguistic matrix – it is tapping into the roots of things. If you consider that language came out of our primal response to the world around us, the way we felt, what frightened us, what we desired, what we perceived as ours, as other – emotionally-loaded sound that eventually settled into specific word-sounds, a sign denoting its signifier – then words do echo the 'primal sound' of things, its keynote. Some words – modern words, technical jargon often doesn't – they feel as dry as dust in our mouths. The best words are often short and to the point. Good Anglo-Saxon nouns. Calling a spade a spade. Saxons knew words had power – it gave you power over a person, an object, if you knew its name – and so they developed kennings for things: a rich metaphorical language, e.g. 'whale's road' for the sea. This indirect way of referring to something lives on in Cockney Slang, which can often be as elliptical as an Anglo-Saxon riddle as well as providing cultural signifiers – a badge of membership, as with any gang and its slang. You're either in the know, or you're not. Every workplace, every profession, every clique has the same dynamic – a secret knowledge imparted through initiation. You have to 'earn it'. And once known, it defines and differentiates you from those not in that social group: those who are 'hip' from those who are 'square' – to use very old-fashioned slang words. Once it enters the public domain it often looses its 'cool', as any parent discovers when they try to speak their children's 'lingo' and just end up sounding 'naff' [out-of-fashion slang words can be like that embarrassing item of clothing at the back of the wardrobe – only brought out for retro parties, for comic effect]. Yet language, at its root, when tapping into the core identity of a thing, is incredibly powerful. It is revealing its quintessence.

As I wrote this on the train on the way home from London [typing it up afterwards] I looked out of the window and beheld the white horse of Uffington: this seemed to provide an apt visual metaphor. It was made not by imposing structure on top of the turf, but by cutting away the turf to reveal the chalk underneath – the inmost form. Good poetry, good prose emulates this: it reveals the core of things. Good writing strikes a deep chord in us – telling us what we have always known, but expressing it in a way we've been unable to do before. It has been on the tip of our tongue, but it takes a bard to express it – to capture and articulate it 'perfectly', or at least aspire to. To expose the white chalk underneath. Poor writing obscures. Good writing reveals. Naked words. Strong. Simple. Direct. Always more powerful. Amateur writers tend to overwrite. Experienced writers strip back. The elegant economy of the Uffington white horse is what all writers should aspire to. Such an icon expresses so much more about the isness of a horse, or the soul of a people, than any prosaic rendering. Look for the lean words and let them run.

Chop Wood, Carry Water
1st September 2008

A new moon and a new month – starting on moon-day, Monday, aptly. And what feels like an overnight change of season: from glorious sunshine at the weekend to grey rainy days. Time to turn to the final third of the year – the inward spiral, yet seldom a time for peaceful reflection in the mad run-up to Yule. It's going to be very busy for me these coming months, with all the teaching lined up, but at least I have a trusty steed now, rather than a rusty unreliable one! Today I've been starting to knuckle down to the tasks ahead. A million and one things to do it seems. Hard work, this gathering in the harvest, yet satisfying. Time to put my house in order for the months ahead will take up my time and I need things in place and low maintenance when they all kick off.

The Way of Awen is very much akin to the Oriental idea of enlightenment: *before* enlightenment, chop wood, carry water. *After* enlightenment, chop wood, carry water. One cannot live in an ivory tower, not expecting to get one's hands dirty, after 'seeing the light'. If the shadow is not embraced, it will fester and influence everything you do anyway. Better to give voice to it, dance with it. Rejoice in it. And also, attend to practical details. The nitty gritty. Get stuck in. Clean that toilet, that cupboard; empty those bins; scrub the floor. Cleaning the house or your vehicle can be very cathartic. If things are neglected, they fall apart. The natural way of things is dissolution. Everything leads to entropy – unless fresh energy is invested. This goes for all aspects of one's life: finances, relationships, the home, work. A stitch in time saves nine, is a wise phrase. Be proactive, rather than reactive. Monitor and maintain. Don't wait for things to go pear-shape, and then do something. Keep on top of things and you won't be fire-fighting, or playing catch up. It's not rocket science. Alas, most of us have a tendency to be lazy, to forget, to postpone and procrastinate. There are always excuses not to do something: these are called displacement activities. Be mindful of them. Watch the way you react when faced with a task – do you attend to it when it crops up, or put it off 'until later'?

Sacred Creativity
4th September 2008
This is a concept I coined today, but it has been part of my methodology for some time – really since 1991, when I started to work on my Fine Art dissertation, 'Illumination: the divine experience of art,' bucking the trend for egocentric and secular concept art popular in the art world. For me, my bardism is my sacred path. When I'm journeying deep into a story, that is my pathworking; when I perform a story that is my ceremony; when

I perform a poem, that is my spell. Yet it is in every waking moment also – immanent awe – there is no separation. That is why I don't feel a particular need to perform ritual or ceremony – for my work already includes it. I don't mind joining in the odd one, but mainly by contributing a poem or tale. I can see their benefit – to create sacred time, to focus intent, to create change, but I'm no ritualist. Some seem to revel in the whole experience of rituals and ceremonies – the dressing up, the formal structure, the sacred play – but this is all incorporated into my performances, and into my private time, researching, musing, meditating upon a theme, often in 'darkness'; the first blind gropings towards clarity, or the flash of illumination, then the long hours – days, nights, manifesting it. Every work of art I create is my small act of magic. To create something that wasn't there before out of pure will and honed skill. To give it vitality, its own autonomy – life! Books, albums, performances, festivals, films – art forms that often take on a life of their own. A good sign. All we can do is bring them through and set them on their way. Give them their wings. Yet there is a responsibility in this – about what we bring through and how we share it. We have to be prepared to stand by our words. In each act of creation we are nailing our colours to the mast. We expose our soul – that's why it can be terrifying to share our dreams. And liberating. We are being true to ourselves – we are honouring the 'god within', the divine spark.

We shine and, in doing so, give others permission to do the same.

Knowing Your Limits
5th September 2008

Part of the Way of Awen is about knowing your limits and reading the signs – being sensitised to the 'web', not just bludgeoning ahead regardless. This morning, I was all set to go off to the Mercian Gathering, having rehearsed and packed the night before – but I awoke to heavy rains and checking the BBC weather website confirmed the worst: flood warnings in the West Midlands, where the festival was due to take place. I didn't fancy riding up in the lashing rain (poor visibility, less grip – and, no matter how waterproof your gear the rain eventually gets in somewhere). Riding a new bike (1 week old) I didn't want to push my luck, make it worse. Although I hate cancelling or letting folk down, it made sense. Besides, my original slot was nabbed by my friend Philip Carr-Gomm no less, (who, because of other commitments, could only make that slot) thus pushing me back from 6.30pm to 5pm, when I'm sure half would still be making there way there (or not, with the weather the way it is). This programme 'cock-up' was a sign. Besides, I didn't like being bottom of the bill anyway – call me vain if you like! One has to weigh up the reasons for going – it's not something I'm getting paid for – just expenses. In truth I'm not that particularly keen on going. Last year I had a pretty dismal time there. There's nothing wrong with the camp – it's nice to be asked – but I felt somewhat on the fringes and I missed my friends/partner not being there (she dropped me off, but couldn't stay, which meant I was stuck there, when I would've rather have been at the Umbrella Fayre in my old town forty odd miles down the road). After a summer of seeing and hearing the same old same old I was well, frankly, bored. Even the prospect of the wicker man failed to kindle any enthusiasm – it seems to have become a 'tradition', when it really is just quoting the Hardy/Schaffer cult film, and has become a pagan cliché. It seems to me a lot of rituals are comparable to the condition known as Obsessive Compulsive Disorder – people feel compelled to do them, because if they don't something terrible will befall them, the crops will fail! Even if folk don't literally believe that these days, people still do odd things like avoid stepping on cracks, or walking under ladders. Generally because to do otherwise would damage one's luck – and yet like the desperate inhabitants of Summer Isle, if their sacrifice fails then next year then, as the unfortunate PC warns, it will be Lord Summer Isle himself. Basically, we only have ourselves to blame. We can make or break our luck. Rather than project and expect things to work out through the agency of an outside power, we need to take the onus and initiative. Often OCD sufferers/ritualists are not conscious of doing them, they simply must, *because it's always been done that way*. And something you don't do consciously becomes the equivalent of chewing gum – a mindless motor action, devoid of meaning. I've seen too many ceremonies like this, with insipid invocations to the quarters – like some dodgy am-dram show. So, if there's no monetary gain (I'll be getting expenses but it hardly reciprocates the effort of getting there and being there in the rain), no intellectual or emotional gain, then why go? I guess there's a chance of making connections and reaffirming old friendships. Last year I did meet a young bardling called Chrissy Derbyshire and I have just ordered the proof copy today of her book I'm publishing (*Mysteries*, a collection of short stories and poems). It's been a productive week, bookwise: Simon's *The Signature of Kisses*, Chrissy's *Mysteries*, and proofing *The Book of the Bardic Chair* (posted to the designer in Portland, Oregon). Maybe I'm just burnt out – like the shell of a torched wicker man. Tired and crabby. A bear being forced out of his cave when all he wants to do is hibernate! I was hoping for a bardic retreat this month – ideally on Iona – but now it's all kicking off. Next week certainly has the feel of 'back to work' – an evening class, meetings, an interview… And then there's the Out of the Ordinary Festival in East Sussex next weekend. Maybe I simply need to take it easy. Staying in is sometimes the best option.

Mercian Gathering
7th September 2008

Made it up in the end – felt a lot better yesterday morning. The weather was looking better. The 'flow' was with me. And so I hit the road north – seeing it in the spirit of a quest, an adventure. And just as well! It was fine until I hit the A45 then the rain came in earnest – lashing gales along the dual carriageway. Not fun. To my horror, I found myself heading into Brum. Turned around when I could and stopped off at a petrol station, taking shelter from the deluge. Thawed out over a coffee to get my bearings. Shaking and dripping. Bit of a miserable state. Asked directions from the attendant. Girding my loins, I set off into the squall. I wasn't far off. I started to recognise things and finally made it there, to much relief. The Dagda were at the gate doing security as usual. I asked then to let the organiser know I had arrived on their 'tin on a string'. He misunderstood me and said 'tin on a string' is here!' which could have been my CB radio moniker I suppose, an alternative bardic name! [an amusing variant of Tallyessin] I certainly felt a bit threadbare by that point and in need of a cuppa. I wasn't the only one who needed morale boost. The site was predictably a complete mudfest (I cautiously parked near the entrance so I wouldn't get stuck) yet the atmosphere was surprisingly pleasant. There was the classic British 'blitz' spirit – everyone mucking in and making do. The site looked like a pagan refugee camp. Sad saggy dwellings, with despondent denizens nursing spluttering stoves. Behold, the mud people! I touched base with the organisers, at least one of them, but the queen of the camp, Anna, was sleeping like something from a fairy tale. I bumped into her right hand man, Ron, and organised a slot, which took some negotiating. Unfortunately, when I was due to start Gary's bardic workshop was still running, so I decided to go into the pavilion next door, arranging that Gary finished at 6.30pm to let the rune guy take over (he was due to speak in P2 then). When he turned up in the middle of my set he seemed fine with this, but afterwards I heard he wasn't happy (Gary's workshop overran and he was left in the rain). Unfortunate, but you have to make decisions 'in the field'. At festivals, you have to be pretty flexible because everything is 'organic'. Any fixed ideas will be met with the usual chaos! It's a nightmare for a control freak. And with the weather the way it was, one had to make even more allowances. Relentless rain, everything soaked. If we as pagans, don't listen to nature, ignoring its strong messages, then are we really true to our creed, being 'at one with the Earth'? Trying to make something happen in the face of such conditions is not really being sensitive to Mother Nature, is it? Unfortunately, we have to plan things, and endure the consequences, which is a real shame for the countless events ruined this 'summer'. You can do everything right, but you can't plan the weather! The climate is the wild card of creation – even more so at present. The main thing in such situations is to maintain a cheerful, fluid attitude. It is only when you have opinions and attitudes set in stone that they come a-cropper, in collision with what the universe has in mind! These events are always loss-leaders. It is a trade-off between one's effort and the contacts and conversations one has. If you make one new friend, or get a booking, or someone signs up for one of your courses, then it has been worth it. But it's important to value what one is offering – otherwise, others unfortunately may not. If you were being paid a considerable fee, you can guarantee the organisers would bend over backwards to get you in the best venue at the optimum time with the maximum bums on seat. If you're being paid zilch then they aren't going to lose anything by not trying – only you have, by making the effort to come all of the way there. It's not about being a prima donna, simply honouring one's effort and creativity. Yet it's been fun in a masochistic way – mud, glorious mud!

Back in the Cauldron
7th September 2008

Back in the Cauldron. Part of the joy of going away is coming home again. To enjoy the comfort's of one's own hearth. A hot meal. A warm fire. Peace. Solitude after the festival atmosphere, the tribal gathering. It was hard work but definitely worth it. A gathering such as the Mercian is like a pyre – each person a log added to the conflagration. A congregation of fire. Hopefully the thing catches light and everybody has a merry time, as happened last night. After a dismally wet day the rain held off just enough to get the fire labyrinth going – with extra sawdust and petrol, courtesy of Maid Marian and her Merry Arsonists – and amazingly the wicker man too, after lots of persuasion! There was a large crowd of celebrants – nearly 700 – many in ritual garb, many in just warm, waterproof clothing. It all came together in the end – a true team effort and credit to the Hearth of Arianrhod for making it happen. What's special about these gatherings is connecting with people – dancing raises the spirits and breaks the ice! There was a great gipsy band last night who got folk 'shaking their feathers' – a good morale boost. Getting rained on can really sap the spirits. Dancing releases endorphins – and is fun! The dance of life is a great leveller! It is possible to do this alone – but it's not as much fun. Collective joy is wonderful to experience. When the whole is greater than the sum of its parts. Something is released, transformed. A quickening can occur. And also, it bolsters a sense of community – something that can keep us going through the long winter nights. We don't have to feel alone. When it rains hard at a festival it can bring out that Dunkirk spirit – we all pull together, huddled in café or marquee, sharing shelter, helping people out of the mud. It all depends on attitude, on how you handle these things. There's no point preserving firm boundaries when the elements conspire to break them down. Water! Mud! Wind! Everything blurs together. We're all one in the goo! When we leave the festival, often after the closing circle, the circle becomes a line again. We resume our journey. The wheels turn once more.

The journey home is easier, as we carry back with us good memories. Moments that make us smile along the way, even burst out laughing, or sing with joy.

Being Taliesin
8th September 2008

Taliesin means the world to me – he has inspired me for over a decade, playing a large part in my life – but what is it to 'be' Taliesin, that is, to reach the final stage of the initiatory phase of the bardic journey? This is when you step up to the mark, to use an Olympian phrase. When you enter the public arena and become a professional bard. You have won your Bardic Chair in open contest – now it is time to go forth and versify! It isn't easy – one has to juggle many things, some aspects of which seem far removed from the romantic image of the bard: money matters, insurance, CRB checks, transport, invoicing, marketing, negotiation, billing, audience, venue, etc... Basically, its like running a small business – you are going self-employed (if you wish to take it professionally) and as a result you will have to be prepared to deal with the Maelgwns of the world. It is entering his realm – the 'master of the world', the Devil if you like – and dancing with it. Not succumbing to it. Not being exploited or becoming too enamoured with accruing wealth, or the other accoutrements of 'success'. Otherwise, you end up like Fafnir, gloating over his Glitaheid – the glittering heath of gold, cursed by Andvari the dark elf, whose hoard it once was. All that glisters is not gold. The best one can gain from making the effort to travel often arduous conditions, 'harp on back', is renown. Be heard, be seen, and hope the word is passed on – for the next booking, and so on, and so on. The words keep the wheels turning, the wolf from the door. If you've food in your belly, a roof over your head, a soft bed, then you're not doing too badly – that's more than half the world. Although it was an effort to run the gauntlet of a deluge to get to the Mercian Gathering, I had given my word. And if a bard is not as good as their word, then he or she is not worthy of their title. And so one must be careful before committing, before agreeing to an engagement. In one's bardic career there will be times when your services will be asked freely – but remember it is your livelihood. Bards have to eat, to pay the rent. Don't devalue what you do. Everyone wants a freebie. The odd tale around the fire is fine; see it as practice, or a taster. A charity gig, a good cause, is always worth the effort (but make sure it's a bona fide registered charity). The bardic path is seldom one to riches. It shouldn't be your motivation – otherwise your sacred art will end up like everything else in this world done for cynical commercial gain: shoddy work with no love, no spirit. You'll end up like the countless pub acts and tribute bands, the modern equivalent of the 'minstrels' Taliesin mocked, the bardic version of hacks, whoring your art. And at the end of the day you must do it with joy, otherwise what's the point? But, at the same time, don't let others exploit your talents. Would you expect a plumber to do a job for nothing? A bespoke tailored suit or dress for free? Or any other professional service, for that is in effect what you are offering. Take pride in your 'work' and others will too. Denigrate it and they will also. Of course, some will want to do it just for a laugh, which is fine, but if that's your attitude then you probably won't be reading this book. It'll be just something you do now and again just for the gas – in a pub, at a party, at the drop of a hat. Your party trick. Nothing more.

What was it like, to have been an itinerant bard of the so-called Dark Ages? Attached to a royal retinue or travelling from hall to hall. The going of it must have been hard – journeys of length must have been time-consuming and perilous. The roads, what few there were, must have been often atrocious. Ambush, disease, hardship. Simply getting warm and dry. Inside the hall the bard was often given one of the best seats and best portions. He had privileges and liberty granted and enjoyed by few. The freedom to move between courts, the freedom to speak his mind, or his patrons (like the cutting jests of the royal fool, in effect the official state satirist – the idiot savant, hiding in his method-madness in plain sight, able to cut through the court etiquette and cock-a-snook at one and all). It was a perilous profession –

to tread carefully between powerful warlords and courtiers with inflated egos. To negotiate the Machiavellian maze of court. To play the game. Perhaps in this respect things have changed little. We still need to seek patrons, to be politic, aware, and canny. To be able to work with people, and the 'ways of the world' without being corrupted or destroyed by it. It's a delicate balancing act, as though juggling grenades.

Awen and the Art of Motorcycle Maintenance
11th September 2008

Awen can be applied in many ways – it is eminently practical, not confined to bardic esoteric lore. If it cannot be used in every aspect of life what use is it? For me, riding a motorbike is awen in motion – it's all about maintaining one's equipoise (as on the road, as on the stage, as in life). Going with the flow, and not just the traffic. This applies to the running of the engine, the changing of gears, road position, acceleration, braking, steering, progress, route, arrival, and parking. If in any of these aspects blockages occur – the flow is broken – that's when the problems start to occur. Clunky gear changes, clutch control, poor handling, sudden breaking or turning, annoying other drivers, etc... there's always idiots out there on the road, who have a chip on their shoulders about bikes/horses/cyclists/lorries/small cars/pedestrians – you name it. Something to prove – overcompensating by the size of their engine, by aggressive driving. Good driving is among other things about consideration for other road-users – respecting the road and all life upon it, including your own. Not taking foolish risks. What is a couple of seconds gained compared to a human life? Is it worth it, rushing? Often the people who overtake you are stuck at the next lights as you roll up behind them. Tortoise and hare. I was told on my bike training 'assume everybody on the road is an idiot, including yourself'. Good advice in principle, but this has to be measured by the common truth that most people want to get to where they are going safely and swiftly. Riding slow is just going to hold people up – and not win you friends. Move ahead at a sensible speed. The great thing on a bike is you can often push ahead when others are stuck in jams, filtering through traffic, cutting to the front of a queue at the lights, overtaking slow vehicles, especially on hills and on the flat, squeezing by the unlikeliest of places – whereas motorists are constrained by the box they're in. A biker feels the elements around him. He or she has no comfort zone – where as in the car you can have the air conditioning on, be eating or drinking, listening to music, on the phone. It's complete concentration on the bike. You have to be fully present. Alert. Living with full awareness, moment by moment. You can't be complacent, you can't drift off. You have to watch the road surface carefully. Make sure you are seen. Keep an eye out for trouble. Be one step ahead of the driver in front. And the one in front of him. Expect the unexpected. Yet it is living in the flow of awen. Moment by moment, making split decisions, acting with alacrity and skill. Dancing on two wheels. It is very similar to a live performance. Good training for a bard!

The Transparent World
12th September 2008

Walking to the station early this morning the flash of a kingfisher caught my eye – a Mediterranean blue against the subtle tones of a late summer morning that felt distinctly autumnal. The natural world has a languid air – leaves hang heavy on the trees, curling fire, or soundlessly falling. Blackberry bushes are ripe with dew. On one boat with 'free Tibet' in the window the end of a line of teapots planted with flowers was a small mast of cobwebs – which made me imagine a fairy ship with such sails, catching a rare breeze, too subtle for heavier canvas – but one that could carry the intrepid mariner to the otherworld upon the trade winds of the imagination.

As I crossed the iron footbridge to the station I noticed the pollution on the river – it looked as though the clouds had been torn from the sky and drowned in the river. Yet it had an ugly reality – pesticides. In contrast, two swans glided on the Kennet, pristine against its brown sludge – largely the product of canal boat waste-product. Someone had left a pair of paddles open and one of the doglegs was drained to its brick lining. I tried to imagine the canal-water completely clear – so you could see right to the bottom, as when Manannan's realm is revealed beneath the disconcerted imrammans. Sometimes it seems the world has become transparent and we can see to its heart's core.

Along the Avon valley – rattling to Bristol accompanied by Ringo on drums – the edges of the world were still being defined. The sun was glimmering through the gap of night and day. A cobweb veil hung over the meadows. The caul of dreams had not yet been removed from reality and magic still seemed possible. Perhaps this wonder is always to be gained by those able to rise early enough – a waking lucidity. A revelation unveiled.

A Mostly Discarded Concept

An article in today's *Independent* ('Curse of the Writer's Block' John Walsh, 12/09/08) said rather categorically: "'inspiration' is a mostly discarded concept...' I am always suspicious of things that validate themselves in terms of popularity – mass appeal is seldom an indicator of quality, think of the popular tabloids. Another article in the same paper debated whether 'Creationism' should be taught in science at school. One of the arguments cited was: 'how can you discard outright something that a large section of the population believe?' By the same argument National Socialism was a good thing. It is important for the individual to follow their consciences, not the herd. Often it feels like the world is going one way, and I the other. And sometimes I'm glad of that, when I see how people are. Yet the bard in me wants to share the wonder, and show them the way. Not leave them floundering in their own world without vision. This notion of inspiration no longer being a valid concept seems a terrible crime against the Muse – a form of imaginative genocide. With imagination, anything is possible. Another world even. Without it, the Holocaust is possible. As a bard I refute Walsh's refutation – awen is all about inspiration – but it's not an excuse to be lazy, to wait for it to strike. Go hunting for it!

One Man's Utopia
13th-14th September 2008

A beautiful sunny (!) morning at the Out of the Ordinary Festival in East Sussex. Decided to go in the end because, for once, the weather reports were promising and it seemed a shame to waste one of the only decent weekends we've had all summer. It was a long ride down – 160 miles (plus more for 'detours'!) which took me approximately four hours in the end. I decided to invest the effort by making it a pilgrimage to the Long Man of Wilmington – a sacred icon to me. It has loomed large in my life.

The journey was a slog – until I hit the A272, which is apparently an old ridge road. It felt like I was on a leyline and whizzed along through the pretty South Downs landscape, a proposed National Park. At the other end I was so fatigue I started to make stupid mistakes and got lost, doubling back to Cuckfield when I was nearly there. I should have trusted my instincts, and pushed on.

But what of the festival? It's charming – all wind, solar and pedal-powered, zero waste and fluffy – a little green gathering. At six I walked onto the small colourful field with its familiar aesthetic of fluttering flags, tipis, yurts, stall tents, cafes, Indian wedding marquees, sculptures, solar panels, fire circles, and ubiquitous drumming circle, made beautiful in the precious golden sunlight. There was a chilled out ambience (the sun makes everyone feel good). I wandered over to the main stage and managed to catch some of Katherine Blake and her band of velvet elves – an enchanting introduction to the festival. After, I took in the lovely evening, letting my senses enjoy the magical sights and sounds: two giant middle eastern featured puppets 'raving', a large metallic spider sculpture platform, stalls selling guarana balls and chai, old hippies, crusties, pikies, rastas, New Agers, respectable middle class greenies, families, femme fatales, bikers... The works. Bumped into an old friend from Northampton – Steve, a sometime DJ, and his two companions, a lovely fox and a badger woman, the foxy lady being his partner. It was nice to be recognised and remembered, to see a friendly face in the crowd. Of course, I could have walked up to anyone and started chatting, but they were my 'way in', they were well in the groove and their bonhomie was infectious. I walked with them whilst they handed out flyers about a circus for Iraq initiative. This is typical of the mixture of the practical and the visionary, the aesthetic and didactic, the wacky and the grounded. The MC – a performance poet in shiny space gear, did a rap from Mother Earth's POV, to trance music. Another starlet did a sacred drama about Lilith with ritual dance and poetry. After a mad but brilliant nu-punk band called the Drookit Dogs there was a peace prayer for the planet. We held hands in a circle and 'ommed' for peace. Led by a priestess on stage like a female pope, a feminist bishop. Earlier there was some impressive co-ordinated fire dancing – synchronised poi-swinging! It was a beautiful clear night, with the nearly full equinox moon glowing apricot in the star-strewn sky – like the sparks of iron wool that nearly set the audience alight! It could have all been made to trip too – as some indeed were. I found a magical set of candlelit steps leading down into an 'enchanted woods', the trunks illuminated as though by their respective plant devas. This illuminated brilliantly the talk I'd just been to in the Shamanism of Light tent – 'the sacred vine of the soul' – which warned of the perils of using and abusing powerful plant medicines, chiefly Ayahuasca. You didn't need to be on anything to enjoy the heady atmosphere – although plainly some were, amusingly dancing their chemical madness to trippy light displays. More organically-enhanced was the djembe dancers, strutting their stuff around the main fire around midnight, until a man in a tutu and bowler asked us to turn it down: to be the 'quietest, loudest space on site', because the local inspectors were on site, recording sound levels. And amazingly, it was kept quiet. And the music didn't go on all night, finishing at a respectable time for once (although I found out from a friend, Rebecca, whom I had chai with around the fire, that she had kept going until daybreak!) Overall though it was quieter than some campsites I've stayed on – an advantage of camping in the carpark near the dry ski slope! Awoken early to bird song after a chilly but generally comfortable night's sleep. Then the usual feral festival children kicked off, effing and blinding as though that made them mature.

Time to go to the coast!

Beautiful ride down to the coast – stopped on the seafront at Eastbourne and drank a good cup of Fair Trade coffee, and availed myself of the nice toilets (as opposed to dodgy festival ones) before heading along the coast road up to Beachy Head, where there was some kind of 'speed rally'. I just pulled up and enjoyed the view over the bay before wending my way down towards Seaford and up the Cuckmere Valley, through the charming village of Alfriston to Wilmington, via steep and windy backroads which a few bikers were out enjoying, including a 'school of scooters' – Brighton mods? On a day like today it's a joy to be on two wheels, especially on such roads. Stunning.

Long Man of Wilmington
14th September 2008

I made it! I look at him from the Priory car park to the timeless figure of the Long Man of Wilmington – it is very moving being here. The impact of a pilgrimage is directly proportional to the amount of effort and ardour of the journey. Mine wasn't too taxing in the great scheme of things but it was tiring (riding on fast, busy road; concentrating for hours on end as though my life depended on it – which it did) yet it was definitely worth it. The feeling of satisfaction is immense – to get here under my own steam for the first time, on my own two wheels. I've been several times now – the first in 2003 I think, so maybe this is my fifth time which is very appropriate as I come here just as I embark upon the fifth and final Windsmith book, *The Wounded Kingdom*, and, as I write this a single-prop plane flies overhead, resembling a spitfire! I watched its silhouette in astonishment through the gaps in the willow tree. This is how TWK ends. From the First World War to the Second, from the Otherworld and back, Kerne has walked between the worlds, as I must: a mundane example of this is the dramatic difference between my day on Friday in the austere academic atmosphere of Walton Hall (all procedural proper-and-correct stuff, with little warmth/humour or colour) to the creative chaos of OOTO. I like the contrast more than the individual events. They are all 'bubbles' – each with their respective bubble-monarchs – paradigms to shift in and out of, not to be stuck in. That's what the long man shows me, (holding a staff in each hand). How to hold opposites in equilibrium, how to negotiate extremes and find a middle way. How not to get crushed between such 'clashing rocks' that life presents – holding the pillars of the temple apart but in balance.

[As I write up this onto the computer back home, there was a UPS delivery of two proof-copies of Awen titles and a big box of *Lost Islands* – my 'harvest' for the year!].

There is richness still in the land. The trees are still green, yet leaves fall upon my journal as I write this. The hill the long man stands upon is verdant with green sward, yet the fields below have been ploughed bare – the chalk in the soil makes it almost white – a post-harvest's tabula rasa. At one point it was thought the long man held farming implements, a scythe and a rake, yet these were probably added by whimsical farmhands, as the 'tool' which seems to be present today (on closer inspection it appears to be a couple of the painted breeze-blocks, moved and added between his legs*) – a pathetic little joke. The long man weathers all of these incursions, including the recent one perpetuated by fashionistas Trinny and Susannah, dressing the hill figure up as a woman – literally a fashion victim! The local druid group, the Anderida Gorsedd, protested against this, bravely appearing on the TV show to defend it. They were mocked for thinking they 'own it', but they more than most can lay 'claim' to it, as good stewards, since they have been gathering there in open celebration since the early Noughties at every festival and will be here next weekend celebrating the equinox – but for now, it's nice to have it 'to myself'. I feel a strong connection with it, yet like the druids I don't claim to own it. We, if anything, belong to the land. All we can do is try and live in harmony with it and such a place helps us to attune to its rhythms, and to honour what it gives us. This is a fecund place, in many ways. The folk tale attached to the Long Man, 'Dru the Windsmith' created by the late Ronald Millar, talks of how the monks of Wilmington Priory needed a windmill to grind their grain. The miller-monks lived off of the fat of the land. A murder of crows caw in the bare field as I wended my way up the footpath, past the bushes of black-berries, rosehips and scarlet haws which make the hawthorns more red than green, so laden they are – perhaps foreshadowing a hard winter.

[*see 'Unmanning the Long Man', by Kevan Manwaring, *The Druid's Voice*]

I lie here in the sun on the mound at the Long Man's feet: prone like Kerne after his odyssey in the Afterlands. It's been a challenging, tiring year – the outline of the Long Man reminds me of the absence my father's death has caused, a negative space in my life.

The outline looks like white chalk in the sunlight (although I know it is in fact, rather prosaically, yellow breeze-blocks) like that of a murder victim last position like in a crime movie. Who dunnit? Who killed Cock Robin? John Barleycorn? Baldur? Llew Llaw Gyffes? All these are solar heroes who are doomed, as is the summer itself. It must end (although this year it didn't really get going – with the wettest August on record). For once the sun is shining, reminding us of what we've been missing for months.

Above Windover hill a windhover waits, poised, like fate itself – to strike at any moment. Who knows when it will fall, that mortal blow? The gods have been kind to me so far (an angel must be looking out for me) but it will happen one day – that's the only certainty. Yet I am glad to have made it this far. I'm glad to be here on this benign day – to feel the warmth of the sun on my skin, hear the buzz of a fly, a plane overhead, the distant rumble of bikes, the chirrup of insects. Peace.

Sitting above the Long Man now – lying on the slope of Windover Hill, same angle as the figure, watching the clouds make shapes (dragons...people...) shaped by the wind – all the struggles, all the conflict for this or that configuration of reality always eventually dissipating. And lying here – in this state of serenity, of surrender – I could embrace my own dissolution. Finally, after all the sound and fury, peace, stillness, silence... But not quite, not yet. Crows land on the figure, black and white and green. I look across the Weald and it's like looking across the world. I must turn back to it now – well, almost – firstly to give my talk at OOTO, then to hit the road back home: a 160 miles 'north by north west'. Back into the craziness of the world – the consensus reality of Elsinore. The rotten state. And then it's down to work. The autumn term. Courses. Book launches. Workshops. Events. The wheel of the world keeps turning. Time to rejoin it. Long man, guide me – help me to walk between the worlds and keep my centre. Adieu!

Home, later

The important thing about a journey is completing it. It's the same as writing a book – many start, few finish. There is something immensely satisfying about completion – and setting out and returning, having hopefully gained something. I feel my trek to East Sussex was worth it – to make the most of this late blast of summer, to make pilgrimage to the Long Man, see the sea and check out OOTO (although the latter was the least of it). It felt good to make the effort, rather than stay at home in my comfort zone. I feel 'buzzy' from it, and feel confident about undertaking longer trips.

Keeping the Faith

The Long Man, with his staves could be seen as a symbol of balance, of tolerance. An equinoctial god, light and dark poised in his hands. Like his brother at Cerne Abbas, the pagan Long Man would not still exist without the goodwill of the local clergy, in this case the monks of Wilmington Priory. They could have easily destroyed him, as could anyone in the area. A local 'folk tale', Dru the Windsmith, postulates how they could have even created him...

I first heard the remarkable tale of Dru the Windsmith from Derek the Storyteller at Eastbourne Lammas Festival 2003. Derek had taken it from Ronald Millar's book *The Green Man Gazetteer*, SB Publications 1997, which he recommended to me. I bought the book and began telling it myself. It excited me, because here seemed to be an echo of Taliesin's wind-summoning, and a term which summed up the bardic art so well: windsmith (in the original story it means a dowser of windmills, yet the protagonist, Dru, could actually summon and banish winds like Taliesin. I took this notion and ran with it). I included a version in my novel *The Long Woman* (awen 2004) and then explored its many nuances in *Windsmith* and its subsequent sequels, which will eventually comprise *The Windsmith Elegy*. I originally thought Millar had stumbled upon a unique piece of folklore. As it turns out, according to Derek, he made the whole thing up (he wouldn't be the first or last whose fictions prove self-fulfilling prophecies, e.g. Arthur Machen's short story 'The Bowmen' and James Hilton's Shangri-La in *Lost Horizons* – both of which impacted upon reality, i.e. people believe them true. They both have created 'phenomenon': Machen's story is entangled with the legend of the Angel of Mons, whileas Hilton's neologism Shangri-La has become synonymous with such places). A poignant footnote to all this is: I bumped into Derek the storyteller at the Society for Storytelling Gathering in Exeter April 2008 and he told me Ronald Millar had died recently. I would like to help keep his memory and work alive with my sequence of novels and by telling his story of Dru the Windsmith. This is the bardic tradition in action and is a good example of how the awen works. It inspires one person and they pass it on, inspiring others. As bards, often all that survives us are our stories, songs and poems. It is a form of immortality, perhaps the only kind. Not that we should seek this – it is the connections that we make in this life that matter. They will be our immediate legacy. Without the goodwill of those who keep our contributions to the canon alive, we soon fade away. Without them, we are voices in the void.

Circles Without End
16th September 2008

Last night I handed over the tiller of the Bath Storytelling Circle after five years as 'skipper' – hosting it one last time, for the foreseeable future at least, because of teaching commitments (a Monday night creative writing evening class on top of a heavy workload) I'm unable to run it anymore, so I gave the 'bells of power' as we jokingly call the Tibetan chimes we use to David Metcalfe and Richard Selby – fellow members of Fire Springs and experienced performers, so I know the circle is in safe hands. It was a poignant night, because of this – seldom do we get to experience something or someone for the last time consciously. For all we know that might be the last time we ever see them, or experience that particular sensation. Perhaps this is just as so. Complete prescience might be a curse. It could drive you mad – like the unfortunate Dr James Xavier in *The Man with the X-Ray Eyes* who eventually was able to see to the centre of the universe. If time became transparent this would be equally maddening. And yet we should act as though every moment is priceless – what could be called 'diamond time'. Instead we squander it, we 'kill time', instead of living it. We wade through life heavy-footed, blundering through these fragile exquisite moments, giants in a flower garden.

Running a story circle requires sensitivity. The Raven has diners upstairs so I went around putting flyers on the table and mentioning the circle was due to start at 8pm, to give them fair warning – emphasising they were welcome to stay and listen, which some did. After collecting names of contributors, I gently got things going, by making a 'trumpet sound' with my hands! This got the room's attention. Then I introduced myself as host, and outlined the nature of the circle (a platform for story, song and poetry – performed, not read). Then I kicked things off with a tale I had just learnt that day, about Eilmer, the flying monk of Malmesbury. After this I picked names as appropriate, alternating tales, tunes and poetry to keep the variety and energy up. The awen began to flow and we had another great night of bardic sharing. Between each contribution I added a quip or comment of praise, to keep things light. These foolish, but heartfelt improvisations keep you on your bardic feet – generating material on the spot. They stop you getting rusty, and it keeps things 'live and direct', encouraging an air of spontaneity and inspiration. Svanur, an Icelandic friend, ended the first half with a medley of stories about the humour of giants. Just before the break, we had announcements – they ended up being all mine, as I've got a lot coming up (hence not being able to continue as co-ordinator). In the break I had several offers of drinks – I always make a joke of 'buying your poor host one' at the start, and for once it paid off!

We resumed in fine fettle with an amusing wonder tale from Richard, channelling a seanachie with his Irish accent. Checking there were no 'hidden voices' out there bursting to share something, I finished off the night's telling with another monk tale: of Dru the Windsmith. This was my way of honouring the Long Man, after my pilgrimage the day before. David ended with a moving song to send us home with melody in our hearts.

Touchingly, as I wrapped things up, Richard asked everyone to thank me for my efforts. It closed the circle, wishing everyone to 'travel well in your own story until we next meet.'

Afterwards, more drinks were bought me and there followed a lively discussion between the remaining few (mainly men) about the nature and difference of truth, truthfulness and honesty – an admirable attempt to be intellectual at a late hour when feeling a little worse for wear! Bidding adieu to my friends I walked home – it was a clear night and the full moon loomed down, a suitable symbol of completion. I stopped at the Rec to pay my respects. Here the view was relatively unimpeded. It felt like a 'ripe' moment. It was a good night to finish on, although circles of course have no beginning or end, and no doubt I will return to the Raven at some point. Yet it was good to end on a high note, with goodwill all around and a positive experience to remember it by. The circle has been a big part of my life, from when I first started going (turning up at its second one end of 1999 as a fledgling storyteller). Then I hadn't been allowed to perform by Anthony the founder, as they apparently ran out of time (ironically I was going to tell my timely tale, The Millennium Gnome). I was put out at the time, but subsequently I became good friends with the host, and ended up taking it over when he went to spend a year and half in the Peloponnese. And out of it came our group Fire Springs – in 2000 we performed our first show, Arthur's Dream at the Rondo: in at the deep end! Next year will be the circle's tenth anniversary and we should do something to mark it. It deserves to be celebrated, for being such an excellent platform for creativity. Long may it continue.

Riding in the Sun: Autumn Equinox trip
20th-22nd September 2008

I set out for another long bardic trip, glad to be making the most of the fine sunshine – a late blast of summer. After the washout we've had every last drop deserves to be savoured. I packed the iron horse once again – tank bag, tail bag, panniers and tent bungeed to the end-bar. The previous day I had given my Zuki a good clean and polish, adjusted the chain, checked the oil, and made sure everything looked okay. I was ready to hit the road, again. A bard on a bike!

I set off at 10.30am. The AA routeplanner said 90 minutes but I allowed for traffic and the 'unforeseen', (e.g. getting lost!). The walk-thru was planned for 1pm so I had given myself plenty of time – the worst thing is to be rushing somewhere [for the wedding gig], that's when accidents happen.

I had ridden the route to Winchester the previous weekend, so I was happy that I knew where I was going. It's a nice run, down the A36 and onto the A303, going past Stonehenge – which always looks dramatic. The hay bales were stacked in the fields like monoliths as the tail of traffic approached the famous stone circle – looking bigger than the actual megaliths.

The traffic flowed and I got to Winchester in good time, rolling up at the King Alfred statue in the centre, where I rang Jane, the hostess, to ask for directions. Amazingly she managed to talk me in through the complicated one way system, and with only a brief stop at a garage to check I was going in the right direction I found myself at the venue, round the back of Cross St, along a private drive past St Cross hospital, which was holding a Michaelmas fair. It was a very charming part of Winchester. A leet flowed past the side of the house, the original part of which was twelfth century. The owners were obviously wellheeled, but not snobbish or overly posh. They welcomed me in an informal way – I was offered a cuppa and some fish and chips pulled from the oven.

It was to be the handfasting of Melody and Andrew and I had been asked to perform. There was a company called Catspaw who were co-ordinating everything and providing other entertainment – juggling, medieval music, and more storytelling. They all seemed like a nice bunch. Jo was the 'matriarch' organiser, Cliff ('the travelling talesman') a fellow storyteller, Justin Time was the fool/juggler, and a couple whose names I didn't catch played medieval instruments and sang songs from that period. The whole set-up was very impressive. The garden, which was extensive, had been decorated in a medieval fashion with a whole suit of armour, and other helms adorned with dripped candles, shields, standards, mock-flamboys, the works. The caterers had provided goblets, platters, kegs and suitable cuisine. All the guests were in medieval costume (well, fancy dress). And the glorious sun shone down upon all. It was beautiful.

Oh, to be in England now that summer's (finally) here!

I watched the handfasting ceremony, as I knew the couple and had been invited to enjoy the day as a guest as well as performer. As the wedding entourage left the bottom part of the garden we, the entertainers, welcomed them, with music and juggling. I shook a tambourine! I wasn't expecting to be part of an ensemble but you have to be prepared to be spontaneous and flexible in such situations.

The wedding proceeded as planned, but for once without the speeches, the lame jokes, etc. After the photo opportunities we ate. I made sure I got something down me so I didn't suffer 'bardic droop' later. There was plenty of ale but I restricted myself to a half, because I had to perform and ride later. Just when I had gone off to start warming-up I was told I was on! Everything was running half an hour early. So it pays to be prepared! I limbered up and raised my energy and went on, announced by Cliff, who was acting as MC. I performed my wedding set, which lasted half an hour, and it seemed to go well, although it felt brief. Considering what I was being paid I would've been happier to have performed another thirty minute slot later on, but Cliff was doing the honours then. So after my performance, I reluctantly hit the road – as I had to make it to the New Forest and find a campsite. Shame I couldn't have stayed but I had nowhere to stay in Winchester, and I had to make it to Maiden Castle the following morning, so I felt it was best to be half way there at least.

And so bidding my discreet adieus, as everything was still in full progress, I donned my helm and headed for the forest, feeling every bit the wandering minstrel forced to spend a night under the stars as I wend my way between towns. Then it wouldn't have been such a problem – although you'd have to be careful of bandits! Now, its private landowners and National Park regulations you have to be more wary of. I didn't want to have to pay to stay in a noisy campsite when there was a huge forest to camp in, and so I hunted for a suitable place – a picnic area. This was harder than it should've been because by the time I had eaten some hot food from a chippy in Lyndhurst and bought supplies – a bottle of wine and some cereal bars – it was getting dark. I headed out along what I thought was the A35 to Christchurch- but it turned out to be heading the other way, towards Southampton. I found a campsite at Ashurst, but the woman at reception was grumpy and charged too much, so I carried on, preferring to take my chances. Things were looking desperate when I ended up in an estate in Hithe, I think, with gangs of teenagers on the prowl. So I got some gas, girded my loins and turned around. I was getting tired and started to feel a little unsafe on the road as by now it was pitch black. But I kept going, I had to. I ended up going back through Lyndhurst and out the other side, this time finding the right road. Along here I spotted a sign for another campsite, because by that time I was getting desperate, but before I came to it I found a picnic area, which I gratefully pulled into: it looked perfect. I found a bay under some oak trees and put my tent up using my headlamp beam. I chucked in my sleeping stuff and with great relief cracked open the wine and poured myself a glass. Shelter! It was nine by now. It had taken me three hours! (one to get to the forest, one of those was spent in Lyndhurst ordering and eating my chips, and one wandering about lost!) I was shattered, but happy. It was clear night and the glittering firmament could be seen through the canopy. Perfect. I felt a fire would have been too risky, and even my candle made me a little paranoid – but what harm was I doing? At one point a car pulled in and I blew the flame out, but they would've seen the bike. However they, whoever they were, simply pulled away. This happened a couple of times (in the morning I discovered there were toilets there, so this could've been the reason). At one point some boy racers whizzed into the picnic area, disappeared down a track then emerged a little while later at speed. Someone bellowed from a loud-hailer something daft like 'beware of the dogger!' then, as they departed 'sleep well'. You could hear the electronic bleep and distorted voice in the distance for some time. Just local 'yoofs' raising hell, but not really doing any harm. A van had pulled in, and it looked like I was going to be in for a noisy night, but they parked up some distance away and were no bother. I seemed I was not the only one who wanted to avail myself of the free shelter. The night was actually peaceful, if chilly, and my airbed seemed to give up the ghost – so it wasn't the most comfortable of nights, but it was satisfying to 'wild camp', a wolfhead bard, and to awake in the morning to a beautiful dawn chorus and sun-dappled glade. Yet I wasn't far from the 'human race' – for a 'fun run' was taking place along the road and hundreds of determined competitors jogged along. Daytime visitors to the forest were arriving as well. It was time to strike camp and go. I packed while the kettle boiled, which took ages. It seems everything is packing up at the moment (last week, my modem; now my airbed and stove – time for some new gear, a new injection of energy). Knocking back my tepid coffee to wash down the gritty cereal bar, I headed off, following some fellow bikers past the runners and out of the forest. Found the A35 easily and was soon heading towards Dorchester. I had a peace ceremony to make!

Stopped off at Bournemouth prom to have a decent coffee and a muffin. It really felt like the height of summer – everybody in shades and summer wear. It was a dazzling contrast to the muddy shade of the forest. I didn't feel 'chic' enough, but it mattered not. I was soon on my way...to the Maiden!

Maidens and Islands
21st September 2008

I arrived at Maiden Castle at midday. The sky was chalk blue. I pulled into the carpark finding a space amongst the scattering of vehicles. There was a large circle of people sitting nearby I thought maybe that was the peace ceremony which Lisa Schneidau from The Druid Network had organised, but walking closer – once I had locked the bike and plucked the half-full bottle of wine and half-empty packet of biscuits from my pannier – I saw it was a party of school children. And so I hiked up the hill to the ramparts of the hill-fort, a formidable killing zone of bank and trench, a maze to disorientate and exhaust the enemy. I entered the enclosure without opposition – it was now a zone of peace. The grass hummed with insects. It was hot in my leather jacket, but I hadn't been able to lock it on the bike. My tough suede trousers weren't good for walking in either. I couldn't see any likely gatherings. In the distance, visitors walked along the ramparts, but there were no obvious 'druids'. I carried on, across the top of the hill-fort, starting to suspect no one had made it. Still, it was a stunning place to be on a sunny day – vastly different from the only other time I had been here, when it had been lashing down diagonal rain. At the furthest end of the hill-top enclosure I found a small cluster of people, sitting or standing in stillness, meditating. This, I realised, must be the peace ceremony. I sat next to a couple on a small mound and checked. It was. The guy explained what was happening – everyone was working on their own 'peace'. So this is what I did, laying out against the curve of the mound and feeling the warm sun on my face, glad to have made it, glad to be still. I let things rise and fade in my mind. The strong silence of the hill absorbed them all, until only peace was left. Lisa came over and welcomed me. We gathered in a circle and shared what had come up. People looked beatific in their peace and spoke from the heart. We awenned, for ourselves, for the earth, for world peace – connecting with others holding peace ceremonies and events around the planet on that day, Peace One Day, initiated by Jeremy Gilley in 2001, ten days after 9/11. Bobcat and her group were holding their peace event outside Parliament. We stood on the eastern edge of the hillfort and sent out our awen to them, to all, noticing a pair of buzzards circling close by. Then we returned to our circle and shared bread and mead, partaking of its goodness with mindfulness. Everything was done slowly and respectfully. It was hard to do more than whisper. The silence was sacred. Afterwards, having closed the quarters, we shared a picnic and talked more informally. There was a lovely atmosphere of gentleness and openness. People were warm and friendly. My fellow biker Nigel made it halfway through and it was good to catch up with him and Lisa and Wilf. Connections were made or deepened. There was talk of a possible event at the Cranbourne earthhouse (Ancient Technology Centre), and maybe a follow-up event in November. It felt good, holding ceremony with these lovely people. There was no pontificating or posturing. None of the usual egomancy of some large-scale public ceremonies. It was truly a ceremony of peace.

Nigel and I had to depart – for we had to get to Totnes and Plymouth respectively. We bid our farewells, and walked down to the bikes. It was great to share the journey with a fellow rider for a change. I see many guys on the road, out and about in twos and threes, but I have not really experienced that: a ride-out with others. The ride was stunning over the coastal road, passed Lyme Regis, Sidmouth, Beer and so on. We didn't have time to stop, but we did enjoy the spectacular views over the shining sea, and we made Totnes by 5ish. Riding through the golden hills of Devon in the late afternoon sun was a real pleasure. This land is beautiful. It felt good to be alive, good to be a bard on a bike.

Nigel left me in Totnes – he had to return to Plymouth because of domestic obligations, but was coming back later. I made my way to a café for a much-needed cuppa. I found the Red Wizard café, tucked away by the Happy Apples green-grocers. It was a gem of a place, with a bohemian vibe – posters, flyers and notices covering one wall; paintings another. It was run by a great character called Tyrone whose huge presence filled the place, but didn't dominate it. He asked me if I was hungry. I replied yes. Veggie. I nodded. I'll fix you something, he said. And that was that. No menu! He called out from the back, something couscousy, with courgettes…sounded good. Spicy, no spice? Spicy. Good man. Salad? Nice. While I thawed out over a cuppa, soaking in the vibe – music playing from a laptop – Tyrone set to work. I didn't even know how much it was going to cost. I estimated from the board a main meal must be a very reasonable 4.50. But with tea, a sidesalad and a coffee to finish with I was expecting a tenner at least. But no, 4.50 it was. Incredible value. And excellent service. I wish there was a place like the Red Wizard in Bath, and I told him so. We got chatting. I said I was in town for a talk and he asked me what about and the next thing, he was excitedly playing me this obscure interview on his laptop about a guy who had a theory that the US had discovered evidence of Atlantis under Cuba and had covered it up! I listened with as much genuine interest as I could muster. It was just nice to connect with somebody and share some of their enthusiasm, even if I didn't agree with the wacky theories. Feeling refreshed, I got my bag of books from the bike – discovering I had left the key in the ignition – although it had been wheel-locked. Totnes is the kind of place you can do that. It has its share of social problems – drunks on the street – but it has a fluffy vibe in general. A place for English eccentricity, of all ethnicities. And walking up the street was a great example of that – Jeffrey Gale, the organiser of the local Wessex Research Group. An artist and bona fide eccentric. I had first met him on the side of Glastonbury Tor, summer solstice 1991, in a ceremony. We had all gone back to the Lightship for breakfast. I remember watching hypnotised as Jeffrey spent what seemed like a long time preparing some muesli with meditative care – mixing the exact proportion of ingredients, stirring in the yoghurt like Gwion Bach stirring Ceridwen's cauldron for a year and a day.

We greeted each other, on the surface presenting a striking contrast, the biker and the aesthete. And yet this was my third visit to Jeffrey's group. It's nice to be welcomed back. This time I had a few more, but not many – a dozen – but it felt a lot better than the previous Sunday at OOTO. I structured the talk well, I think, and it felt well received. There were some questions at the end, although Jeffrey used his to just talk about a poem he had written! Afterwards, people chatted over tea and coffee, Jeffrey making a big deal of me drinking 'real' coffee (actually horrible instant stuff). I definitely needed some by that point, feeling the effects of the tiring day and weekend. A beer would've been nice, but I had to wait until we got back to Mark and Lian's, who were kindly putting me up, which was just as well, as the roads were windy and the night was dark. It was like following the white rabbit down the rabbit hole, keeping up with Mark's car as it whizzed along the back lanes between Totnes and Denbury, where they currently reside in a lovely one storey house. Mark is a fellow Bard of Bath and has gone on to set up the Bardic Chair of Caer Wyse, Exeter, although he's encountered resistance and problems with local nutters [since resolved, with fine performance poet Liv Torc taking on the mantle]. He now co-runs the Totnes ghost walks with Bob Mann, a local 'bard'.

It was nice to see Lian, Mark's partner, and catch up with them all informally, over a much needed pint or two. Everyone was tired but it was nice to see them both. They are both very creative and sensitive people. Lian is an artist, and her art adorned the walls and her artist's eye was apparent in the lovely rooms. I got to sleep on a blissfully soft foldout bed, and slipped into wonderful slumber. In the morning I had a coffee with Lian before hitting the road back home. The day was clear, although cooler than the weekend. There was a distinct autumnal tang in the air. Leaves whirled on the road before the bike. There was a greyer light, but at least the roads were dry. The journey home flowed well. Coming off the A38 by Exeter I felt vastly different to when I rode the bike up from Plymouth three weeks earlier. No longer a bag of nerves, tearing down the dual carriageway at high speed! And this time, I didn't get lost in the backroads of Somerset, finding the A37 and A367, which took me all the way home.

Later that day I was to retrace my steps along the last leg of the journey to Midsomer Norton, for my new evening class, but for now, I was glad to be back. It had been a satisfyingly full equinox weekend, riding in the sun.

Awen and the Information Age
24th September 2008

I've been in limbo for the last week. I haven't existed. I've lived in a virtual void because my internet connection went down at home. It made me realise how dependent I am upon it. How much logging on has become second nature. Checking my emails. Surfing the web. Watching movies. I am not a leisure-surfer – primarily I use the internet for work – mainly for the OU and so my connection is essential. The new term was starting. All my courses were kicking off. Books were due at printers. And I couldn't get online. It was incredibly frustrating and demoralising but it taught me a lesson. Not to take it or anything for granted. Not to be cyber-dependent.

For millennia we have managed to communicate with each other without the internet. We've managed to find out things without the World Wide Web. We don't need it, however useful it may seem. A phonecall, a letter, better still a conversation – real communication. That is what matters.

But I'm glad my mouse has found virtual cheese to nibble again!

Creative People

There's a wonderful old fellow I often bump into when I'm walking into town along Great Pulteney Street – he's called Jasper Rose, a former Professor of Art and the spitting image of an elderly JRR Tolkien. Whenever he spies me, he exclaims: 'My dear boy!' acosts me, shakes my hand warmly – and while keeping hold of it recites a clerihew, a kind of limerick based upon a famous person's name. He has a new one each time. He has two sons: one's a painter – my friend, William Balthazar Rose – who lives in Italy. The other is an actor who lives in California. I have yet to browse properly Jasper's extensive library in their five storey Georgian house next to the Holburne Museum but no doubt it contains many treasures.

Another friend of mine, Marko, is a man you don't meet every day. He is something of a West Country wizard with his silver-topped cane, long white hair and beard, black velvet hat, and leprechaun twinkle in his eye. He wears only black clothes of good quality, often a waistcoat and a fine pair of shoes, an arsenal of rings and always a penny whistle in his breast pocket and a pint of Guinness or glass of wine at hand. I met him on my first night in Bath when he led the ghost walk I went on, and I've been friends with him ever since, getting to know something of his 'mystery'. He trained in Fine Art and he has made his life his magnum opus: his eye for design, which he employed in book illustration, leatherwork and stone carving, has helped forge his distinctive style. And his tiny flat on Lansdown hill is his master-piece – a veritable occult museum, crammed with esoteric object d'art: a skull on the dresser, candlesticks, witchballs, mirrors, spooky portraits, horse-brasses, statues and effigies, Masonic and druidic regalia, picture frames of past lovers, stacks of books, video tapes and cassettes, his various 'costumes' hanging up and artwork – his own and from friends. The curtains are always closed, a joss-stick is always burning and some Irish air is wafting out onto the landing along with the fumes of Bacchus if guests are visiting.

Peter Alfred Please cycles around the British Isles and mainland Europe, recording all the encounters and little epiphanies he has in his journals – moments captured with a journalist's eye and a storyteller's heart, finding inspiration on the wayside, in the quiet, marginal places. He sculpts totem-like icons, with which he tells stories or 'plants' in obscure places for people to come across. He travels through an organisation called SERVAS, staying with fellow members who offer a bed and a meal for the night. He exchanges copies of his books as he goes, and uses his experiences to write more.

These three and many more I know lead creative lives. For them, there is no separation between their lives and their art. There is no stage, except life itself. They are never anything other than what they appear – they don't adopt an artistic persona to impress, for special occasions. They are deep within their own story. They inspire those who know them with their creative presence. For them art isn't something they do in an evening class or while on holiday. An artistic possibility is present in every moment. In a conversation on the street, in a choice of clothes, mode of transport, road less travelled.

How can you live creatively? You don't have to make your life a performance as Dali did, or use your art to treat people horren-dously as Picasso and Capote seem to have. You don't have to try and live like a rock star. You can be still modest in your behaviour and appearance, discreet in your actions and attitudes and still be living your creativity. It manifests in different ways for different people. It could be in your cooking, in your gardening, your handwriting, your hair. Think how creative energy can enrich every aspect of your life. We often allow others to make the choices – leading busy lives, we opt for 'off-the-peg' lifestyles, ready made for mass consumption, rather than ploughing our own furrow, coming up with our own style, our own way of going about the world. Design a new personal transport system. Go to work on a pogo-stick! Wear snorkels and flippers on the bus! Swim against the mainstream. Make each day an act of creative defiance, a positive act of living.

A Cornish Wedding
4th-5th October 2008

We were going to a friends' wedding in Mevagissey, Cornwall – a tiny fishing village named after its two local saints (there's a super-abundance of them in this narrow leg of England, as though an endemic native species) Saints Meva and Issey. Getting there was touch and go but we made it with fifteen minutes to spare, parking behind St Andrews church hall, where the reception was to be held after the ceremony at 3pm – the wedding of Suzanne Marie Dabbs and Svanur Gisli Thorkelsson, my skaldic friend from Iceland. They had held a Bahai ceremony earlier so this Christian ceremony was mainly for the bride's family benefit, but it was charming nonetheless with readings from *Captain Corelli's Mandolin* by the bride's brother, Malcolm, and the Song of Solomon from the vicar who espoused enthusi-astically about the fire of love. Afterwards there was tea, cake and mead in the hall as guests mingled and photographs were taken. There were none of the usual speeches. Indeed, it was no ordinary wedding. None of the bridegroom's family were there – as they all live in Iceland (an event will be held for their benefit later in the year) – and instead of a best man, Svanur had his mother-in-law as best woman! This was in keeping with the couple, who are distinctively original. Suzanne, something of a clothes-junky, went for a Jackie-O retro look full white wedding dress with straight satin lines, and a Russian style trail. Svanur wore a bardic blue silk waistcoat. They both looked happy and pretty relaxed. We were guided back to the guest house we were staying in, courtesy of the family, by JR, the American that we were sharing with along with his Canadian partner, Sharon – both lovely, genuine people.

After we had freshened up, we headed for the Rising Sun, were the evening's reception was to be held, starting with a sit down meal in the restaurant part of this charming Cornish smuggler's inn at the tiny cove of Portmellon. After the first course I was asked to get up and share something. I had planned to do a story, but felt this would've been too long before the main meal, so did my love poem instead – originally written for a friends' wedding at Comlongon Castle, Scotland, but composed in Cornwall in the summer of the eclipse, 1999 at a place called Wheal Rose, which inspired the title, 'The Wheel of the Rose'. I didn't make this Cornish connection until I stood up – but adrenalin can make you think fast! I had wanted to go to the loo to run it through in my head, as I hadn't practised it. With all the speeches and conversation I wasn't able to concentrate, and couldn't remember the second verse! Fortunately, it all flowed out as it should – your tongue remembers what to do, even when you don't! It left a stunned silence, which I hope was good. 'Now, follow that!' joked Svanur. Afterwards, a guest came up wanting a copy – so she could circulate it to everyone (writing it out in calligraphy no less). After the main meal the band started –

beginning with Tom Corneil solo before he was joined by his friends. During a break in their set I was asked to do my story – I chose to do my Welsh version of Tristan and Isolde, Trystan and Esyllt. This seemed to go down well enough, although I wasn't as eloquent as I should have been, because of the pint of local ale and glass of wine, and having just eaten – not ideal conditions for me, but I did my best and it served its purpose. Afterwards, folk thanked me and said it was a good choice. I felt I had 'done my bit' and was able to kick back, joining in a round of rum bought by JR! This served to turn us into pirates, and the evening got merrier after that! We decamped to the bar, where we chatted more informally until my partner wished to go back, feeling tired. It had been a good wedding, despite the weather. At one point in the evening I had stepped out into the wet blackness – the restless sea lapped at the quayside. The rain sent streams of water down the roadside and ramp, seeking to become one with their salt-brothers, dissolution in the saline solution. Such events break down barriers, forge alliances – between families, between friends. Everyone is forced together. Such rites of passage generate social cohesion. The guests were asked to vow to help maintain Suzanne and Svanur's wedding vows. The collective witnessing creates a moral boundary, a framework of taboo. All know the couple have made a sacred commitment to each other and are asked to honour that equally. Two families, and their many narratives, are joined. And, staying with JR and Sharon, we are forced to loosen our barriers and it feels like some kind of bridge is built over the Atlantic. Generations come together also on such occasions – elderly relatives, new additions, young and old. And also, different belief systems and backgrounds. My partner and I ended up talking to the vicar and his wife. Worlds apart normally, but over a cup of tea we found something in common. Another lady asked me about why I called myself a bard – I explained it was a title conferred on me by my community, and I outlined the Bard of Bath competition. She, being local, was familiar with Gorseth Kernow – I explained there were Bardic Chairs popping up all over the country, indeed, over the world. The boundaries blur. We merge.

We couldn't leave Cornwall without seeing some of its stunning landscape – without connecting to its spirit of place. And so the following morning, after breakfast and a pleasant chat with JR and Sharon, we headed down to the quay after Mevagissey for coffee and a stroll around the seafront, taking in the sights and smells of a classic Cornish fishing village – the colourful boats and houses perched on the hills around the small cove, the tang of fish and tobacco, the acrid aroma of good coffee. As it was nearly midday I bought a pasty (of course) to compensate for the meagre bowl of cornflakes I had for breakfast. Briefly, we enjoyed a break in the clouds. It had been forecast heavy rain, so it something of a blessed contrast. The day had threatened to be a washout, but now our plan to go walking wasn't so unwelcoming. We bid farewell to this charming spot and headed to the north coast, to visit Tintagel.

We parked in the village and walked down to the base of the dramatic headland. Despite the gaudy commercialism that surrounds it, the actual landmark retains its magic. Even though its connection with Arthur is as slim as the isthmus which connects it to Cornwall (thirteenth century ruins are scattered across its exposed top. A sixth century fragment has been found, and obviously it was of strategic importance, but...) one can see why generations have been inspired to see this savage outpost as a backdrop for the early stages of the Arthurian story. It is usually the location for Arthur's conception and birth – devised by Merlin's conjurations upon Igraine, wife of Gorlois, Duke of Cornwall. And it is the perfect setting for it. One imagines the 'dragon's breath' conjured up by Nicol Williamson in the wonderful Boorman treatment, *Excalibur*, is quite common around these cliffs. Today it was grey and the waves pounded in suitably dramatic way, little to the comfort of my partner who has a mortal dread of 'tsunamis'. I assured her these were quite rare in Cornish waters, but that did little to assuage her fears, although she managed to summon up courage to scramble down to the shoreline, exploring a less-visited cave which I called Morgen's Cave – as it lay opposite what is commonly referred to as Merlin's Cave, without a shred of evidence. However, upon entering it, one could see why it is associated with Britain's tutelary magician. Its long chamber, dark, dank and booming with the sea, had the tang of magic about it. I entered alone and connected with Merlin, asking for his wisdom to guide me and his blessing upon my Windsmith series, in which he features with increasing prominence (coming into his own in the final volume, which I plan to work on this winter, and so this experience was good fuel for the imagination – it certainly stirred the embers). Sometimes the Matter of Britain wearies me and feels distant – I get 'Arthurian fatigue' – then the passion is rekindled and I get swept away by its magic once more. At the moment, a playful retelling of Merlin is being broadcast on Saturday nights – one which takes liberties with the story – but tells the over-familiar story in a new and inventive way. It seems there is yet more gold to be mined from its deep seams. I am hoping there is some left for me!

From Tintagel, we headed for St Nectan's Glen – probably following a well-trodden pagan pilgrim trail (ending up at the Boscastle Witchcraft Museum, no doubt). My partner hadn't visited here before, so I took pleasure in guiding her up to the enchanting waterfall that pours through a hole in the rock, an organic symbol of awen. I imagined the water as inspiration, pouring into me and through me, but also wealth – receiving enough to be comfortable and sharing the excess. If the hole wasn't there, the pressure would build up until something would burst – a geological coronary. As with life. We need to let things flow – feelings, good luck, etc. Open and receive, but also release and share. My partner was busy taking photographs of orbs, while I was happy to feel the water droplets on my face that obviously cause them as they dapple camera lenses. People want to see the mystical and mysterious in things, when things are magical in themselves. Water is a miracle: without it we wouldn't be here on this planet. Nothing living would. And consisting of seventy percent water, the planet Earth is like a giant drop of water in space (in zero gravity it is possible to make perfect spheres), a blue pearl. Within it is contained six billions plus human lives and countless other kinds, insects by far outnumbering everything else like stars in a galaxy. We are a drop in the ocean in the great scheme of things. Yet such places as St Nectan's Glen make us feel connected to the mystery. Pilgrims had left offerings – creating quite a midden of meaningful litter, including plastic ID cards, photos, scribbled notes and the usual feathers, crystals, ribbons tied to the trees and, distinctively, piles of little stones everywhere. A fallen log was covered in coins, hammered in sideways, half-sticking out and creating an interesting 'armoured' effect. This looked like an intentional piece of 'earth art', a la Andy Goldsworthy, but the custodian of the site told me it was just something started by one visitor and taken up ever since. Thus traditions start. The place seems to be bring out the creative in people, and the credulous – photos of orbs were displayed back at the tearooms. It's not surprising – it is a gateway of dreams. Such places alter our brainwaves and make us more susceptible to lateral thoughts and stuff from the subconscious which floats to the surface. It brings up all kinds of things. In the case of my partner, it brought her to tears – ostensibly triggered by a postcard about Paxo the chicken, the tearoom's long-term resident who died last year. She had a cry about this with the owner, even though it seemed to be a positive thing – Paxo had a far better life than her feathered fellows in the battery farms – and too trivial a thing to waste tears on. Yet it was just a trigger, acting as a catalyst for a necessary catharsis – a build up of emotion and tension brought about by the strain of the journey and the time of the month. It made me burst into a fit of giggles – another kind of release! We left, subdued, depleted, after this eruption of emotion – like a fire, it had burnt us out. Water in such abundance can purify up to a point, but too much of it can leave you feeling washed out. Now we needed a hot meal, a warm house and a soft bed – but first, the long ride home. Yet, without succumbing to the tourist tat, we were not leaving empty-handed. The best treasures are invisible.

Dead Poets Sobriety
18th October 2008

Today would have been the fifty-second birthday of Simon Miles, a Bath-based poet and personal friend. To mark this occasion myself, his brother John Miles and Helen Elwes, another close friend, decided to publish his collection *The Signature of Kisses* posthumously. Simon handed me the manuscript of it a year before he died. I edited it, typeset it and designed it. Helen, a local artist and personal friend of Simon's, did the cover based upon the title poem, and John underwrote the whole thing through his business Ankerbold International Ltd. It was a team effort, although at times it felt like a case of 'too many chefs'! Helen, the archetypal perfectionist artist, decided the cover of the proof cover wasn't good enough and through a spanner in the works – so we had to print a separate wrap around cover to please her, used to artist book quality – whileas this was being done on a limited budget. The meetings required painful negotiation, and there was a dysfunctional communication chain of Chinese whispers – I would ring John, John would ring Helen, I would hear from Helen...

Despite all the birthpangs, the book was finished and arrived on time. However well these things are planned it always feels fraught right up to the last minute! It has often felt like 'hot water and towels' in the middle of the night – with the editor or typesetter acting as midwife. And when it arrives, it's like being the nervously critical parent, counting fingers and toes. Any typos seem ten feet tall.

The day before Simon's posthumous launch another book arrived – hot off the press – *The Book of the Bardic Chair*! It was truly wonderful to finally see it. A note of joy at the end of a tough week. I had handed the manuscript to RJ Stewart at Hawkwood the end of last summer, and only now, two weeks before Samhain (14 months later) it arrives. But that's because we did a thorough job on it – I worked closely with Arisha Wenneson in the States – combing thru proof after proof of the 237-page manuscript. Enough to send you goggle-eyed. Now I want others to see it with fresh eyes and tell me it's good. It was done with love to honour all those involved, especially Tim – another posthumous publication...

The night finally came. I was there on time, 5pm, as arranged and no one showed. I waited a whole hour – putting out all of the chairs – until John turned up. He had been told by Helen that we couldn't get in, which was plainly not the case. This seemed almost like deliberate sabotage. We rushed everything up stairs and set it all out in a great hurry – rather in the relaxed manner we should have done if everyone had turned up on time... John and Helen were stressed. I strived not to be annoyed by these final vexations. It was the finale – and after this night I need not have anything to do with these people ever again! The thought of this gave me considerable solace. However crazy the night proves to be, it wouldn't last forever. It would soon all be over.

It was poignant to launch a book for a friend no longer here – something I seem to do more than I choose to (Tim's was launched on what would have been his 60th; and, had I known it, a year later we would be holding a book launch for fellow poet and creative writing tutor, Mary Palmer, who tragically died of cancer). Perhaps an apt thing to do as we approach Samhain.

The woman doing the lights said Helen wanted the performers to be on stage – news to me, as I had arranged the room to allow for speakers in front of the stage, as this is more intimate, avoids stage fright and awkward pauses as people climb up and down the steps (some might be infirm like Simon's mother). This seemed to be more control freakery going on – who was running the show here? I took a deep breath and carried on regardless.

Things finally kicked off – and already the atmosphere was lively thanks to Pete, Simon's old college friend and now professional drunk. John started the evening off with introductions – I was meant to follow, but he had Micalef (aka Steve from Brixton) up – Helen's poet partner from London – to read one of Simon's poems, another annoying 'intervention' but I tried not to let it 'derail' me. When I got up to speak some called for me to go on the stage but I ignored them. I was there to be heard, not seen – and as I pointed out, the only star this evening was Simon (hopefully this punctured some egos). I just started – and my clear authoritative tone created respectful silence. It was heartfelt and emotional and set the mood for readings from friends – a selection of poems from the book.

It was a suitably bipolar night – I likened it to Simon's Apollonian and Dionysian impulses – light, music, art and darkness and wild ecstatic poetic frenzy. Pete got increasingly drunker and louder – the devil in the vault – much to the annoyance of John (perhaps a mirror of the relationship with his late brother?). Ironically, downstairs an AA meeting was taking place – perhaps Pete had come to the wrong room by mistake? The whole thing was hysterical: Pete did a convincing impression of the main actor from *Shameless* as he read out a David Gascoyne poem, most of it shouted in hoarse drunken bellows – the cries of a wounded beast – and ending in tears. A tale told by idiots, indeed. By that point I was beyond caring, and actually enjoying the whole mad show. We had launched the book – that's what mattered. I hope Simon enjoyed it, appreciated the gesture. It was certainly an occasion fitting of the late poet – a poem in itself.

Interesting how I attract such people and such experiences – perhaps a weakness on my part to drunken fools because of growing up with one? My blind spot – like Amelia Earhart's. Maybe this gives me more tolerance than I would have otherwise.

Afterwards, we repaired to the Rising Sun, which used to be home of the Bath Storytelling Circle. Now it has been done up and has a very different atmosphere. The former landlady, who was an old soak, would bring out her crystal ball at the drop of a hat and insist on giving people a drunken reading, still runs the B&B there. Marko was in his cups by this point, but fortunately didn't turn belligerent – perhaps that energy had been exorcised by 'Pisshead Pete'. Instead, we had a pleasant 'wind-down' session with the 'inner circle'. At one point an endless round was ordered and nobody knew who was going to pay for it. Somehow the tab got cleared. By this point I reverted to water, to limit the damage and I was glad of it the next day. Drinks were finished off quickly as we were chucked out onto the dark streets. At least we all parted as friends.

Simon, happy birthday. Rest in peace.

The Lighting of a Fire
20th October 2008

I am currently up to my eyeballs with teaching – I have about a hundred students a week. It's a dismal rainy Monday and it seems like a million light years away from my summer peregrinations, out on the road, following the awen. And yet teaching is very much part of the bardic path, an intrinsic part I would say. What is the point of wisdom unless it is passed on? True education is about illumination, not indoctrination, as WB Yeats epitomised:

Education is not the filling of a pail, but the lighting of a fire.

As bards we should empower – enable people to express

themselves, to tap into their own awen, find their own spark. It's not about having 'followers' or delusions of grandeur. We should be on the Way of Awen for the 'art in us', not 'us in the art'. As a say to my writing students, are you interested in being a writer, or in the writing? If it's the former – stop here, you're deluding yourself if you think you'll get far without a deep passion for the medium itself. This enthusiasm, this joy in the 'journey, not the destination' will sustain you longer than any false dream of success. What is true wealth? Doing what you love doing, day in, day out, comes pretty close. Fame and fortune brings attendant problems – hence so much disease and dysfunction amongst the rich and well known. How many 'celebrities' seem happy to you?

From this place of passionate commitment to one's craft you will be a stronger position to teach – for you'll be practising what you preach. Dan Millman, author of *The Way of the Peaceful Warrior*, says: 'You must teach what you've realized through your own experiences.' This is the approach I've adopted in this book, and one I generally employ in my pedagogy. If it works for me, if I actually use it, then my students might find it useful to. This anchors the teaching in a solid place – authentic, tried and tested: proof-of-the-pudding stuff.

Teaching can seem exhausting at times, dealing with all of the admin and clashing personalities – behind the scenes and in the classroom, but it has its rewards, as captured in the ancient Celtic verse, The Cauldron of Vocation: 'one gives and is replenished'.

I never thought I would be a teacher – but then I had a mistaken impression as a boy that you had to only teach school-children, which promised to be nightmarish, going by my schooling! However, around my Saturn Return I discovered Adult Education, and realised it was something I could possibly do, having reached a certain point in my career (winning the Bardic Chair of Bath and a national ghost story competition). I duly undertook the required training and came out clutching the necessary certificate. I started to run workshops – mainly in storytelling – until I consolidated my pedagogy with an MA in the Teaching and Practice of Creative Writing. And since then – five years ago – I have been teaching on a freelance basis for various institutions, both Further and Higher Education. Mostly part-time contracts, it has allowed me time to continue in my own practice, which I think is essential. My priority is following my own creative path – in doing so I'm in a more genuine position to help others, as I'm tackling the problems they will encounter pretty much every day. I'm not lost in an academic ivory tower, removed from the world, but engaging with it all the time. I go out into my community and teach in all kinds of places, to all ages and abilities: primary school children, homeless, mental health service users, Senior Citizens, postgraduates, professionals. This is rewarding in the way it allows me a healthy cross-section of humanity – I don't get stuck in my bubble as I don't get a chance to! I am forced to meet people halfway – reaching out and connecting with all sorts. As Dan Millman adds: 'Respect others. Give them what they want (to learn) at first and, perhaps eventually, a few of them will want what you want to give them.' Being a teacher is certainly about remembering it's more about the 'us' than the 'I'. Everyone in the class needs to be considered, above the issues of the individual (i.e. you don't want one student taking over or biasing the class in his or her direction). You get all sorts of projection – you are seen as an authority figure and this can bring up a student's issues around their parents, their boss, an older sibling or a teacher at school. They may be habitually late, or wilfully disregarding of set activities, disrespectful to the tutor or fellow students, disruptive, over-demanding ... you get it all and need to have a thick skin and the patience of a saint. Then one student tells you it has meant the world to them, or they contact you a couple of years later to tell you they've got published or started getting paid gigs – and it all feels worth while.

One thing is for sure – you learn as much from the students as they hopefully will from you. It is a two-way process. And of course, you never stop learning. As Blake said, 'he who never changes his opinions breeds reptiles of the mind'. If a student challenges you, well and good, it keeps you on your toes – stops you resting on your laurels. And you never know, one day, someone may leave you an apple.

Ghost Story
24th October 2008

I have a dark cautionary tale to tell, a week before Samhain – a salutary lesson for all storytellers, hence I include it here. One year (2004) I performed at Chalice Well Gardens in Glastonbury at their Samhain Celebration. I told an Irish myth of Nera and the noose, which for me ultimately is about the affirmation of life beyond death, and love beyond death. It has a powerful kissing the corpse on the gallows moment (in my version at least). Afterwards I went into town to catch up with my friend, who was performing in a play that night at the Assembly Rooms. I took a photograph in the street for some reason – later, when it was developed, it revealed two ghostly footprints in the middle of the high street ... I discovered a couple of days later that a man in Glastonbury had hung himself that night. I was shaken, having told a story about hanging in my set. I was chilled to think the tormented soul might have seen my performance, and, in his deranged state, been influenced in his method of suicide. I wanted to find out for sure this was not so. I left a message with my friend, who, with his local contacts, would be able to check (he was living in town at the time).

Yet that was not the worst of it.

A couple of days later I heard of another suicide in Glastonbury.

Another hanging.

I began to feel I was in a nightmare.

A couple of weeks later another tragic death was announced

in Glastonbury.

A never-ending nightmare.

This time I wasn't sure if it was a hanging, but by then I really didn't want to know.

Had I unleashed some awful curse?

Yet I had other things on my mind – a month-long book tour was about to start. I was to be on the road for practically the whole of October, with my partner, giving readings in all the places where the novel is set – a story about a lover laying to rest the ghost of her husband.

On the final date of the tour we were returning to Bath late at night – around pub closing time, when we recognised a figure drunkenly staggering along the London Road into town. It was my friend Richard Wilde. We stopped.

The last time I had seen him, it was at my book launch and he seemed in a strange mood. He ranted on about Nazis, for some reason – to him the ornamental stone eagles in the Countess of Huntingdon's Chapel [The Building of Bath Museum, showing an exhibition on Bath's Georgian druid architect, John Wood the Elder, called 'Obsession' at the time] which I had hired for the event, were Nazi-like in some way. He had stormed off.

I wanted to show I wasn't bothered and we offered him a lift home – he was obviously in his cups.

He asked just to be dropped off at the Porter Butt – the next pub along – although he plainly didn't need any more.

Yet, we obliged and, as he departed, I gave him a fraternal hug. We bid each other good night.

About a week later I heard from his distraught partner, Liz McCaig-Scott, that he had committed suicide.

Apparently, he had been found hanging in his flat, suspended by a hemp rope he had made himself.

This was devastating. Richard was, I like to think, a good friend. Earlier that year we had walked across the Quantocks in the footsteps of Coleridge and Wordsworth. I had encouraged him to write, and to take up teaching again (he had been a PhD student, but had had some kind breakdown, and had turned to gardening and dry stone walling instead. He said he was happy, yet spent most of his days drunk).

I was numb. Lost in a world of death. A self-fulfilling prophecy.

After this I found it impossible to tell stories. I was terrified that what I narrated would in some way come true. Irrational I know, but I had experienced a spate of suicides and was in shock at the loss of a dear friend. I could not perform – I just wanted to crawl inside myself and hide.

This feeling stayed with me into the new year. We held a ceremony for Richard at Folly Farm, a Wildlife Trust place he had worked at the end of January. A moving experience. I read out a poem I wrote for Richard, 'Walking with Richard', or simply, 'My Friend' (a favourite phrase of his). Yet I was unable to perform stories. The Bath Literature Festival was coming up and we were planning a show, but I stepped back. I had lost my nerve completely. Rationally, I knew I had nothing to do with Richard's death – but friends and family always blame themselves when a loved one commits suicide. We all ask ourselves – could we have done something? Why didn't we notice? It seems likely Richard's death was caused by the side-effects of the anti-depressants he was taking. The heavy drinking obviously didn't help – but there has been a record incidence of suicides of young men taking this particular drug in recent years. However, I was, to say the least, rattled.

This was my raison d'être – but if this was the results? I couldn't bear it.

Then my friend, Justin, informed me that the first man who hung himself had not gone to the Chalice Well that night. I felt enormous relief.

Slowly, I rebuilt my confidence and returned to the stage,

chastened by my experiences.

A truly chilling ghost story.

***

[It seemed ironic I had spent a year writing a book about a woman suffering from grief – yet in some strange way it helped me to prepare for this experience. I had empathised with it so closely that I was able to cope far better.

Since then my life has been marked by other deaths. Yet I have been able to use my bardism to work through the aftermath – to honour, to remember, to express and release. I believe every act of creativity defeats death. By being creative we can be most fully alive. It is the opposite of destruction, of decay, of oblivion, of nothingness – that will come, but in the meantime, sing, dance, paint, write, tell stories.

It is for me the only antidote.]

Dark Shift
26th-27th October 2008

Saturday I performed in a show with fellow Fire Springs member, Kirsty Hartsiotis, at Victoria Art Gallery, Bath. We had gone along to the Bath Storytelling Circle together, December 1999, met storytellers and formed Fire Springs. And now here we were, performing professionally together eight years later. It was an hour show we had devised called 'Sea of Light' based on the Peter Lanyon exhibition in the main gallery – Lanyon was a Cornish artist, and his major work – a sixty-foot mural was there. We had created the show with his art and themes in mind. But when we arrived we were told we'd be performing in the upstairs gallery in the permanent exhibition – all terribly nice but not relevant to our tales. It would have been far more effective in situ – surrounded by Lanyon's art. The reason we were given was it was the first day of the show and it would probably be 'too busy'! So obviously they wanted as few as possible to come and see us... Having us upstairs meant people had to come and find us. It's always best to go where the people are. We had a dismal turn out – about ten at the most, and nearly half of those were young kids, when we had planned a show for all ages. Once again, it seemed we were being set up as 'children's entertainers' when we'd created a show with intelligent threads echoing Lanyon's themes, all pretty much wasted on the under sevens. I always avoid gigs for kids – I am not a children's entertainer – I'm happy to perform to mixed audiences ('children of all ages') but struggle and flounder with the younger end of the spectrum. Nothing wrong with them, just something I choose not to do. And once again, it seemed like we'd been let down by a venue – although they had done all the necessary marketing. It's the actual performance space that makes the world of difference – it can make or break a show. The gallery we performed in was very large and echoing. And had little relevance to our nautical set. Yet we put on a brave face and did our best – it hung together well considering we hadn't rehearsed it together, mainly drawing on existing repertoire. I told a new tale (for me) Jason and the Golden Fleece, because it features in Lanyon's mural. Also did my Ys story and Alcyone and Ceryx. So the show was a mixture of Celtic and Mediterranean. We put in good enough performances – but without a decent sized audience you can really start to flounder. Basically it's demoralising and exhausting. You're giving out a lot and getting little back. I found my first story was not as smooth as I wanted, because it was the first time I'd done it, and was my 'warm up'. But by Ys I was in full flow, and the tale really took me over, and I really felt the audience was captivated. By the last story I had run out of energy and made stupid mistakes because my brain was tired. I really needed some Red Bull or something to keep going – to avoid those mid-set dips. It shows perhaps how tired I am these days (lots of teaching draining my energy). Compare my thirty minute set to the two hour stint I did once at Peat Moors Visitor Centre…

Today I went on a whim to the Samhain Storyfest at the Peat Moors Visitor Centre on the Somerset Levels, a partial reconstruction of the Glastonbury Lake Village with its three round houses (though one has collapsed – due to the extreme weather?). It was overcast when I set out – a pathetic fallacy, matching my melancholy mood – but the rain held off as I rode to the isolated location, over the Mendips, following my familiar route passed the Mast down thru Wells to Glastonbury. There were half a dozen storytellers entering. When I arrived I was asked if I was one – which of course I am – but that day I was happy to be in the audience. I wanted to support the event and those who entered it, not try and steal their chance for glory. I wasn't hungry for another title.

Standing in the shop was Eddie Wills, who runs the centre, Jem Dick and the previous year's winner. I almost immediately got into a discussion with them about running such a contest – they chose to draw lots, which I disagreed with. It seems too random, and doesn't honour the quality of the better performers. Basically anyone can win. In which case, you don't need to try your best. Winning based upon the merit of your performance is a real incentive to do your best – this is how the Olympics work. Folk don't seem to have a problem with that, or most sport. Exam results. School tables. Pop and film charts. Book lists. Popular culture is rife with lists, with an inevitable winner. A bardic chair can be more considered than that. I cited the example of poetry slams, based upon the most popular performer winning – basically, whoever turns up with the most mates, or makes the crowd laugh the most. I see this as a dumbing down of poetry – playing to the gallery. Poetry can be accessible without having to be crowd-pleasing. Many things in life are popular, but that doesn't make them good. The National Socialists were popular in Thirties' Germany. George W Bush, incredibly, was voted in for a second term. The mainstream, like the mob are not reliable indicators of quality. So, the shortest straw method doesn't, I feel, do the performers justice. It absolves responsibility, leaving it in the lap of the gods. As conscious human beings we are able to make intelligent choices, I feel, without relying on oracles. One may say it's cool to 'let the Fates decide' as Eddie put it, but this can be exploited. The winners (Unlimited Company of Storytellers) had three entrants out of the six, so they had a fifty per cent chance of winning…(it turns out they will use their win to secure more funding, which is great – and it will obviously mean the world to the members, who have learning disabilities, a real achievement for them. But…) Yet, despite my gripes, I believe it is healthy for each chair to do it in its own way. There should be no orthodoxy. As long as it's done openly and fairly. That should be the only benchmark. A level playing field.

All the entrants had something to offer, but my money would have gone on Beth, who did an excellent version of the Taliesin story – including details which I normally leave out. Perhaps being a woman, and possibly of Welsh origin (going by her pronunciation) she focussed more on Ceridwen's point of view, whileas I focus on Taliesin's. There's always room for a plethora of interpretation. That's the great thing about these stories. Nobody 'owns' them. They are our common wealth.

It has been interesting to see how this Chair has developed. It is now seven years old. Eight years ago – the year before the contest began – I performed at the first Samhain Fair as the guest storyteller, billed as the Winner of the Bardic Chair of Caer Badon. The following year Eddie launched the Bardic Chair of the Avalon Marshes. That proto-year, I performed a marathon set – one hour of mixed stories, and then, after a break, an hour of Beowulf! I am astounded, now I think of how tired I get after thirty minutes of performing! What made it extra special was – I got to sleep over in one of the round houses by myself. Curled up on the fur-lined bench in my 3-4 season sleeping bag by the embers of the fire, I was snug as the proverbial bug. It was thrilling to stay there on Samhain. A time when the veil is thin, yet I slept soundly. Outside a storm raged and it felt like Grendel's mother raking the thatched roof of the roundhouse – but they are so well designed that, blow as it may (unlike the straw house built by the three little pigs – an amusing variant Eddie told today) it didn't blow down. It didn't have a door, but fortunately the entrance was on the leeward. In the morning I awoke to scenes of devastation. The Levels were flooded. Trees were down. But the round house was intact, and I'd had a pretty good night's sleep. I feel that, by honouring the ancestors with my tales, and especially the story of Beowulf, I placated the katabolic forces of Samhain. I had fended off the monster 'death' – like Scheherazade – with my fabulation.

The lots were drawn and the winner/s were selected – the whole of the Unlimited Company of Storytellers, who were understandably jubilant. Afterwards, emerging blinking and stiff from the roundhouse where we had sat in the chilly twilight for two hours (no real fire, because of bloody health and safety), punters gratefully queued for hot punch as they stretched their limbs. And then we awaited the burning of the wicker man (who looked more like a wicker womble or a craft fair artoo detoo in its watery ditch, lacking much in the way of humanoid limbs or head!). Still, it served its cathartic purpose. People were encouraged to burn a withy in memory of a lost loved one, so I put one on for my Dad. I'd had a week of grief of another kind, and it was into this direction I channelled my intent. The death of love is perhaps the most painful of all to endure.

One of the most satisfying things about being a bard is being able to express these feelings, to nail them. It is said, 'Physician, heal thyself.' Bardism is our own medicine and magic. We can provide this service for others – expressing and epitomising – but also for ourselves.

Broken Trails

The trees give up their ghost.
Another bough is shook naked
With each melancholy sigh
Of the October winds.
The forest path is covered
In the year's screwed up drafts.
A walk alone,
With her.
Shadowing my foot steps.
A deer races ahead,
The forest yields up its beauty
And only I am there to witness –
A pauper amongst such riches.
Emptied I drift
Light as leaves
Along these broken trails.

Rocks East Woodland

Walking to London (footnotes)
23rd October 2008

Flash of blue fire – spying a kingfisher along the Kennet and Avon Canal gives me courage. On the train, my eyes scan along the tracks of text, then look up to see the white horse, proud on the Ridgeway. Walking through Hyde Park, three swans land like a Celtic myth. A rabbit, twitchily alert to my presence, fixes me with its sloe eye. Squirrel on an iron fence, its eye like a dark nut. Joggers puff by in rhythm to their i-pods as I briefly sit on a bench dedicated to Rudolf Steiner, enjoying the view over the lake, framed by willows. Wild wind carols through the city street, whipping away my hat. London business, the hustle and bustle, the designer boutiques of Knightsbridge. Rushing to the campus, racing up to the fifth floor, breathless and thirsty. Twenty-two people eager to write, sharing dreams. Afterwards a beer with new friends. In the belly of the beast, jewels can be found.

Samhain Dark Moon
28th October 2008

Unless I make that melody, how can the dead have rest?
The Feather, Vernon Watkins

The above quote by the 'bard of the Gower', Vernon Watkins, sums up one of the key functions of the bard. To honour the dead – ancestors, loved ones, heroes and heroines of the tribe – with words of deep intent. This ancient purpose, as relevant as ever, is especially resonant at this time of year, when the veil is said to be thin and it would be foolhardy to do otherwise. To reverse Watkins phrase, would we have rest if we don't?

The dead scream in my ears and it feels like my life has been taken over by them – as I dedicate my energies to telling their stories, their arrested narratives.

This Saturday sees the launch of *The Book of the Bardic Chair*, initially published in a limited edition to honour the founder of the Bardic Chair of Caer Badon, Tim Sebastion Woodman, who died Imbolc 2007. It features profiles and winning poems by all the Chaired Bards of Bath, plus Ovates, Druids and all those involved with what has become the most successfully revived English Bardic Chair to date. It has now been revised and expanded to celebrate Bardic Chairs across Britain and around the world. It is my way of honouring all those who are making this a living tradition. It seems very appropriate to launch it at Samhain. It was originally meant to come out at Imbolc, a year on from Tim's passing, and I organised an Imbolc Bardic Showcase in Glastonbury for that purpose – but the book wasn't ready. It seemed Tim was having a last laugh in the afterlife! Yet perhaps it wasn't the right time anyway. Now seems to be, and it has finally manifested – I have the book here. When things flow it is a good sign that the time is right. The event encountered a snag when I discovered the venue had been mistakenly double-booked for original date, October 31st. And so I had to move it to the Saturday, 1st November – which is still Samhain, and perhaps better, since it's the Celtic New Year. A good time for new ventures. I have a sneaking feeling that the 'Good Folk' were making their presence felt – just to remind us who's in charge! Samhain is always a busy time, so this new date is probably better for most. There's going to be performances from Bards of Bath and special guests, with some floor spots – so a chance for everyone to shine.

But before then, tonight is Samhain 'proper' – dark moon. The nadir of the year – the ultimate 'death' time, more so than the winter solstice I feel, which is redeemed by the rebirth of light. We have some hard walking ahead before we reach the light at the end of the tunnel: the underworld journey of winter. Yet this katabolic tide has its place. A time to strip away all that is unnecessary, all that is uncertain. The Cailleach is abroad – the fierce mountain mother sweeps across the land (snow fell in the North yesterday for the first time this season, and it feels like the true start of winter), testing all – like Lady Ragnall at King Arthur's court. Anything weak will not last the winter. Lame livestock culled, meat salted and stored. The rest driven to winter pastures. This is Nature at its cruellest, but most honest.

It looks like the world is experiencing this 'winnowing' at present, with the escalating financial crisis. Global economic meltdown. Who knows when it will bottom out – how far the house of cards will fall? It shows 'the fragility of everything revealed at last', to use Cormac Mccarthy's words from his haunting post-apocalyptic novel, *The Road*. Hopefully it will make people realise the vacuity of materialism, the flaw of Capitalism, and the meaning of true wealth – friendship, health, the generosity and beauty of the natural world, freedom of expression, community. We live in terrifying times. Nothing feels safe. So we need to hold onto what is nearest and dearest to weather the storm. Yet it is important to look at these 'winter wounds' as Watkins called them, hard in the face. This is the ugly reality of life revealed at last. The skull beneath the smile. What is of value? What is false? We will all be tested in the times ahead – will it bring out the best in us, or the worst? As the world's resources dwindle, will those who have widen the gulf more, become increasingly selfish and paranoid? The only consolation seems no one is immune to this – even the fattest cats – and this may level the playing field somewhat and make us find common ground. We may bond through this peril.

On a personal level, this stripping back is extremely healthy. Time to take stock. What do you need in your life? What don't you need? What will sustain you through the dark months? It is time to batten down the hatches, to survive on our reserves like bears in hibernation. This 'wintering' can be exceptionally productive. I love the deep dreaming of winter, when the seeds of summer are sown in the imagination. I often embark on a new book over the winter, having more head-space than the busier summer months allow, although this is generally not until after Yuletide: things get crazier until then. It is the dead of winter – January – that things begin to blossom for me. Revelling in the quietus, I can get my head down and write. The austerity of the season is a blessed relief after the jangling frippery of Christmas and Hogmanay. We can hear ourselves think, and our feelings are our own, rather than colonised and manipulated by the cloying sentiments of the season when we are expected to feel and act in certain ways. A bardic humbug on it all! Saying that, I do like certain aspects of Yuletide – the carolling and wassailing, the holly and ivy, mistletoe and mulled wine, the merriment and misrule. Perhaps I'm not as much of a Scrooge-like curmudgeon as I sound! Every Twelfth Night I hold a wassail in my back garden to my apple trees – my favourite way to celebrate after the tinsel has settled.

Before then, it is time to listen to the night and hear the ghost songs. It is a time for ghost stories, prognostications by flickering firelight, rituals of appeasement, days of remembrance and nights of sacrificial fires.

Samhain Bardic Showcase
1st-2nd November 2008

The Book of the Bardic Chair was launched last night at a Samhain Bardic Showcase I organised. The Good Folk were certainly making their presence felt: first there was a double-booking, thanks to a mistake by the booking secretary; then the keyholder didn't turn up to let me in (thinking it was another day – appropriately, he's called Wally). I had to stand for forty minutes in the pouring rain, waiting outside the venue (I had meant to meet a friend arriving from Oxford, but he failed to turn up to!). It truly felt like the 'dead of the year' – over the last couple of days it had turned bitterly cold. Suddenly, it felt like winter, for once synchronising with the actual festival, although after a very mild autumn it was something of a shock to the system. Amazingly, I managed to keep my spirits up – whistling the Gene Kelly song. Must have looked a creepy sight, loitering in the doorway with my raincoat and trilby, like a character from a detective story on surveillance, or Harry Lime in *The Third Man*. No cat came crawling round my ankle to give me away. Fortunately, Richard Carder turned up – Druid of Caer Badon and another key-holder. We were on. I helped bring in the stuff, although I was shivering by that point, and annoyed that the keyholder had let me down. Still, I took a deep breath – I adopted a smile and decided to take whatever the night threw at me in good grace. I had to dash back to the train station to see if my partially-sighted friend had arrived – another stress-inducing detail to consider – but he didn't show. I had an event to run, so had to go back. He'd had three chances. I hoped he was alright (and he was – much to my relief I heard a message from him when I got in, saying he'd missed his connection and had decided to go back). I returned to the venue and set up the book stall. Moyra Caldecott had been brought by Richard and Misha and was the first to buy a copy. After much hard work and a false start it had finally manifested.

I tried to thaw out with a black coffee, and play the congenial host. I introduce the evening, and invited Richard and Misha up to run an opening ceremony. They both did poems (Richard also played the clarinet, which sounded good in the old church hall of St Marks). Then I got, as third Bard of Bath, to perform Dragon Dance. For some reason I was nervous – though I've done it several times over the summer – but I closed my eyes and just immersed myself in it. The main thing is to get into the zone. A certain look, sound or movement in the audience may distract you and break the spell – in this respect poetry recital is very different from storytelling, where you work such distractions into the performance. I had to concentrate fully on remembering the fourteen page epic. The drumming helped, as did the refrains and other mnemonic devices I had woven into it. I went into a kind of a trance, and if it seemed shamanic – with my drum and tassles, wolf jewellery and skins – then it was the desired effect. I 'warmed up' and was soon in the zone – and then it poured out of me. I was able to open my eyes at times, to check the audience was with me, but many closed their eyes to listen. Afterwards, Brendan said he'd like to listen to it in his car. Must do a recording some time!

With much relief that it had gone well, I left the pumpkin-lined stage, and introduced the next performer – another Bard of Bath. We had seven in the end: Richard, myself, Mark, Brendan, Ash and Thommie. Plus Moyra, honorary bard. A good showing. After the break, when the audience gratefully warmed up (it was chilly in the hall, despite the heaters) with hot apple punch, we had our special guest bard, Dearbhaile Bradley from Glastonbury, second bard of Ynys Witrin, who did a great set.

Brendan brought us back down to earth in an amusing way with his droll northern comic verse. Then we had Anthony and Kirsty up to end the evening in fine style with two fantastic ghostly tales. We finished with a closing ceremony, burning small pieces of paper with things we wanted to let go off. Afterwards, we mingled and chatted. Some books were sold, and connections made/reaffirmed. A couple of ladies from Oregon said they might set a Chair up back home. And so the word is spread. We packed up and left about eleven. Fortunately Richard and Misha gave me a lift home – as it was still raining. I was glad, being very tired by that point, but happy with how it had gone. It had been a moving and magical evening of bardism. It felt like we had honoured the ancestors with our voices, our hearts. I'd made some to cover the hall hire, and to help with the books, but the real measure of the success of an evening like this was the 'emotional capital' gained. The community had come together and the awen had been shared.

Mysteries in Cardiff
8th November 2008

Tonight I travelled over to Cardiff to launch the first book by Chrissy Derbyshire – a rising star if ever there was one. It was the first time I had been back to Cardiff since my graduation in 2004. It felt satisfying to be returning as a publisher – I wouldn't have conceived it at the time, even though I had launched Awen Publications a year before. But my small press hasn't really taken off until this year – with a flurry of seven titles! This month has seen a hat-trick of launches – Bath, Stroud and now Cardiff.

I made my way through the rain to Chapter Arts Centre, negotiating the buses and the strange accents. Just getting out of Cardiff Central station was a challenge, as it had all been barricaded off as hordes of rugby fans were being funnelled to their respective coaches and trains. I seemed to be the only one going the other way, and not dressed in colours.

I arrived early and had a pint of Rev. James and a lite bite of Welsh rarebit in the café. Finally, Chrissy's entourage turned up and, after introductions to her folks, we set to work, setting the place up. Chrissy's family and friends were very supportive, taking care of refreshments and a generous bar – with lots of mead! I held back as I was due to introduce the evening. I recalled how special my first book launch was – you never forget it. Afterwards, Chrissy said it had been one of the best nights of her life!

After my introduction, which wasn't as eloquent or as focused as I wanted to be (guess my bardic energies were flagging) Chrissy impressed everyone with a good talk and a series of readings from her book. She seemed to take to the 'stage' naturally and is a good speaker. She also sings, but I haven't heard her yet – fulfilling the Awen author criteria to be a spoken word performer as well, our USP. You could say we're a bardic publisher.

It was very satisfying to see people queuing up around the room waiting to get their books signed by Chrissy. Virtually all were family and friends but it was still good to see. Chrissy must have been buzzing. Unfortunately I wasn't able to stay and continue celebrating with her and the others as I had a train to catch! I had to dash and luckily a bus came just at the right time to get me to the station. Unfortunately, this 'last train to England' was packed with drunken revellers, and there was one or two altercations – one bloke being collared by a policeman for being lippy. Two gay bicyclists standing by me were getting hassled by an odious rugby fan, who objected to their bikes taking up seating space, even though that part of the carriage was dedicated to bikes. He was being far more objectionable, but when other fans piled on, they chatted away to the gay guys without a problem – it was clear who had 'the problem' here, and he was marginalised in his loathsome opinions. It was a sour note to end on, after a good night. But the contrast could not have been more striking. I wish I could have stayed and shared Chrissy's success – but I'd already booked my return. This was an echo of the problem when I was studying at Cardiff. Sometimes I would stay over, but often I came back – and missed out on the social element. Chrissy's circle, which has largely come out of the Cardiff Uni Pagan Society shows what college life can be like. Lifetime friendships can be forged. Chrissy's circle of friends showed their support admirably – whilst I felt the 'lone wolf', slinking back to my solitary lair. Sometimes a bardic life can be isolated – it is not always possible to share the path we walk with others.

Mist Over Pendle
16th November 2008

(Mostly written in Gloucester Station)

Boots still damp from bog-trotting on Pendle Hill today – walked up there with Anthony Nanson, fellow writer and storyteller. He had arranged a joint reading in his old home town of Clitheroe, Lancashire, where he went to Grammar School ('Like *The History Boys*, but without the homosexuality!'). We stayed with his parents, Simon (ex-headmaster) and Cynthia (ceramicist and mean cook), who were most hospitable. I even got to sleep in Anthony's old room [he crashed in his sister's old room]. It was really special to let me into his past like this.

The next morning we dropped some books off at the shop, looking perhaps a little bohemian for a small northern town with Anthony's Aslan-ish mane and my devilish hat. Afterwards, as we had a few hours to kill before the gig, Anthony took me up to 'the Cut', a notch in Pendle Hill frequented by revellers on Halloween (not a place to hang about, according to Anthony's schooldays reminiscences, but very much part of the mythic landscape of his childhood). Here, with a dramatic vista either side we rehearsed our stories, slightly apart from one another.

Failing to raise Old Nick with our 'incantations', (our mythic mumblings would have probably had us burnt two or three centuries earlier) we drove into 'witch country' – now clearly sign-posted (as the Pendle Witches have been marketed as local heritage) although we still managed to have a moment of 'navigational uncertainty', at a suitably bleak crossroads, where the signs seemed to point all the wrong way (which, as it turned out, they did – having been bent round! It was all getting a bit 'Blair Witch'...) We found the village, which seemed rather pleasant and harmless, as no doubt the 'witches' were – persecuted for political ends or local grudges. With the temperature dropping, we wended our way back to the town. Time to get to work.

The 'reading' (more a performance, as we didn't use the texts) took place in Kaydee Bookshop – where Anthony worked for a year. We were co-promoting Anthony's short story collection *Exotic Excursion* and my non-fiction tome, *Lost Islands* – a good combination. We told thirty minutes of material each, alternating ten minute slots. After Anthony's introduction I started my set with the opening of Oisín and Niamh, including the poem, 'Delightful is the land beyond all dreams'. In the middle I did The Spirit Bride, an Algonquin tale (which I last performed in Malta last November at Metageum). I ended with two modern stories – a Climate Change one about the 'discovery' of a found island, Nymark, in the Arctic, due to melting ice; the other was about how the Onge tribe of Little Andaman survived the Indian Ocean Tsunami thanks to the thirty to fifty thousand years of folklore. Anthony was thoroughly professional and engaging as usual. He hesitated doing his last 'spoken fiction' story from *Exotic Excursions* – because of an incursion by mainly teenage girls halfway through the event, but after apparently listening to Spirit Bride they upped sticks and left, so luckily we got to hear Anthony's movingly subtle rendition of his lakeside epiphany – an experience perhaps you appreciate far more the older you get. It would be nice to have someone to share such a moment with.

Indirectly, I supposed we had – a small but committed audience listened attentively (mostly Anthony's family and friends, including an old Primary school teacher). We sold three books each, and they took six more of Anthony's title on sale or return. The long trip certainly wasn't reciprocated financially – most of it went on petrol and trains – but in other ways it felt worth the effort. It was great to have a break away from Bath after a heavy fortnight of teaching and marking. I hadn't really been away from Bath properly since late September (OOTO/Long Man). Also, I have had a hard time lately – separating from my partner and, earlier in the week, having a motorcycle crash. I survived (a bruised knee and bank balance) but my beloved Zuki is in the garage awaiting repairs – the last thing I needed in these difficult times.

I was appreciative that Anthony was allowing me into the precious territory of his formative years – as we walked streets ghosted with memory. Later that evening, after the gig, we went into town with Andrew, an old Grammar School friend of his. We holed up in the Castle, by a merry fire. The old friends got caught up in a discussion about economics, while I yearned for some more feminine company. I find a political debate not that relaxing, whileas some love to argue the toss (they had both been members of the school's debating society and you could tell). I wished I'd gone into the other room to watch the musician, but by the time I decided to do this, he had finished. When we got back, I just hit the sack. It had been a tiring day.

Sunday, the weather miraculously cleared up after an overcast start. Togged up, we set off with some basic supplies – from Anthony's 'iron rations'. We parked in the pretty village of Barley and followed the line of reservoirs up – the effort warming us up, as it was chilly. We stopped to savour the black lines of bare trees against the silver water, the steep flanks of green hills beyond, the reddish bracken in the foreground. It was cold, clear – with a Celtic clarity about it, like one of those Medieval vignettes, perhaps the Gawain poem – one could have easily imagined the Green Knight dwelling up one of the cloughs, the sound of him sharpening his axe ringing in the brassy air. We carried on up passed Wembory Clough, a jagged gulley down which iron knots of water gurgled. We were meant to follow the V of the main beck all the way up but the path seemed to vanish into muddy, rocky slopes – so we struck out across country, hoping to intersect the lost track, but found ourselves bogtrotting over spongy ground riddled with treacherous 'holes' of brackish water. It was tiring slog, but at least it was sunny. It would have been grim going in wind and raining. This wasn't a place to linger in such conditions. It had a wildness about it, an abode of trolls. After a determined yomp we hit the stone slab pathways – what bliss – which led to the top, the 'Big End'. After ritualistically touching the trig point we went to the brow of the steep side to enjoy the spectacular view over the Ribble Valley. It had been certainly worth the effort. We enjoyed the prospect despite the noisy group of ramblers nearby, stopping for their summit snack like us, before the temperature made them move on. It was a clear day, and the Big End afforded fine views. We scoffed some crisps and chocolate and got moving again, making a small diversion at my request to Robin Hood's Well, from which we both sipped. It was a romantic place, one could imagine the wolfshead slaking his thirst here as he looked back to his possibly native Yorkshire. I asked for cunning and agility, for it was also known as Fox's well, but this was probably after George Fox, the founder of the Quakers, who had a vision on Pendle which inspired him to found his new religion. It was easy to see why – this place lent itself easily to noble thoughts, to vision. We now stood on Mount Epiphany, in the footsteps of prophets, and drank from those same waters... Having supped from the source, we gladly descended, body temperature plummeting. Down the steep rock steps passed the hordes of visitors flocking up, some ill-attired for the heights or a sudden turn in the weather. It was good to descend to milder climes now, although the land retained its wonderful rugged quality. We followed a merry beck lined with tangled hawthorns back down to the carpark, and, after purchasing some placatory jam (a token gesture to my kindly hospitable hosts) we wended our way home to Anthony's parents for a lovely lunch, before hitting the road in earnest – South, a long but agreeable ride down the Welsh Marches. Anthony dropped me off at Gloucester station, where a dull long train ride home awaited (3 hours!). I wearily made it back to the Cauldron, ready to collapse – but first I finished off the stew I'd made earlier in the week, and hit the sack with toddy and bottle. A tiring jaunt, but I was certainly better for it than if I'd stewed at home all weekend. Nature is most certainly the best medicine. I agree with GM Trevelyan, who said: 'I have two doctors, my left leg and my right.'

I am grateful to have both.

Bardic Busy-ness
25th-30th November 2008

A triptych of bardic engagements this week. The first one was at St Andrews Primary School, Congresbury, on Tuesday afternoon. I was to perform Greek Myths with two classes of Years Five and Six. One of their teachers, Dan Wilson, had booked me after finding my website via a search. (It's nice to know the website pays off now and again!)

I had to go by train, still being bikeless – shame because it was a beautiful cold, clear sunny day. Dan picked me up from Yatton station at lunchtime. I grabbed a roll from a nearby shop, ate it on the way back, and prepared myself for the first class, warming up in a spare classroom.

I performed three tales: Phaethön and the Sun Chariot, The Judgement of Paris, and Jason & the Golden Fleece (approx. 30 minutes in total) before fielding general questions about being a storyteller. Then I repeated this all over again for the second class (about 30 each time). The kids were respectful and pretty attentive, although it was the afternoon, and energy levels/attention spans were probably not at their best. Still, they asked some good questions. Some were clearly in awe of me – sitting wide-eyed at the front, right under my feet!

I had to get a taxi back to the station and the driver asked what I did. Sitting at Yatton station, gazing at the tracks, diminishing to their vanishing point into the west, I had time to reflect upon my life as a bard on the road. It was good to be getting gigs again, although the teaching is demanding virtually all of my time and energy, and so I'm not at my best when I perform at the moment – I'm low on battery and virtual memory!

The teacher sent me this email message later: *'Thanks for coming today – the kids really enjoyed it. I've had a look at the resources that you sent – they look really useful, thanks very much!'*

Dancing for the Earth, an event co-organised between Jay Ramsay and Anthony Nanson, took place on Friday, 28th November – in honour of William Blake – at the 'Bristol Old School', Stroud. There were a plethora of performers contributing: Fire Springs – Anthony, Kirsty, David and myself. Phoenix members – Jay and Gabriel Millar. Plus Helen Moore, a fellow Bard of Bath; a poet called Jeff who recited his 'Valentine's to Albion', and Kirsten Morrison, who performed a 20 minute set with her brother – a showcase for her extraordinary operatic voice. There wasn't a huge turn out (the hall was half full or half empty depending on your point of view, although we did get a few more in the second half) but it still felt worth it – a coming together of bardic kindred spirits and 'Children of Albion'. We ended with dancing, with music supplied by Jay's friend, Christina McLaughlin. It was a great chance to 'shake the feathers' and to break down the artificial demarcation of audience and performers. It helped to 'shift' my mood a little – releasing some endorphins. Alas, it was over all too soon, and the music wasn't all my cup of tea (lots of frantic trance stuff). It was bit like being at a school disco, being a wallflower, waiting for a good track to come on! Oh, for some good ole' rock and roll!

I got a lift back with David and despite both being tired, we had one of our lovely chats – one of the joys of such 'adventures'. When he dropped me off I gave him a wee present to show my appreciation – he has been a rock to Fire Springs, and as a friend, throughout all of life's ups and downs – *The Drovers' Roads of Wales* (in our first show, Arthur's Dream, he created a framing narrative about Dafydd the Drover who stumbles upon the once and future king and his knights, slumbering under a Welsh mountain until Albion needs them once again...).

Afterwards, Anthony described it thus: '*Every act was magnificently professional, passionate, and committed. Despite the small and delayed turnout of the audience, I think we did something really significant together. I hope the relationships between us all will continue to deepen and lead to other things.*'

I had to get up early the next morning (6.15am) to catch the train to my next engagement – a big stately home called Compton Verney – which involved catching three trains to Banbury, then a taxi, shared with Kirsty Hartsiotis, my co-performer, who had set these gigs up (3 weekends' worth – I was standing in for her partner Anthony today who had a prior engagement in Yate, at the Heritage Centre, where I've performed before).

The themes of the stories were meant to allude to the various exhibitions in the house. We had plenty of scope... North, Winter, hunting, animals, forest, etc. I focussed on tales from the North, and animal tales. I did three sets – Mabon and the Oldest of Animals in set one; Raven's tale and Fenris the Wolf in set two; then two solar myths, Bladud and Baldur, in set three. The first two went well, but the third was disappointing – we were down to two by the end (a mum and her five year old son) although Bladud and his swine went down well. The problem with all of the slots was the really young members of the audience – five and under (!) playing on the 'Once Upon a Time' rug like it was a kindergarten. It is difficult to perform to under sevens, you have to do something especially tailored for them (e.g. balloon-puppetry, clowning, tricks, etc) and we are not trying to be children's entertainers. Time and time again this has happened, despite us pointing out the fact we offer entertainment for adults and older children. We happily accommodate a mixed age audience, as long as the majority are adults, and children are seven plus. Otherwise, you're just wasting energy trying to fruit-lessly engage the youngest and end up losing the rest of the audience. I spent the majority of my performance time staring down at the carpet of toddlers, trying to keep them interested – rather than maintaining eye contact with everyone. It's hard to, as you can in a normal mixed audience.

Kirsty was better at engaging the really young ones – perhaps less scary than a tall, shaggy man! She is really shining these days. And to think how nervous she had been when she first performed at the Bath Storytelling Circle eight years ago, when we did Thomas the Rhymer and Tam Lin together (after I had persuaded her to give it a go – it was to be her first storytelling performance). And now we're professional storytellers – Kirsty mainly performing with her partner, Anthony, the founder of the circle.

We were both tired afterwards. I was glad not to be doing it five more days, to be honest – although Compton Verney staff looked after us, and the place is very impressive. The gardens were designed by Capability Brown and it was a shame there wasn't an opportunity to explore them.

Our erstwhile taxi driver turned up – we were relieved to see him, thinking he may have got lost again! – but it was merely the time of day and the conditions. I was happy not to be riding today, as it was a real pea-souper outside, like some Hammer horror story about a couple who take a wrong turning and end up in a village that doesn't exist... The taxi driver made his slowly cautious way back along the narrow windy lanes, each turn giving us palpitations as he seemed to only notice it at the last minute! Finally arriving at the station he asked if he should make the receipt out for £30 not £27 (the actual fare), but Kirsty refused. He had charged us £30 before on the way there, after getting lost, so he had conned us out of a tip anyway (we had been quoted £25). Good job Compton Verney were paying travel expenses – but the taxi cost as much as the train, more in Kirsty's case. Fortunately, Anthony will be driving the rest of the time.

By the time I got home I was too tired to go out again, or even do anything much at home – I had popped into On the Video Front on the way back from the station, and just stared at the rows of films like a zombie. Uninspired by any, I left. The story-teller had wanted a tale told to *him* for a change… Instead, I went to bed early with a good book – the most reliable entertainment!

Natural Contests
14th December 2008

A kestrel hovers in the wind, wings wavering then knife-edged, against a cold winter sky. In perfect equilibrium with its element – its will and skill counterpoised with the icy contours of air. It drops a dozen feet, but keeps air-borne – a sword of Damocles hanging on a thread, keeping me on tenterhooks. I dare not move. A little closer and I could scare it off, break its concentration. Then it plunges, wings tucked in – beak first, a deadly arrow out of the blue. It disappears briefly from sight amongst the frost-bitten tussocks, then it emerges triumphantly, a black limp parcel clutched in its talons. It flies away to devour its prey, justly plucked from the austere larder of the land.

Further on, I watch three crows harangue a buzzard above a naked forest. They heckle it, attack it, yet it bears their assault with a stoic grace – flying away, out of sight, pursued by the black-hooded hoodlums.

I was walking on Bathhampton Down, enjoying the cold sunlight, peace and space, after last night's Battle of the Bards.

Nature is red and tooth and claw – it is part of life. That doesn't mean we have to be cruel to each other, but that we should accept that a certain healthy competitiveness is also part of life (from the quickest sperm to the most successful predator – evolution encourages excellence. Nature isn't sentimental. If you don't make the grade, you don't endure).

The contest for the thirteenth Bard of Bath took place at the Mission Theatre on the edge of the city. I was asked to be one of the judges by the outgoing bard, Thommie Gillow, along with fellow Bard of Bath, Brendan Georgeson, and Sulyen Richard Caradon, Druid of Bath. There were five entrants, all who made a good effort. The theme, chosen by Thommie, was appropriately for the 13th Bard, 'Superstition'. Most chose to simply list superstitions in verse, but a couple interpreted the theme more imaginatively – local screenwriter Dave Lassman performed a clever story about 'The Cursed Screenplay', which got the audience involved; but he was pipped at the post by an impressive performance by up-and-coming bard, Master Duncan. He entered last year, but was hampered by nerves and a joky approach that didn't do him justice, but this year he had plainly taken it more seriously and had put some real thought into his piece. He deconstructed the theme with some intelligence and ingenuity. He couched the core message within an amusing framing narrative, but the heart of the piece, with its very bardic song, showed his true colours. He has a good folk voice – which, combined with his hip-hop style and satirical style offers an interesting hybrid. A bard should be able to walk between the worlds, and it sounds like Master Duncan might be able to reach out to younger audiences, as he has been doing to a certain extent already with his fortnightly Speakeasy open mics. He plans to continue his work, spreading the word – and he's got off to a good start, with Channel Four trailing him yesterday on the run up to the contest (as one of the contestants). Amazingly, C4's choice won. The other participants were interviewed before the winner was announced and some of the evening was filmed – to feature in one of the '3 Minute Wonder' broadcasts. It seems Andy Warhol's 15 minutes of fame has been down-sized – another victim of the credit crunch? It was a good evening, professionally hosted by Simon, of Emporium Cabaret. Ironically, it took place on the same night as the 'X Factor' finals (yawn). What a contrast! There seems to be a tendency in popular culture to dumb things down, so it was good to see the winner of our contest wasn't the ones who simply played it for laughs. Although his style is accessible, Master Duncan had a serious message with his poem, 'The Idiots are in Charge', which he performed on receiving the Chair showed.

Some people dislike the nature of such contests – preferring a wishy-washy hippy approach, usually to avoid making hard, but critically valid, qualitative judgements (as at the Peat Moors Centre Bard of the Avalon Marshes contest, where the winner was drawn from lots). Certainly everyone who enters any contest is a 'winner' in the sense that the fact of entering is an achievement. It takes some pluck to stand up there and be 'judged'. Not pleasant, but as they say – 'you have to be in it, to win it'. Obviously the desire to win the accolade (of Bard of Bath) is sufficient to push the participants beyond the 'fear' threshold. It is good to rise to a challenge. It helps us to grow. Such contests encourage excellence in the arts, rather than rewards mediocrity. Many prefer mediocrity – perhaps because it makes them feel better about themselves, but actually most of us intuitively respond to excellence – when we see a true 'star' perform, in a film, in a play; or when we behold a work of art by a genius – a painting, a book. I don't think this appreciation of the finer things is elitism, it is simply a respect for true craftsmanship, for mastery of a form. Virtuosity is dazzling. It shows what human beings are capable of. Surely we should strive for our highest potential? Certainly the Bard of Bath isn't elitist, as last night proved. The winner seemed to be a popular choice – and Master

Duncan's success sends out a clear message, that the Bardic Tradition is something for everyone and at home in the Twenty First Century. As he pointed out we must 'evolve or die'. This is what I've been striving for these last ten years, since winning the Chair myself in 1998.

And it occured to me, as I watched the 22 year old Master Duncan perform – standing up there and shining – that we was watching a modern re-enacment of the Taliesin legend. The youthful bard wins the contest, defeating the older bards of King Maelgwn's court. The awen shone out of him, and Taliesin's spirit lives on.

Richard, Brendan, Thommie and myself 'initiated' Master Duncan into the Gorsedd with the Druid's Vow and an awen on stage; and then I presented our youngest, newest member with a reference copy of *The Book of the Bardic Chair* – which should give him all the background he needs to fulfil his bardic duties over the coming year.

May the Awen flow for him, and may many be encouraged to come forth to enter (or re-enter) next year.

Full Circle
16th December 2008

Last night at the Bath Storytelling Circle, Fire Springs – the Bath and Stroud based storytelling troupe I belong to along with Anthony, Kirsty, David and Richard – launched *An Ecobardic Manifesto*: a vision for the arts in a time of environmental crisis. We each performed – (Richard, hosting, did his Cow wonder tale and a version of Alan Garner's mummers' play; I did Baldur and the Golden Bough; Anthony, The Story of People on Earth; David, a ballad of Scottish pirates; and Kirsty, an amusing Jack tale). It was really special having us all there – a rare occasion these days, due to the demands of our busy lives. We all met at the circle, became friends and shortly after formed Fire Springs. The Bath Storytelling Circle was founded by Anthony Nanson in late 1999 – I hosted for five years when Anthony and Kirsty left for a spell in the Peloponnese, but had to hand over due to somewhat more prosaic teaching commitments, which I was finally free from after 12 weeks. And after nearly ten years (we celebrate the first decade next winter) it is still going strong – we get on average forty people, and that's without even a listing in the local paper. Word of mouth brings newcomers every month. Yet there is a bedrock of core regulars who have provided a through-line of quality and consistency over the years. It was nice to see some of them last night – considering it's a busy time of year, socially, we had a healthy turn out and the atmosphere was merry, enhanced by some excellent performances, both seasonal and timeless. David provided an introduction to the manifesto shortly before the interval – it seemed to do the trick, as 18 were sold (albeit with special circle discount). We gathered briefly for a hasty photo shoot – for the press release. Afterwards, we finally managed to gather around the same table and raise a glass to our collective 'baby'. It was a satisfying and affirming conclusion to the year. Fire Springs' journey has run parallel with the circle's – they started within six months of each other, the former emerging from the latter (like, I quipped to Anthony, an away-team from the Starship Enterprise). As with the Bard of Bath and *The Book of the Bardic Chair*, it is good to have something to show for the time, but in this instance it feel like not the end of a chapter, but a new beginning. After a pleasant chat after the 'business' of the evening had ended – over a mug of a local seasonal ale called 'Bristletoe' – we departed on a feel-good high. After a tough year, when the integrity of many things have been challenged (and continue to be) it's heartening to feel that our tiny vessel and its 'mothership' feels stronger than ever.

Solstice Celebrations
22nd December 2008

After a busy week, tying up loose ends and completing projects –

last classes, admin, the first draft of my radio drama, 'The Rabbit Room' – a flurry of seasonal celebrations this weekend, from which I'm still recovering!

Saturday, Helen (8th Bard of Bath) and her partner, John the blacksmith, held a gathering at their new shared house over at Southstoke, a large house on the edge of Bath owned by Phil and Jenny. There's about 8 living in this 'unintentional community', which has a green ethos as it's bedrock. Helen read from her new children's book, *Hope and the Magic Martian*, plus a couple of her poems by candlelight, and then there were open floor spots. I did a couple – my mistletoe poem ('All heal') and 'Follow the sun road home', which I wrote after visiting the nearby long barrow at Stoney Littleton on 21st December 2005. Jay Ramsay was also present and performed some of his profound, heart-felt poems. We also had a good heart-to-heart. And it was lovely to connect with Helen and John again – it's been quite a while, although I saw Helen at 'Dancing for the Earth' late November. As with Jay, Helen is completely committed to her path – and performs with absolute conviction.

As often happens this time of year there was more than one party happening on the same night, and I wanted to pop into Kim and Phil's later – but the taxi driver had some trouble finding me, out in the sticks, due to being misdirected by his office. He finally caught up with me as I hiked along the road back to 'civilisation'. I made it to the second party, high above Bath on Richmond Place at about 11.30pm! Although folk were surprised to see me, the party was still very much in full swing and it was nice to see folk. I didn't stay too long as I was seriously flagging by this point, and there was alot to do the next day…

As was glad I had done the bulk of preparation for my solstice celebration the day before, as I woke a little late and a little delicate! Still, I managed to give the place a quick clean and have everything ready for when guests would arrive after the solstice ceremony in the Circus, which I dashed to. Here we publicly declared 'in the eye of the sun', Master Duncan as the new Bard of Bath, and celebrated the turning of the wheel with a good ceremony from Sulyen Richard Caradon and his partner, Misha, former Ovate of Bath. There was only eight of us but we did the works, and it felt good – especially as the sun came out in the middle of David's story, right on cue! Hearing Master Duncan perform one of his poems which started 'There's too many poets…!' was great as well – his voice booming around the three crescents of the Circus. I wonder if Nicolas Cage was listening in? [a sometime resident of the city, he owned a house on The Circus until recently]

Afterwards, I swiftly made my way back to flat, joined almost straight away by Richard, Misha, Lizzie and Mairead – and so the party began! It was a relaxed afternoon affair – which was just as well after the night before! There was a lovely atmosphere created as folk gathered around my hearth and shared stories, songs and poems on light, rebirth, renewal and winter in general. Mairead led us in some singing 'rounds'. Sheila sang some beautiful Gaelic carols. Richard shared his 'green song'. Svanur arrived later to share with us an Icelandic tale, which was a treat. Also had Mika, a Finnish research student and his wife, Maarit, present – so with all our 'tales from the North' we had a distinctly Arctic feel. Anthony told the amusing story of how the bear lost its tale, and his partner, Kirsty, shared her own funny story. I asked a couple of people to recite 'Spring Fall', my Bardic Chair winning poem, (10 years old!) and David and Misha kindly obliged. It was a real thrill to hear it being performed by other voices for the first time. It was designed for two actors, a man and a woman, and was originally performed by myself and Emily at 'Enchanted Wood', Walcot Chapel, Summer '98. I have just produced a tenth anniversary edition of the booklet, and today was the launch. In the spirit of MR James, I read out the previously unpublished ghost story, 'Taking the Waters', from the new edition. All I needed was a smoking jacket!

The gathering slowly wound down by about 7 or 8, which was my intent. The final stragglers left and I cleared up the aftermath – well worth the mess! It was great to have a gathering at the Cauldron again – I haven't felt like it since last Twelfth Night (my Dad dying five days after). It was wonderful for the house to be filled with awen and good cheer again – the lovely warm atmosphere in the room after everyone had departed was a clear sign it had been a successful event. Forging such memories fills one's heart.

After a dark, difficult year in many ways, for many of us it really felt like a rekindling of the light.

I felt so fired up afterwards, that I typed out my old mummers' play, 'The Head of Winter', also performed ten years ago at the first Bardic Festival of Bath in a commedia dell arte style by local friends – it had been hand-written back then and needed tidying up. Having worked on drama for stage, screen and radio lately I found it easy to lick it into shape. The next morning I posted it on the Silver Branch forum – offering my merry contribution for midwinter amusement.

Mummery on Boxing Day
26th December 2008

Boxing Day (so-named because servants and tradesfolk were given gift-boxes on this day by the larger houses – although now it seems synonymous with sales at places like Ikea – different kinds of boxes! Perhaps it should be renamed Flat-pack Day), AKA St Stephen's Day is a traditional time for Mummers Play, at least round these parts. The oldest is in the Cotswold village of Marshfield, just north of Bath – now famed for its icecream and flapjacks! – where at noon today the Old Time Paper Boys gather to perform their seasonal rite at five locations along the High Street (which is just as well, because it's often hard to catch what they're saying if they happen to face the wrong way, or if the wind is up – none are professional performers, so we shouldn't expect them to project). The cast is drawn from a motley of real local characters – the butcher, the baker, a farmer, a postman, etc. They become such memorable moochers as Saucy Jack 'with his family on his back', Beelzebub with his club, Ten Penny Nit, Old Father Christmas, St George of course, and the Doctor (Who is now I regular feature on Xmas TV and is in many ways a modern Mummers – with its lively battle between light and dark enacted every year). I once shared a flat with a guy – Marshfield born and bred – whose grandfather used to take part: the costume of paper rags was stored in their house, along with the script, such as it is (at one point, apparently, the costumes were made of leaves – which thrilled me with the thought of some primal fertility rite taking place in a forest clearing; this notion was somewhat disabused when I discovered the Mummers, the oldest in the region, probably only date from the 19th Century like alot of 'ancient' folklore). Authenticity and antiquity aside, it is nevertheless wonderful to behold and gives Yuletide a refreshingly real, earthy quality after the tinsel and 2-D entertainment of Christmas – a sobering shock to the system, standing in the rain or freezing fog, watching a death and resurrection show. The script is fabulously nonsensical, tantalisingly fragmentary – like some half-understood radio transmission, cultural Chinese whispers (rather like the *Mabinogion*, the 13th Century collection of older oral Welsh tales written down by unwitting monks). There's other Boxing Day Mummers locally in Southstoke and Keynsham. And on New Years Day the Widcombe Mummers perform their play – this has only been going for five years, and is open in its 'newness', featuring an anachronistic cast of traffic wardens, hobby horses, fools, and local figures such as 'the King of the Beggars of Holloway' (which my friend the late Tim Sebastion Woodman researched and first performed; indeed the last time I saw him fully conscious was in the Widcombe Social Club, New Year's Day, 2006, when he had just watched the Mummers – too ill to perform that year, my friend Ian Davidson stepped into the role. Tim allowed the Mummers to use his Wassail Bowl – which was passed onto me after he died a month later). Every year, the Widcombe Mummers incorporate some topical issues, for instance a satirical stab at the Spa fiasco. This year they plan to bring in King Bladud's Pigs, which stormed the city this summer.

I've been working on my own plays recently – dusting off the Mummers Play I wrote in 1994 ('The Head of Winter') which has only been performed once publicly so far, at the first Bardic Festival of Bath in 1998 in a chilly Walcot Chapel. My Bardic Chair winning poem, *Spring Fall*, was inspired by the ancient Mummers mask found under Stall Street, and now on display in the Roman Baths museum. It got me wondering what kind of play would have been performed in the Temple Precinct (a theatre was also discovered). And so I set about writing a mystery play about the springs – *Spring Fall: the story of Sulis and Bladud of Bath* was the result.

I also dug out a play I wrote about the perils of genetic engineering – an updated version of the Taliesin legend called 'The Child of Everything'. This I typed up and sent off to a script competition at the Bristol Old Vic. I love the idea of grafting modern themes onto ancient myths (and vice versa). Mummers have always brought in topical references – witty asides to cock-a-snook at whoever deserves public mockery, usually those with too much money and power and too little sense. Guised in their shaggy costumes, often with blacked up faces, their anonymity allowed the Mummers a degree of satirical freedom. Their identities were kept 'mum'. The pantomime is a later derivation of the Mummers Play and indeed the Mummers – relating right back to early Greek tragedy, performed in static masks – could be seen as the prototype of theatre. The masks of tragedy and comedy are still the symbol of theatre, summing up the most ancient repetoire and the bittersweetness of life. (Incidentally, on Christmas Eve, the playwright Harold Pinter died of cancer of the liver, aged 76. One of the greats of modern theatre).

Yesterday, enjoying a quiet Christmas, I wrote the first draft of a new play, 'Wassailing Avalon', which dramatises the wassailing traditions of the West Country, which commonly take place on Old Twelfth Night, 17th January, weaving in local mythology... I hope one day to see all of these performed!

A friend gave me a copy of Hugh Lupton's and Chris Wood's 'Christmas Champions', which I heard when first broadcast on Radio 4 a couple of years ago and I highly recommend it – an enchanting and moving evocation of a tradition that connects people and place, combining storytelling, poetry, song and archive recordings of the original players. Put it on, pour yourself a glass of good cheer, sit back and enjoy.

Long live the Mummers!

Winter Walking
January 2nd 2009

The first day of the New Year. The land white like a clean sheet of paper. A heavy overnight frost had transformed my corner of England into Narnia. My friend, fellow writer and all round good egg, Anthony Nanson, was staying over – we went to a New Year's Eve party together at Mairead's the night before, watched fireworks exploded over the city while toasting in the new year with champagne (later we had both shared bardic efforts, along with Marko Gallaidhe). After a hearty hobbity breakfast we headed for the hills – 'into the wild' as Strider would say, or into the Mendips at least, which usually seem tame, but today felt like more like Dartmoor: slightly edgy. A wildernessed zone of white death.

We put on our boots, drank some edifying coffee from our flasks and set off – following a bridleway up to our first destination, the 375 m. of Beacon Hill. The hawfrost was half an inch thick on the branches and evergreen foliage. Nature's attention to detail was, once again, astonishing. No film set could mimic this so completely. Coleridge called it 'the secret ministry of frost', and I mentioned the pleasing notion that we may be walking in the Romantic poet's footsteps – as he and Southey (who became Poet Laureate) used to walk across the Mendips. Here they hatched their plans for a pantisocracy – a utopian society based upon the idea that two hours work a day is all man needs to survive, the rest of his day spent in creative or leisure pursuts, the ultimate idler's paradise. Anthony and I are no slackers – indeed we are both close to certified workaholics (when it comes to our writing, teaching and publishing), but the idea of a lifestyle where one's own creative endeavours took precedence over the treadmill of existence sounds tantalising. We both endure the grind of marking – it's somewhat heartening to discover that Tolkien did to. My mind was saturated with Tolkienian arcana, having just finished my radio drama, 'The Rabbit Room'. To anyone else, my harping on would have been a bore, but Anthony shares my enthusiasm, and indeed our whole walk had an Inklings-ish feel to it, discussing matters literary, philosophical and spiritual as we traversed the bewintered landscape.

From the trig point, where we were surprised to discover a cluster of other hard-core walkers, who'd had similar notions of New Year's Day walks – we made our way down into the forest of Rowberrow – which had its own micro-climate, lacking the frost and being noticeably milder. We then ascended to Dolebury Warren – using a convenient break in the stone wall, like the gap in the border between this world and Faerie in *Stardust*. No threshold guardian appeared, although barbed wire halted our progress when, breathless, we got to the brow. Instead, we followed the ridge along to a proper gate and stopped for a chilly lunch on the lee of the hillfort; some honeydew mushrooms our 'hearth', cheering us with their bright orange colour in the bleak landscape. I found the wintry vista sublimely beautiful and for a while we just stood and stared at the muted tones, fading into visual oblivion. I observed how 'grey' can have so many nuances. All the vibrant shades of the natural world were softened by the pervading whiteness. Soothingly gentle after the often garish nonsense of Christmas and New Year – a true stillpoint. Blissful stasis. The wheel, it seemed, had mercifully stopped. Fellow Fire Springs David Metcalfe described it as 'a day outside time' – having driven over the Mendips to Wells that day. It did us both good, Anthony and I, to have a day off – having both worked over Yuletide, either on teaching obligations or our own projects. It was salubrious to be forced to focus on the physical, on simple needs – food, warmth, shelter. This was hardly a survival situation, although it easily could have become so – if one of us had slipped and broken something. But we were both suitably equipped for such predicaments, although it fortunately didn't come to that. It was only a hike in the hills – and plenty of other people were around: mountain-bikers, motor-trikers, families… It was hardly Antarctica! What I loved was the way the frozen landscape had its own acoustic: the brittle crunch of ice beneath one's boot, the satisfying crack of an ice-pane in a puddle, the scittering of ice-shards, the dull thud of our progress on the iron hard ground. Our words were as distinct as cold pebbles, forced from blood-sluggish mouths. The frost-world muted sound as well as colour, but at the same time made them stand out even more. At one point we followed a path of ruddy soil, strangely exposed and unfrozen, flanked by endless white heathland – like a trail of blood in the snow. It could have been a scene from *Fargo*. Yet this was a Mendips Nifleheim and our conversation was 'the director's commentary' of a different DVD. Two writers in search of a pen in a world of endless paper – the land a tabula rasa of our imaginations and ambitions. Swinging back east towards our starting point as the brief hours of daylight began to wane, we passed the magical dell of Rod's Pot – where Old Man Willow himself seemed to guard a stream-crossing, his mighty limbs covered in moss – and further on, Goat-church Cavern, hidden amongst the downy folds of the hills. We arrived back at the car after a good three and a half hour yomp. Gratefully back inside its artificial warm cocoon we drove through Burrington Combe, passed Aveline's Hole and the Rock of Ages, which inspired the famous hymn after a passing Reverend Augustus Montague Toplady took shelter there in 1763. Nature had similarly provided our sanctuary that day.

Rock of Ages
Rock of Ages, cleft for me,
Let me hide myself in Thee;
Let the water and the blood,
From Thy riven side which flowed,
Be of sin the double cure;
Save from wrath and make me pure.

Old Hobbits Die Hard
4th January 2009

Yesterday I decided to hold a birthday party of 'special magnificence' in honour of JRR Tolkien, born on January 3rd 1892 – exactly one hundred and seventeen years ago. I invited a select group of 'elf-friends' around to join me in raising a glass to the Gandalf of Fantasy, and to test-read my new radio play based upon the Inklings called 'The Rabbit Room'. This is the only way to gauge whether something works or not – with a live reading. David Metcalfe played 'Tollers' (Lewis' nickname for Tolkien); Anthony Nanson played 'Jack' (CS Lewis), Mika Lassander played Owen Barfield and Svanur Gisli Thorkelsson Charles Williams. David's partner, artist Ione Parkin, was VO – the voice of the Rabbit Room, Anna Dougherty was the BBC announcer, and Maarit – Mika's wife – the landlord and the Minister of Health (or Elf, as I punned). It was thrilling to hear the play come alive after slaving away on it in solitude since November. To write it I immersed myself in Inklings lore – and tinkered with it obsessively over the holidays, finishing it just in time for the party, which provided an appropriate deadline.

After providing a hearty feast for my guests – piles of good plain English fare, which both Bilbo and Tolkien would have liked – I recited an extract from the opening chapter of *The Fellowship of the Ring* – about Bilbo's eleventy first birthday party and disappearing act. For this, I asked my guests to take off their shoes and socks, so we could all be Hobbits together! Bare-footed and waist-coated, I read out the text in a suitably merry fashion. We toasted JRR, and then we attended to the main after dinner entertainment. I assigned roles, handed out scripts and we begun. It took a hundred minutes (perhaps it should have been 111) but it was a cold reading and slower than it would be when rehearsed. Some sections really flowed, others were perhaps inevitably murdered, and some evidently need work – but it was wonderful to hear it out loud. I was filled with feelings of loving warmth for such a lovely fellowship. Truly friendship is one of the most important things of life. Without it, a man is impoverished. But last night I felt 'wealthy' from having such beautiful talented souls as my friends.

Tolkien extolled the virtues of simple pleasures ('fire and lamp and meat and bread, and then to bed, and then to bed') and Lewis wrote about friendship as one of the Four Loves – and I whole-heartedly agree: there is very little better than gathering around the hearth with good friends, sharing good food, drink and conversation. The home is a sacred thing and true fellowship is divine – together they forge a piece of heaven on Earth.

Afterwards, there was useful feedback from the group (Svanur is a playwright and director; Anthony fellow creative writing teacher; David fellow performer in Fire Springs; Mika Religious Studies research student; Maarit child psychologist and Anna an Oxford English graduate). Tolkien I think would've liked hearing the Anglo-Saxon, Finnish and Icelandic spoken that evening in my living room (his three favourite languages, except his own invented ones!) – although he might have corrected some of us on pronunciation (but not the native speakers, of course).

The hour was getting late and David and Ione departed – to relieve their babysitter from her duties. We tucked into some late Xmas pud, and then Anthony shared a sample of Tolkien's 'manifesto' poem – Mythopoeia. There followed a suitably Inklings-ish discussion on a number of subjects (art, politics, popular culture) before the alcohol and awen ran out. Around midnight folk departed, except Anthony who crashed over – saving the drive back to Stroud for the morning. He agreed that we had well and truly celebrated the unique anniversary. I was pleased to have 'premiered' my play on Tolkien's birthday – my way of honouring such a huge inspiration to many. The world is richer for his contribution. His vast imagination and unparalled elven-skill has provided a gateway for us all.

Long may his name and the fellowship live on!

Twelfth Night Wassail
5th January 2009

This evening I held my annual Twelfth Night Wassail – to thank the orchards for their fruits and to mark the end of Yuletide. This is a lot nicer than just taking down the decorations, as we are meant to do by the 6th (Epiphany). When so many Christmas trees lie discarded by the roadside, and the pavements are heaped with blackbags destined for landfill sites I think it is more important than ever to thank the Earth, rather than take from it. Certainly, the credit crunch has made people more circumspect in their consumerism although the impact upon the environment of Christmas was probably just as devastating. Still, rather than get all preachy about it, I think it is far more positive just to thank the Earth, and that's literally what we do at my wassail – braving the freezing temperatures to gather round my apple tree at the bottom of the garden and wassailing it, that is toasting its health. I ushered my guests out into the darkness, equipped with the necessary wassailing regalia. I got the fire going dramatically with a little help from a petrol can – not ideal, but it was a freezing night. I asked people to imagine what dreams they wanted to bring through this year and to visualise them as apples on the branches. Then, taking up my old black-thorn shelaghley (formed, according to antique cane dealer Geoffrey Breeze – who gave it to me as a birthday present – from 'a Gloucestershire wodwose') with its gold nob, I rapped the trunk of the tree chosen to be our Apple Tree Man. I asked my guests to call out, 'Wake up, wake up, Apple Tree Man!' three times. Then I poured a whole bottle of 'Wurzel Me' Somerset cider onto the roots. Next we toasted the tree, literally, with triangles of toasted bread dipped in the steaming wassail bowl impaled on the bare branches of the tree. These offerings were to thank the tree for its generous bounty and to welcome in the 'good spirits', i.e. the birds. They had a feast too! To finish our ceremony, we scared away any 'bad spirits' with loud noises – using party poppers instead of the customary shotguns, the weapon of choice in some Somerset orchards (Carhampton being the most famous on 17th January, Old Twelfth Night)! My work done, I asked Richard to lead us in a couple of wassail songs. It was so dark it was hard to see the words, and the temperature was dropping as the fire petered out, but we valiantly carried on carolling. I performed The Song of Wandering Aengus in the interlude, and then we gratefully decamped inside, where we carried on the circle with more singing, poetry and merriment, fuelled by more mulled cider, baked pomme de terre (apples of the earth: potatoes!); and numerous other nibbles: the last of the Yuletide feasting. Chrissy Derbyshire, a budding bard over from Cardiff, was eventually persuaded to sing – and what a lovely voice she had, offering something from Blackmore's Nights repertoire, before she had to dash to catch her train. Mairead led us in some rounds. Richard read out Rose Flint's specially commissioned Wassail poem. Peter Please offered a couple of excellent tales (the one about a wounded bird guiding a friend of his to its trapped mate was especially enthralling) before generously gifting me a copy of his new book *Clattinger: an alphabet of signs from nature* – a beautiful tome made with elven craft. Sheila Broun, arriving late, sang a haunting song. Steven Isaac read out his poem about birch trees from *Writing the Land*, and I recited the poem 'Wheel of the Rose', fortunately remembering the words despite the intake of mulled cider and beer! The conversation flowed, but I was flagging after a sociable few days and was relieved when most departed by midnight. I felt I had done my 'bit' for the season – three gatherings around my place, and was looking forward to taking down the decorations the following day and getting stuck back into things. There's a sense with Twelfth Night that 'illusions must end', an idea which Shakespeare explores in his Comedy of that name. It was a traditional time for 'merrie entertainments', but after being 'cross-gartered' the revels must conclude. Time to strip away the frippery, pack away the tinsel and knuckle down to some work. Yet my heart and my hearth had been warmed by friendship, merriment and awen.

Eulogies & Elegies

The beginning of the year was overshadowed by a tragedy in the family. The phrase 'dead of winter' took on a deeper meaning. I've always enjoyed the austerity of the post-Christmas season, the stripping back, the collective sigh of relief as we leave the intensity of the festivities behind. For some it's depressing, being faced with gloomy January and the return to work. For me it's a chance to take stock and get a perspective on the year ahead. Like a tree stripped of its leaves, I can see the skeleton of my year and plan what I want to channel my energies into, what I hope will bloom, bear fruit – touchwood. But sometimes life runs contra to our expectations. This time last year I was worried sick about my ailing mother. She was seriously ill and had to be taken into hospital. She had a major operation coming up and was given a fifty per cent chance of living. We were all on tenterhooks. But amazingly, thankfully, she pulled through. She wasn't well, but she no longer was at death's door.

But the Grim Reaper would not be so easily cheated.

On the 10th January, 2008 – a day that will always be etched into my memory – I was working as an extra on, of all things, a new BBC TV series written by two Bath-based pensmiths called *Bonekickers*.

Death has a serious sense of humour.

It was the second time I had done work of this nature. The first time, I had to dress up as an Arthurian knight and stand in the rain at Chepstow Castle for some ropey *Tomb Raider* rip-off ('Relic Hunter', I believe). This time, I was to be a modern-day Knights Templar. It sounds glamorous, but it distinctly was not – spending, in the end, thirteen hours, hanging around in rainy Keynsham (a dismal dormitory town between Bath and Bristol). We had been told to arrive on site at 7am. We weren't used until midday, and then only briefly. Then we had to hang around all afternoon, 'because they were going to use us again', which they didn't. It was particularly bleak, lurking in an empty charity shop (our Purgatory for that scene). As people passed by, a couple of the younger 'knights' pretended to be show-room dummies and suddenly came alive. This sorry cluster of TV mannequins attracted the attention of a local gang of hoodies, loitering in the square outside, but even they got bored of us. Supporting Artists – more like 'superfluous'. It was exhausting, doing nothing for so long. There was a good-humoured stoicism amongst the extras, but even the quips started to wear out by the end of the day. We all wanted to be elsewhere.

Finally we were told we could go at 7pm. It was cold and dark, being the middle of winter. I got changed out of my

Templar/Highlander gear (raincoat, longsword) into my biking leathers and, after getting my form signed so I could get paid (peanuts) I left on my bike (eventually – at first the bike refused to start...) With relief I rode home, eager to get back, to thaw out, to eat. I stopped off at a supermarket petrol station to fill up. When I went to start the ignition, it wouldn't start. I tried again and again. No luck. I thought I must be doing something wrong, but couldn't figure it out. It was probably something simple, but I was exhausted. The security guard came over, and I told him my problem. I let him have a go with the key, but to no avail, and so I pushed the bike over to the side of the forecourt and racked my brains. I just wanted to get home!

I thought I could jump-start it, and so I pushed it up out of the petrol station, to a sideroad leading into the supermarket carpark. I tried rolling it and trying the starter button. No good. I was about to give up, when a young man passing by offered to help. What angels appear when we need them! He gave me a push and it got it going! Thanking him I roared off, relieved to be finally getting home.

This strange delay I'll return to later.

And so, after an exhausting thirteen hour day I made it back to the flat, feeling cold, worn out and hungry.

That's when I saw the messages.

Two.

As I pulled off my boots, I listened to them.

The first one was from a woman whose voice I did not recognise. Her voice had an edge of stress to it. It was a poor line. She said: 'Your father's been taken ill. He's collapsed. Could you ring back as soon as possible.'

My chest tight, I played the second message. It was the same woman. Voice breathy this time. 'Ring home as soon as possible. Your dad's been taken to the hospital.'

Stunned, I let it sink in. I needed something inside of me, something to give me strength for this – for my batteries were completely flat. I made myself a cup of tea, and girded myself for the phonecall. It sounded bad.

As I sat down, the phone rang, making me jump. Hands shaking, I picked it up. It was my sister. She said my name, and the tone of the voice conveyed everything.

'He's passed on, hasn't he?' was my reply.

She made a confirming noise.

And my world fell apart.

Within fifteen minutes of returning home, I had gone from having a father, to not having one. Two messages, one phone call. Bang, bang, bang and ... that's it.

I spoke briefly to Julie, and then I called my Mum – or maybe she called me. I can't remember much after this. She was hysterical. I tried to calm her down – told her to breathe. She had a couple of neighbours with her, which was reassuring. I would come up as soon as I could.

That night, I nearly lost it. I quickly reached for a stiff drink, shaking uncontrollably. It felt like my mind was going to split, the floor was going to open up and I was going to fall forever. I went through waves of rage, of near-hysteria. I was overwhelmed with panic as I tried to find a photo of my Dad – a recent one. Everything seemed to hinge on this. Finally, on my computer I found one and put it on my 'wallpaper'. I thought of the last time I saw him, if I had said I loved him. I think I bought him a pint down the Golden Horse. He had looked my new bike outside.

Then with a shudder I reconsidered how I had broken down on the way home – the 'heart of the bike', the engine, had refused to start. I nervously worked out the timing. Information was scant at that time, but later I was able to ascertain that it was at the exact moment of his death.

Around the time he collapsed, my bike had struggled to start, leaving Keynsham. Then at the petrol station, the time of death, it had 'given up the ghost' completely.

My world did indeed stop at that point

Had he been making his presence felt? Had I somehow felt his death? Had he come to say goodbye?

Could he have somehow stalled my bike? I could imagine him doing this...

One immediately thinks about the last time you saw them, and the awful realisation that you won't be able to see them again.

It had been just over a month ago – 5th December – I remember it distinctly because that day I returned to my old school, Mereway, now a community college, to run a couple of creative writing workshops as an ex-pupil turned visiting author. It was the first time in twenty years I had stepped through those doors. I felt, in some ways, like Odysseus. It was a kind of full circle. When I left Northampton the following morning I nearly ran out of petrol. Stopped to fill up – card maxed out. Wished then I could call Dad, wished he was the kind who would come over, sort it out. But I know he wouldn't. If I had made it back to Delapre, he might have subbed me – and, I realise now, was what I was meant to do. See him one last time. Instead, I rang my partner and she paid for the petrol on her credit card, bless her. Yet I felt guilty – my Dad had made a typically odd request. He wanted me to bring up some 'real Cheddar cheese' up with me (from the famous tourist town, 33 miles away from Bath). I mocked him, saying you could buy cheddar in any grocery store! If I had known it was a dying man's request I would have taken more heed. A simple, foolish thing – but one which haunts me. I couldn't make the effort.

Death fills us with regrets, of all the things we should have said or done. I think my Dad knew I loved him. I made an effort to see him, to keep in touch, sending him postcards whenever I travelled. He always said 'We won't be here forever,' and I wearied of the guilt-tripping, though I knew he was right.

But I did not know how close to the truth it was.

I made it up to Northampton two days later, on the earliest, cheapest train I could get (money was very tight then and I knew I was in no fit state for the long ride up). I spent a week making sure Mum was comfortable and blitzing the house, trying to make it half-decent for all the visitors she was having and would have. It was hard work, and I had no one to help.

Julie, my sister, was providing emotional support brilliantly, whileas I was doing all the practical things.

Eventually I would speak at my Dad's funeral – a real vindication of my bardic path – but the 'toughest gig'. I didn't wax lyrical – my Dad wasn't that kind of person. I just shared the plain facts of his life – they were impressive enough. I spoke from the heart, without text, without rehearsal. I felt strangely calm. All my professional experience took over. It was as though I was on 'auto-pilot' (yet paradoxically fully present). The truth was I had to keep it together, I had to stay strong for my Mother (later I could weep, but not then). Afterwards, the vicar said it was the most impressive eulogy he had ever heard. Mourners came up and said how touched they were – that I had 'done him proud'. I felt numb. No words could ever replace the man – a big fella – who had left a large hole in our lives.

Although I was never dependent upon my father, his sudden death was decimating. It felt as though the 'sheltering sky' had been ripped away, to use Paul Bowles' metaphor. I was left with an existential nakedness. I was the 'next in line'. There was no one between me and death now. The death of a family member makes one painfully aware of one's mortality. It makes you scrutinise core beliefs – and one can feel consoled or disillusioned. I felt he was 'up there' somewhere, having a pint in the great pub in the sky, a consoling fiction, perhaps, but a pleasant one.

It wasn't until the summer, six months later, that I was able to have sufficient perspective on it all to write an elegy for Dad – for what would have been his seventieth birthday. I came up, laid the patio for my Mum and wrote poetry. We had a birthday celebration in the garden and I recited it to the small gathering of close friends and family. It felt good to honour his memory in this way. Through the elegy I was able to express my own feelings about Dad – whileas the eulogy at the funeral was more of a public thing. Wounds can be healed with words. They let out the poison. The passion. They cauterize. They acknowledge the impact, the connection. They honour.

A year on, I returned to Northampton to plant a tree for my Dad with my Mother and sister. It was good to do something affirming at this time. A tree is a symbol of growth, of renewal, of longevity. It can be visited and used as a channel of communication between the worlds, a way of connecting with those who have gone on. Here is the sonnet I wrote for the occasion:

Poem for Memorial Tree

Belov'd slender sapling of tender years
Earth-bidden you are to set spirit free.
From this soil, may your soul soar heavenward
Aspiring skywards like limbs of this tree.
In good measure, may the sweet, sweet rain fall
And water with precious tears thy young roots.
Though bewintered and bare be your branches
Memory offers the rarest of fruits.
Soft, soft light of sun smile benign on thee,
In fertile shadows feed deep from good earth.
Spring come! Bring forth bud, shoot, flower and leaf.
And let all who wander here see your worth.
Hallowed corner, with our loyal hearts we lease.
Where kith and kin shall pilgrim, be at peace.

Death and the Awen

Death can be the ultimate creative act. A release of stagnant life energies, enabling catharsis and transformation. This makes it no less tragic and we should rightly grieve if a loved one dies –

especially before their time. But we should also rejoice – they have been freed from the suffering of the Earth. It is we who remain who suffer, to endure – that is the only certainty. And yet awen can dramatically alter our attitude towards death. It is simply a soul flowing on – hopefully back to the Source. We do not grieve when the rain falls because it is simply water returning to the sea – some gets trapped in the land (like the Artesian wells in the Australian outback, formed from 'fossil water', aqueous ghosts trapped in the land) but most finds its way eventually back to Mother Ocean. Death will undoubtedly bring wounds to the surface – all the things said or unsaid, done or undone – but it can heal as well, by giving these things air. Bringing them out into the light. Death only becomes an ordeal when we cling onto old patterns of behaviour. When we try to take control. A bereavement should be a time to honour the spirit of the loved one lost; not to impose our egos – to take over. Conflict occurs when wills lock. Family feuds emerge and the ugly side comes out in people. It is an emotional time – everyone is stressed, upset – and we may come out with cruel things we don't mean: as a knee-jerk reaction to being hurt ourselves. With awen, we can transform death into a positive thing – by honouring the departed – as bards by writing and performing an elegy. Expressing what everyone is feeling. Allowing everyone to pitch in, shoulder the burden, keep busy. People hate to feel helpless at such times – so let them help. If it takes a village to raise a child, maybe it takes one to bury the dead – this would certainly have been the case when mounds were raised for Bronze Age nobility. Indeed a whole nation can be involved, as in the funerary monuments of the Pharoahs. Yet death shouldn't force us into servitude! It should be liberating in every aspect – offering apocastasis: a chance to start again. Old stagnant energies can be overturned, as when a dictator dies. A septic boil is lanced. This is depicted dramatically in *The Return of the King* when the One Ring is finally thrown into Mount Doom, making it erupt.

Sauron's tower crumbles and the rule of the Iron Crown ends. Like a blocked well, a capped spring, suddenly cleared, the waters are released (the Grail-winner was known as the Freer of the Waters – Parsifal 'pierces the veil' and this world is enriched by an infusion of otherworldly magic). The waters are freed, washing away all that was negative. A lifetime of neurosis, dysfunctionality, 'bad blood', denied desires and dreams, unexpressed emotions, rage, fear, sadness … all the poison let out, until finally only the shining soul seed remains – which was there at the start. And, unburdened, it can finish its journey. As free as it wants to be. And now, in its wake, it is up to us how we choose to live. And the greatest insult to a loved one's memory is not to live, to deny life, to shut oneself away. It is important to go through the grieving process, but then, critically, move on. To live in misery, or worse, commit suicide, is an insult to life. Our loved ones would want us to live, to enjoy life, to do all things they can no longer do, removed from the realm of the senses. A death can make us change the habits of lifetime. We can use to jumpstart a new lease of life, to savour things long denied us for whatever reason. A new hobby, a holiday, a new wardrobe, change of diet, renew old acquaintances, make new friends, move house, start a new job, keep the hours and habits we choose – throw away lots of old stuff. Spring clean our lives. That is not to say we shouldn't be sad, or that we'll not miss them. Think of them every day even. It is right to mourn, but not to mope. We'll all die sooner or later, but while you're alive: live!

Use the awen to explore your attitude to death – where does the soul go, if anywhere, and where does that leave you? Make death a doorway, not the end. As Black Elk said: 'Death is merely a change of worlds.'

Banishing the Bad Spirits
18th January 2009

On 17th/18th January across Somerset (and these days, as far afield as America) Old Twelfth Night is celebrated with the wassailing of the apple orchards – from which the famous Somerset cider is made. A libation of cider is poured on the roots of the oldest tree, chosen to represent the Apple Tree Man. The tree is 'toasted' with toast soaked in the Wassail bowl – usually an alcoholic concoction. The Bad Spirits are banished with loud noises and the Good Spirits welcomed in with Wassail carols and general merriment. It's a great community event encouraging people to connect with the land and its natural cycles.

I managed to miss two such events on Saturday – it was lashing down by the evening, which didn't make the prospect that enticing, even to a 'hard-core' apple wassailer. I had also been invited to a 60th birthday celebration to perform, but I still felt a little disappointed to miss out, especially since I was looking forward to seeing the Weston Mummers. But I made up for it the next day – it felt like a very different world. The storm had blown itself out and there were patches of blue sky above, spring shoots pushing through below. What really thrilled me was the prospect of going for a spin on my recently repaired bike (I finally got it back on Friday after two months of nightmarish entanglements). I got suited and booted and, checking everything over, took the bike on one of my favourite short blats – to Stoney Littleton long barrow. The narrow lanes were strewn with storm detritus and flooded in parts, so it was a good back lane test of my rusty riding skills. I got there okay and enjoyed the walk up to the barrow in the sunlight. I ventured inside the ancient Neolithic 'tomb/womb', crawling to the very end chamber. There I crouched in the dripping darkness – savouring its anonymous shadow, silence and stillness, before emerging 'reborn' and ready for what the new year may bring. It felt like a symbolic enactment of my 'Underworld' journey of the last year – a difficult year for many, by all accounts. With a flurry of personal good news last week, it felt like that had finally come to an end and the new cycle was beginning; the Bad Spirits had been banished – and thank goodness! This is happening on a grand scale tomorrow with the inauguration of the new President of the United States, Barack Hussein Obama, and it feels, with the departure of Dubya, that the world is waking up from a bad dream. I ardently hope so. Tomorrow, humanity should rejoice at the dawn of a new era: one that proves, with enough vision and will, another world is possible.

This new 'buzz' seemed to be present in microcosm later when I made it over to Willsbridge Mill, Somerset Wildlife Trust's HQ, which was holding its annual wassail. Hundreds of 'Shire folk' turned up – families with little ones, all wrapped up warm – to enjoy the numerous craft activities. I joined in – carving toast (to make letters of the wassail song to hang on the Apple Tree Man); making a musical shaker (to make noise); and a crown of greenery (to present to my Apple Queen later). I sat around the campfire, toasted bread and enjoyed some spread with local honey (a rare commodity, with the worrying decline in the bee population). A local primary school did some Morris-dancing, complete with hobby horse – it was lovely to see some young 'uns doing it – they looked like little fairy folk (the Morris scene is apparently struggling to recruit new blood and is also in danger of dying out): no wonder I get accosted to join every time I watch some! A wassail queen was chosen to pour the libation, plus a princess and a 'holly lad' to beat the bounds. It was a charming affair, which brought a smile to my face. It felt like the first inklings of Spring, and also wonderfully Hobbity: a scene from the Party Field, beneath the Party Tree, in Hobbiton. By riding there and back again (in the dusk) I too banished my own bad spirits, dispelling any ghosts of November. I enjoyed the freedom my wheels afforded and look forward to ride-outs this coming year.

I can't wait to head for hills. Here's to brighter days ahead.

Return of the King
20th January 2009

A truly historic day, when the world changed: the day President Obama was inaugurated, becoming the first African-American Commander-in-Chief of the United States of America and the first intelligent holder of that post for at least eight years. Eight long hard years that are finally over – the end of a bad dream.

Obama's election is a victory for diversity, for equality, for common sense, for hope. His campaign ticket was 'change' – something this world sorely needs, in its current beleaguered state. It is interesting that this momentous day takes place a day after Martin Luther King Day (an echo which no doubt Obama was deeply aware of) and on the day of St Agnes' Eve – when it is said young women would dream of their future lover (as immortalised in Keats' poem, The Eve of St Agnes). Well today proves dreams can come true. Obama's inauguration earlier in a chilly, but sunny Washington was in many ways the culmination of Luther King's dream.

What pleased me most about today's ceremony – on a micro-cosmic scale – was the inclusion of music and poetry amidst the pomp and ceremony. Four world class musicians performed a piece composed by John Williams; Aretha Franklin sang an 'alternative' National Anthem; and Elizabeth Alexander, Yale Professor of Poetry, performed her Whitmanesque 'Praise-Song for the Day' – these contributions framed the vow-making and made it feel quite bardic. They provided a symbol of a renewed harmony – after nearly a decade of discord – hopefully ushering in a new era, as when Aragon sings at his coronation in Jackson's version of *The Return of the King*, which today's ceremony in Gondor-analogue Washington echoed, visually at least (although there was no bowing to Hobbits, unless you count Obama's charmingly present and colourfully attired daughters, or the fact that Obama began his speech by saying 'I am humbled'... in a similar way to Aragorn's 'this day is not for one man, but for all

Men'). After too many bad kings it seems the Western world may finally have a good king – let's hope Obama achieves all that he sets out to do in his inspiring, but practical speech – for all our sakes. He is a master orator and his eloquence is heartening, especially since it seems matched with ability, commitment and integrity. Here is a man of action as well as words. Yet his fine words show how powerful the ability to express oneself can be – to match one's thoughts and feelings with phrases of pertinence, of eloquence, that do them justice. When words and the world collide, synchronise, make each other real.

Here's to better days ahead: may they be 'the Days of Peace'.

Inklings of Spring
Imbolc, 1st February 2009

Today celebrated what is in the Celtic Calendar the beginnings of Spring – although it feels like long way off yet – the Fire Festival of Imbolc, sacred to the goddess Bridghid, patroness of poetry, smithcraft and healing. We could have done with her sacred flame (which was tended by priestesses and later nuns at her sanctuary in Kildare) today as we held a ceremony outside on a bitterly cold winter's day – the pre-snow (infintesimal flakes like fairy tears) as delicate as the snowdrops pushing through the slumbering earth. Sue Cawthorne, current holder of the Ovate Chair of Caer Badon, called it to take place at the Beazer Garden Maze with its mosaic of Bladud and six Greek Myths by Pulteney Weir. A raggle taggle circle gathered – many canal folk – huddling together like penguins in the Antarctic. After Sue started the proceedings, followed by a song for Imbolc by priestess of Sulis and Nemetona, Sheila Broun, I asked people to remember Tim Sebastion Woodman, the founder of the Gorsedd – who died two years ago on this very day – crossing over, with impeccable druid timing on Imbolc (as though consciously choosing the day of his death): the first time he'd ever been on time for anything, I joked. And Tim was, among other things, a joker. His irreverently wise spirit is missed. He has a way of puncturing the pomposity of much of the 'oaky machoness' (as he wittily put it) you can get at such ceremonies. The posturing and publicity-seeking. Last year I held an Imbolc Bardic Showcase in his memory in Glastonbury. For me, the festival will always be associated with him – and I think of it, with some amusement, as 'Timbolc'! Yet the festival for me has been for a long time the one I associate with Taliesin and Ceridwen. It is a poet's festival and the ideal time to rededicate oneself to one's path – which for me is the Way of Awen, the way of the Bard. And yet this year there is an extra sadness – locally we are mourning the recent loss from cancer of Dave Angus, who was a great poet and singer/guitarist. He set up a popular open mic event called What a Performance! On Friday there was one scheduled which became an emotive tribute night, following close on his passing. I performed my 'Last Rites to John Barleycorn' there – because Dave was something of a Barleycorn figure, as a merry soul who gave of himself freely to his community. Today we made him an honorary Bard of Caer Badon – a gesture to acknowledge his contribution and talent. During the gorsedd I performed my Imbolc poem, Bride of Spring above the roar of the weir. It was a nice visual fix to have swans swimming close by in the Avon.

Things were quickly wrapped up, for it was seriously cold, and I headed back home to prepare for my wee Imbolc 'poetry tea party' – a gentle Sunday afternoon affair. The sharing of poems over tea, cake and other tasties. Folk turned up from about 3pm and it was pleasant chilled out occasion, with contributions of song, verse and tale from some of my talented friends. This is my ideal way to celebrate such times – I'm not one for 'High Church' paganism, preferring bardic sharing around the hearth or campfire to the pomp and ceremony. I like to simply gather in a circle and share. As a bard this is how I engage with the deeper meaning of the festivals – by the reciting and listening the traditional tales and songs. And by the physical experience of visiting appropriate sites – as I did this morning, making a modest pilgrimage to my local woodland spring: a simple Sunday morning stroll on the surface, but for me, a way of reconnecting with the Source.

White Rainbow
5th February 2009

Just walked back from the station through heavy snow – the world turned into a snow-dome. Heavy snowfall in the Bath area over last couple of days. The first wave came on Monday and brought the nation to a standstill – a flurry of snow and it all grinds to a halt! We just can't cope, it seems. I can hear my Icelandic and Finnish friends laughing. But I think it's more than just Anglo-Saxon ineptitude. I think it's just a secret excuse to bunk off work and go and have a snow ball fight. Snow brings out the child in all of us (perhaps because, for people my generation, most memories of decent snow are related to childhood, when we used to have 'proper winters'). Monday saw a wave of 'mass-skiving' strike the country – as evidenced by Facebook confessionals, photoes, videos, texting, twittering, etc. A adultlescent dawn chorus. A snowfall seems to turned even the hardest cynic goofy. It was wonderful, going for an amble up the hill this afternoon – usually a quiet loop around the National Trust slopes overlooking the city – to see it populated by a swathe of snow-junkies, young and old, making snowmen, sledding, throwing snowballs, juggling snowballs, rolling about in it giggling – high on snow. Toddlers pulled on tiny sledges by parents. Teenagers on tea-trays. Three men on a binlid. Snowfolk of various sizes and skill. An inevitable snow-penis, complete with snow-balls – like a white May-pole – around which the snow-children played. We are made innocent again. The world is reminted, layered in broken slabs of Kendal mint cake.

Leaving the slope of fun, I headed for virgin fields to leave my Man Friday prints, the compacting snow making a polystyrene sound. The familiar had become a film set. A special effect. I had to take photoes to remind myself what I was seeing – my neck of the woods, re-rendered as a Brueghel painting.

I saw other snow art on the way to London later that afternoon. A snow-couple – the snowman and his wife, sitting watching the 15:13 to Paddington. Other spirits of the snow sat stoically considering their inevitable dissolution in backyards and parks. Michelin families rolled up winter into a ball, leaving negative slug-trails of naked grass. In Hyde Park, by the Serpentine Gallery, someone had sculpted an impressive snow-head, like the head of Bran the Blessed, singing still, stopping time – as snow seems to – until the strong door of reality is opened once again. Bran's head was taken to London by the heart-weary seven who survived and buried beneath the White Mount, where now the Tower of London stands. The ravens (Bran's bird) there have their wings clipped, because it is prophesied that if they were to ever leave, the country would fall. Bran's head was buried facing France to protect the land from invaders, like the striking oil refinery workers who wished they could hold back the inevitable tide of market forces. 'British jobs for British workers' the protesters cry and yet even Bran's role as tutelary guardian was usurped by another 'foreign' incomer, Arthur, who dug him up. Even magical protectionism can fail. As I passed the statue of Peter Pan, a raven landed nearby and looked at me with its black Odin eye. I doffed my cap to both – the forces of joy and death – and continued onto my evening class at Imperial College, a session on genre-busting with my writing students.

I returned home late. Tired. The night turned into a swirling flurry of TV screen static, stuck between stations, whispering from its glass world.

Exactly a year ago on this day, my Dad was cremated. In the summer, just before what would have been his 70th, my mother, sister and myself took the urn (heavy as mortality) over to one of his favourite haunts – where he used to take us walking the dogs as children. There, on a perfect sunny day we scattered the ashes. They made a summer frost on the green blades. I picked some up and let it run through my fingers, watching the particles dissipate in the light breeze. Then gently, so, so gently, I brushed the dust of my father into the earth, leaving no sign of his passing visible to the world. Only a white absence remained inside of us, as cold and as silent as snow.

Now we have planted a silver birch tree for him there (the first tree to establish itself after the icesheets withdraw) and the whiteness has taken on a new significance – a white of potential, for it is the colour that contains all colours. It is the beginning of the spectrum. A white rainbow.

Snowdrops
27th February 2009

When the snows cleared a couple of weeks ago the snowdrops were there. They had already raised their timorous heads before this Cold Snap and had survived its harshness, despite, or maybe because of their small frailty. Too insignificant to be noticed by the frost giants. And yet easily trod underfoot.

Snowdrops are a welcome sight – the first tenuous signs of Spring, although that may be weeks away. Their white petals add a bright firmament to the gloomy days of winter. There is a collective yearning for the light at this time – in the Northern Hemisphere – as we slowly escape the point of singularity of the solstice. Imbolc seems to be its particular event horizon – once we have crossed it, we are free of winter's gravity. Snowdrops cluster around its edges like stars pulled into a black hole. And yet they reach in the opposite direction, pushing up from the dark earth. Growing out of death, like the Simbelmynë flowers that grow on the barrow graves by Edoras of the Rohan in *The Two Towers*, called in the common speech of men 'Evermind': 'They blossomed in all the seasons, like the bright eyes of Elves, glinting in the starlight.'

At the weekend I met up with a friend at Nympsfield long barrow, high up on the Cotswold escarpment overlooking the Severn plain. Returning for tea and cake to her lovely cottage, similarly situated, we passed a country churchyard at Edge filled with white flowers amongst the stones.

Life determinedly returns, however transient, though its roots cling to mortal clay. Something makes it grow, despite its brief life. Or perhaps because of it. It feels the impulse more urgently. Every day is more precious, and sweeter the dew. Whatever may have befallen us in the past, whatever 'slings and arrows of outrageous fortune' it is hard not to feel some sense of renewal, of a new chance, with the virgin year before us. All things are possible on its tabula rasa. Snowdrops are a symbol of that most precious commodity: hope. In these bleak times, when the economic house of cards crashes down around us, it seems foolhardy to be hopeful and yet more imperative than ever – if we are not succumb to the riptide of gloom. In a speech made by President Obama in the light of the economic crisis, the *Guardian* said that 'he has undammed the springs of hope.' ('The Springs of Hope', *Guardian*, 26.02.09) If we listened to the news every day, with its tales of 'toxic debt', banks going bust, big firms going under, fat cat payoffs, nuclear folly and celebrity cancer, it would be hard not to surrender to despair. But nature quietly, insistently, tells us, not to give up. That the world will keep turning whatever we do to it, or ourselves.

To feel better, all one has to do is walk out into the garden of Spring and enjoy the morning of the year. The world is still beautiful.

'Sing cuccu nu. Sing cuccu.'

Clown-face
27th February 2009

Just saw a sublime piece of theatre, 'Scaramouche Jones', at the

Ustinov in Bath – a one-man show featuring the supremely talented Justin Butcher, who wrote and directed it. It was originally staged to great acclaim with Pete Postlethwaite in the lead role, but Butcher clearly made it his own again in a tour-de-force of tragic-comedy physical theatre, drawing upon the ancient repertoire of clowning – slapstick, Commedia dell Arte, mime. It was about the life of a 'clown' – who acquires, eventually, the name Scaramouche Jones – over the Twentieth Century. He is born when it begins and dies when it finishes, on the New Year's Eve of the Millennium and so his life becomes symbolic of this bloodiest of centuries, when history became a farce. He recreates the seven masks he embodies throughout his life – metaphors for the seven ages of man, and perhaps the different phases of the century, from infantilism to senility.

I found it deeply moving – for it captured the 'tears of a clown' and the way art can redeem life, even at its most harrowing. How a smile and the rictus of death are not far apart. How laughter is a kind of ecstasy – an ec-stasis – when we lose control and finally taste freedom, a moment echoed at death, the ultimate ecstasy, la grande mort, as opposed to the la petite mort of orgasm.

The white mask of the clown is a brilliant leitmotif for many kinds of 'whitenesses' – the white of identity (as Jones seeks to discover his long-lost English father); the white of salt from the high seas; the white of the bleached desert; of goats milk and an albino cobra (called Benjamin Disraeli); the white of lime of the death-pits of the concentration camps; the white of grease-paint of vaudeville... Jones spends fifty years becoming the clown (always depicted as an unfortunate old man with red-nose, pot-belly, tatty clothes, a stoop, bent by life, more unfortunate than us – the fall guy, the immortal fool) and fifty years playing the clown, which becomes his way of 'miming' the tragic comedy of life, having witnessed some of its darkest periods of history. His role is validated is the only response. A kind of adopted madness in an insane world.

But what I realised as I watched this astonishing piece of theatre, was how the 'whiteness' of Scaramouche, the sacred clown, mirrors the 'radiant brow' of Taliesin. At some points Butcher dripped with sweat and glowed with intensity. The amount of energy and concentration, skill and stamina, he had to sustain such a show – in which he played all the parts – was formidable. I sat in awe of his awen.

This is the bardic tradition in full flow – in theatres across the country, big and small, most nights of the week – but especially in cutting edge theatre like this, which shows what humanity can be capable of. Humankind, conscious of itself – able to reflect on and make crazy sense of the great dance of life and death.

I left, wanting to savour the feeling this had created – the hard-won moment of gnosis. I wandered the streets of Bath, on a 'different high' to those around me, filled with beautiful melancholy for all that is sang and how sad it is so few hear the song.

On the Gower
28th February 2009

I am here to connect with the Source: Awen and the spirit of Taliesin, whose mythic presence haunts these shores. According to one version of the legend (from MS 'once in the Havod Uchtryd collection' – see below) it was from here that the Penbeirdd was shanghaied by Irish pirates from whom he escaped – adrift beyond the ninth wave in a coracle until he ends up caught on Gwyddno's weir.

The Gower peninsula, neither fully Welsh or English, surrounded by the sea but connected to the land, seems to be a threshold place – a place of creative possibilities, where the unexpected can happen at any moment; the raiding of free radicals, the lightning bolt of inspiration. The ion-rich air crackles with the nascent energy of the hidden world, ready to burst through. Gower-based poet Vernon Watkins, was acutely aware of this field of potential:

Darkness is not dark, nor sunlight the light of sun
But a double journey of insistent silver hooves.
Light wakes in the foal's blind eyes as lightning illuminates corn
With a rustle of fine-eared grass, where a starling shivers.
(Vernon Watkins, '*Foal*')

While staying in Llangennith I discover a tantalising echo of the Taliesin legend in the apocryphal tale of its local saint (and saint of Gower) St Cenydd.

Saint Cenydd was a Sixth Century hermit monk, founder of the church of Llangennith, which is named after him, although he has connections with Brittany to where he later travelled, where his cultus is centred around Languidic. He also has a chapel at Ploumelin. According to Edward Williams, aka Iolo Morgannwg he was one of the sons of Gildas, who married, had sons, before becoming a monk at Llanilltud Fawr (Llanwit Major) under St Illtud. Yet even the fertile mind of Morgannwg would have been hard-pressed to have come up with this colourful saint's tale.

Cenydd's rather unusual legend was collected in truncated form by John Capgrave from various Welsh sources, and may be found in the *Nova Legenda Angliae*. According to this, the saint was a Breton prince, the son of King 'Dihoc' (presumably Deroch II of Domnonée) born of incest, apparently at Loughor in Glamorgan, while his father attended King Arthur (the first of several interesting links to the Taliesin story). He was born with one leg joined to the opposite thigh – the posture of the Hanged Man from the Major Arcana of the Tarot. As an unwanted cripple, Cenydd was placed in a cradle made of osiers and cast into the Lougher estuary. He was washed out to sea, eventually landing on 'Ynys Weryn' or Worm's Head Island. Here, the local seagulls and a series of angelic interventions, involving a miraculous breast-shaped bell (a cauldron-like source of nourishment, known locally as the 'titty bell') ensured that he survived and was educated as a Christian. He became a hermit, his only companion being an untrustworthy servant, whose dishonesty was revealed when he stole a spear from one of a group of robbers who had been hospitably received by his master. Saint David later cured Cenydd of his deformity while travelling to the Synod of Brefi in 545. The hermit, however, preferred to remain as he was born and prayed for his previous condition to be restored. The story breaks off abruptly at this point.

The pariah-child who is consigned to the fate of the sea in a tiny craft and is saved by a lucky landing in a fortunate place – to become honoured in later life – has echoes with the Taliesin legend. Of course, it has Biblical echoes also – and some might argue that the Christian 'Mabinogion', the Old Testament, is ultimately the source of both – but there is something both more universal here and also very particular to Wales. The Taliesin story could not be more emblematic of Wales and here is a local saint tale echoing it in microcosm, in a place connected to one version of the Penbeirdd's legend. It is as though one had been grafted onto the other. A mythic transfusion has occurred. It could be an attempt to assimilate local pagan practices by appropriating the tutelary wonder tale and making it a saint's tale. Many of these saint 'creation myths' or martyr stories have a pre-Christian air about them, filled with bizarre imagery. Certainly the 'titty bell' seems far removed from anything normally found in imaginations scrubbed clean of healthy sensuality. It is hard to imagine this story being related to prim and proper Sunday parishioners.

Another clue as to St Cenydd's pagan credentials is the fact his feast day is 1st August – the pre-Christian festival of Lammas or Lughnasadh. Throughout the Gower, Mabsant Day – when the local saint is celebrated – was traditionally celebrated on 12th February (the festival died out in the late 19th Century) but Llangennith's was on July 5th and was renowned as being the most lively, lasting for three days ('three days to die in bliss and three weeks to be reborn,' a local would say)!

The fact St Cenydd finds sanctuary on Worm's Head – the 'pen-dragon' – is telling as well. It seems to be either part of a local Dreamtime – mythologizing the landscape – or just a story-teller's wily use of local evocative landmarks. Certainly Worm's Head lends itself to fanciful speculation, looking like a backdrop for a fantasy movie sequence. And the village had its very own fabulist...

Phil Tanner – the Bard of Llangennith

In this book we've looked at the formative years and early career of Taliesin, who was to become Penbeirdd – but what of the bard in his autumn years, whose reputation has been established? While staying in Llangennith I came across mention of a fasci-nating local character, renowned across the Gower and folk circles: Phil Tanner, a farm labourer born in the village in 1862 to a family of seven, he became what the *Picture Post* in an article written just a year before he died (John Ormond Thomas; 19.03.49 edition of *Picture Post*) called: 'one of the finest of Britain's folk-singers...' Phil Tanner was literally the seventh son of Isaac and Jennet Tanner (Isaac worked like a lot of the 'Englishry' of the Gower in the weaving trade – and claimed descent from the 'Flemings', the Flemish Weavers brought over by the conquering Normans to colonise the area). Phil came from a family known locally for their music and dancing – his brothers were singers too – but it is said: 'In him were embodied, somehow, the abilities of the rest.' (Doug Fraser article accessed 08.03.09 http://www.folkwales.org.uk/arcgopt.html). He had an exceptional memory – committing a song to memory as soon as he heard it. He added to his inherited repertoire any song he heard in the area – mainly Victorian ballads – some 80 or 90 in total, a selection of which were fortunately recorded by the English Folk Song Society in 1937 and a later BBC radio programme. Although songs were 'owned' by particular singers in the region, as certain storytellers have 'signature tales', Phil outlived and outsung them all. His reputation grew and grew, so that: 'for the next two generations no celebration within miles was complete without him cracking a song or six.' (Fraser, ibid). He augmented his impressive skills as a singer and mouth musician ('the voice that danced itself' *Picture Post)*, with that of storyteller and a superb mimic. He would have been the proverbial life and soul, and became the 'official entertainer' of the King's Head pub in the village. If his bardic status was in any doubt it was also recorded how: 'Tanner was the authority on what remained of local customs and rituals and is particularly remembered as the last of the bidders at the bidding weddings. The bidder went from house to house, perhaps mounted on a white horse, but always carrying a staff decked with white ribbons, repeating the bidding rhyme at each house. The rhyme was not only a wedding invitation but also served as a splendid panegyric on the fare and entertainment available to the guests.' (Fraser, ibid) Here is the Bidding Rhyme of invitation, which gives a flavour of the man's style:

> *"There will be a fiddle in attendance, for there'll be plenty of music there, and dancing if you'll come and dance. There'll be fiddlers, fifers, drummers and the devil don't know what beside. I don't know what. There'll be plenty of drinkables there, so they tell me, but that I haven't tasted. And if you'll come to the wedding I'll do all that lies in my power to get you a sweetheart apiece if I don't get drunk. But the brides is wishful you should come or send."*

Roy Harris of the Cardiff Folksong Club said of Tanner: 'He lived the song's story and made every word tell.' He was a bard who lived and breathed awen until his dying breath in a nursing home on Penmaen in 1950. He was a tradition-bearer, a 'national treasure' (Roy Harris) and with him died a part of England's folk tradition: 'Phil Tanner is a piece of walking social history, a man who holds a culture that is rapidly disappearing from our life.' (*Picture Post*)

But it seems, for once, a 'prophet was honoured in his own country' and, rarely, in his own lifetime. Tanner's life and remarkable talent shows how important a bard can be to his or her community. He was, indeed, the Grand Old Man of Gower.

St David's Day, College House, Llangennith
1st March 2009

A cock crows. Dawn on St David's Day. A buzzard circles over Raven's well. The urgent song of Spring is sung: an orchestra tuning up. The sun rises over Hardings Down. A horse shakes its mane in the clean sun, then continues nosing dewy tufts of grass. A slight smell of the fields wafts in – a musky animal smell. Trees show a barely discernible fuzz of green, like the first growth on a young man's face – the adolescent Taliesin. With the onset of puberty – in the budding Spring of his life – Taliesin's embryonic power awakens, as with so many shamans who are tested at this age. He is thirteen; his life before him. He has won the Chair of Deganwy. The world is at his feet. He has yet to taste the delights of love. The touch of a lover. The heart aches. The joys and sorrows of life. Often in child prodigies knowledge outstrips experience – they may be clever, but lack the wisdom forged by hard-won life experience. This tempers their potential arrogance, acts as a ballast to their vaulting ambition. Yet Taliesin claims to have lived many lives and has wisdom beyond his years.

Here, in this College House, young monks would learn their Matins. It is a place of deep peace and clarity – 'Ancient music of silence born' (Vernon Watkins, from Taliesin and his Mockers) – like a clear well. A well of knowledge, like the one Odin drinks from at the base of Yggdrasil – Mimir's Spring (with Ravens Well close by it is hard not to make a Nordic connection, with Sweyne's Howe up on Rhossili Down, two stone cysts). One flows into a stone trough outside the lych gate of the church; by its side another flows into the ground from beneath a stone 'trilithon' – I filled my waterbottle with it after seeing an elderly lady come out from the church to fill a watering can, presumably to water the church flowers for the St. David's Day service – one can imagine it being the centre of village life and probably the start of the settlelement here, a spring venerated as sacred by the Celtic ancestors of this land?

It is thrilling to think Celtic Christian holy men dwelt here, contemporary with the historical Taliesin – in 6th Century Wales. Could the Penbeirdd have visited? St Cenydd's story and the pirate narrative certainly seems to suggest so. Perhaps he started like as a monk – the only access to education in those days – before being kidnapped by Hibernian pirates. Like Parsifal/Perceval he could not hide from life. It came and grabbed him. Destiny was on his trail.

Running the Dragon
1st March, 2009

Midday at Worm's Head, Penrhyn-Gwr, on St David's Day. A good place to be, in the Spring sunshine. The gulls and gannets shriek, the withdrawing waves roar in indignation ('you may have won the battle, but not the war...'). The sea is turquoise – sky, a chalk-blue. A few wisps of cloud on the horizon – more over Devon and Somerset, south to England. Visitors seem to be queuing up to 'run the dragon', waiting for the tide to retreat sufficiently for the causeway to be safely exposed. Serendipity is with me today as I arrive at the right time to cross. Low tide is 14:40 and there's a two and half hour window either side of this, so at 12.10 I will cross. For now, a moment to catch my thoughts.

Here at the dragon's head I honour the spirit of Wales and its finest son of song, Taliesin – Penrhyn-Gwr to Penbeirdd ... Hail!

A good place to reflect on my journey of a bard, as I reach the completion of the Way of Awen – may the dragon give me a final burst of awen!

The very end of the Worm's Head – a dramatic stack – is approximately a mile out. Reaching it requires a tricky scramble over jagged rocks and running the gauntlet of the tide. Time it wrong and you can get cut off! It takes me fifty minutes of energetic effort to reach the end – carrying a twenty pound backpack as well, which nearly made me lose my balance and fall into a gulley at one scary point. With enormous relief and satisfaction, I reach my goal...

Sitting in the sun on the head of Worm's Head on a grassy ledge, eating my sandwiches, restoring my energy levels, and watching mighty waves rolling in. Standing on the endstack was literally a peak experience. I realised my nine month journey had come full circle – from Orme's Head to Worm's Head, from the far North of Wales to the far South – a satisfying symmetry. Which one is the head, which the tail? Or does the dragon have two heads? Then it dawned on me – it is Ourobouros, the dragon eating itself. The story does not end. One 'tale' begats another – each ending, another beginning. We have to join the story somewhere, but there is always a before-story and after-story, and many other paths along the way.

My story started back in the East Midlands – which seems like another universe compared to here, to my current life. The landlady of the B&B said, rather presumptuously, 'you're as Welsh as me' – meaning what exactly who knows – but in fact my middle name is Gerald, as in Giraldus Cambrensis: Gerald of Wales (it was also my father's name). Although I have no Welsh blood (as far as I know) this is a reassuring foreshadowing of what has become something of an obsession for me – what could be called Cambria-philia, a love of Wales.

I hail Wales, Cambria and the Cymru on St David's Day and, of course, Taliesin Penbeirdd. May his name endure forever. I felt complete. A good place to 'end' my book, but not my journey along the Way of Awen. Like the dragon encircling the world – it has no end or beginning. A circle with no edges, whose centre is everywhere.

Reaching the end of the Worm's head is like crossing the Bridge of Leaps to Scathach's Isle of Shadows – one has to traverse razor-sharp rocks, perilous pathways and the Devil's Bridge. It has a mythic initiatory quality to it. I imagine Caer Sidi on the end-stack and set off. All the time the clock of the tide is ticking, making the blood pump with excitement. There's an element of Kêr-Ys here, or Cantre'r Gwaelod – the sea is always present, threatening to inundate the land at any moment, jealousy seizing back what it had given. One feels humbly in the lap of the goddess.

Below Rhossili Down in a strip of dunes known as the Warren a lost village was discovered. Briefly revealed in late 1979 after a fierce storm, the unnamed village was excavated. A ruined 6th Century church was uncovered. The medieval village seems to have been the casualty of 'besanding', and was abandoned to the encroaching sands in the 13th or 14th Century, probably after a series of violent sandstorms. When the subsequent dig, which took place in 1980, was finished the lost village was once more covered over for future generations.

On Rhossili beach itself, for some time the rotting hull of a wrecked boat has added a certain melancholic charm to the vista, half-buried by the sand – its timbers like the ribs of a fish, but even that has finally succumbed to the restless processes of tide and brine.

There is a possible allusion to a tutelary goddess in the place name. Rhossili probably gets its name in part from the Welsh word for moorland, *rhos* (the intricate open medieval field system found on the Down is known locally as The Vile – presumably related to Old English words for 'field', as in 'wold' of the Cotswolds). The second part of the name is possibly derived from the word for salt, but may also be a reference to a Saint Sulien or Saint Sili, whom the church of the lost village was dedicated to. Little is known of this saint, but etmologically seems linked to either 'Sil' of Silbury Hill – King Sil was said to be buried beneath it on his horse, amid a hoard of treasure; Sillina, tutelary goddes of the Isles of Scilly; or Sul, goddess of *Aquae Sulis*. Sillina and Sul seem linked (although the latter is indivisibly linked to the hot springs unique to Bath) and it is possible the goddess 'migrated' via tradelinks with the Isles of Scilly and with Aquae Sulis. Bath is not far away on the other side of the Severn and trading links with the West Country were established for some time, with limestone quarried on the Gower shipped over to the coast of Somerset and Devon. Bath, referred to by Morgannwg as Caer Badon, has a hillfort now referred to as Little Solsbury (made famous by Peter Gabriel's song) and Solsbury does not sound a million miles from Rhossili.

Perhaps it is in human nature to find connections with one's home or interests when travelling – in the same way many see human features in nature (simulacra). We project. And this trans-figures our expectations and experience. But nevertheless, my visit to the Gower has uncovered some resonant treasures. Taliesin seems to have found a 'brother' in the unlikely guise of St Cenydd. We should not be surprised that such a legend has other family. No mention is made of a wife, alas, but there is mention of a son. So let us end our journey with speculation on 'the next generation'.

Taliesin's Son

Hast thou heard what Avaon sang,
The son of Taliesin, of the recording verse?
(Englynion y Clyweid. – Myv. Arch. I. 173)

There is reference to a son of Taliesin, Avaon or Adaon, of whom not much is known, except for fragments preserved in the Welsh Triads, above and in the *Mabinogion*, in 'The Dream of Rhonabwy', in which the protagonist, stranded in a storm, lays down upon a 'yellow calf hide' and has a visionary dream of Britain:

> *Then they beheld another troop coming towards the ford, and these from their horses' chests upwards were whiter than the lily, and below blacker than jet. And they saw one of these knights go before the rest, and spur his horse into the ford in such a manner that the water dashed over Arthur and the Bishop, and those holding counsel with them, so that they were as wet as if they had been drenched in the river. And as he turned the head of his horse, the youth who stood before Arthur struck the horse over the nostrils with his sheathed sword, so that, had it been with the bare blade, it would have been a marvel if the bone had not been wounded as well as the flesh. And the knight drew his sword half out of the scabbard, and asked of him, 'Wherefore didst thou strike my horse? Whether was it in insult or in counsel unto me?' 'Thou dost indeed lack counsel. What madness caused thee to ride so furiously as to dash the water of the ford over Arthur, and the consecrated Bishop, and their counsellors, so that they were as wet as if they had been dragged out of the river?' 'As counsel then will I take it.' So he turned his horse's head round towards his army.*
>
> *'Iddawc,' said Rhonabwy, 'who was yonder knight?' 'The most eloquent and the wisest youth that is in this island; Adaon, the son of Taliesin.' 'Who was the man that struck his horse?' 'A youth of forward nature; Elphin, the son of Gwyddno.'*
>
> ('The Dream of Rhonabwy', *The Mabinogion*, Guest)

This portrayal of Taliesin's son depicts him as a reckless, hotheaded youth – the equivalent of a boy-racer; a Celtic Phaethön (the foolish 'son of the sun' who rode his father's solar chariot and lost control, with devastating consequences). In that instance the world was scorched – deserts were created, forests burnt, skins darkened and drought caused as, unable to control his father's mighty horses, the chariot flew too close to the Earth.

But here, it is with water that Avaon immerses the symbols of Church and State – the bishop and the Emperor Arthur himself. Water is a symbol of the intuition, the feminine element, and is perhaps exactly what these figures of patriarchal authority lack. Arthur, in his time, has connected with the Divine Feminine through water, via the Lady of the Lake and later, mortally wounded, he journeys to Avalon on Morgen's psychopompic vessel. Avaon's own name seems to carry the ghost of Avalon, and his presence has an Otherworldly quality to it – as when the Green Knight appears before Arthur's court one midwinter to test their mettle. Then it was Gawain, Arthur's nephew, who rose to the challenge set by the fairy knight. Tellingly, the court in Rhonabwy's dream meet at a ford – a threshold numinous with significance. Arthur's company linger perilously on the borders of Faerie. They seem to be in a limbo of inaction until awoken by first the drubbing of Avaon, then the admonishing of a 'tall and stately man of noble and flowing speech', who points out: 'that it was a marvel that so vast a host should be assembled in so narrow a space, and that it was a still greater marvel that those should be there at that time who had promised to be by midday in the battle of Badon...' The knight said he would proceed there anywhere. Prompted by his words and deeds, Arthur seems to remember his duty and rides out to battle and to victory.

Taliesin's son himself had a fearless reputation, as Triad 73 attests:

> *Adaon or Avaon, son of the chief of the bards, and a bard himself, was also celebrated for his valour. He was one of those three dauntless chieftains who feared nothing in the day of battle and strife, but rushed onwards regardless of death.*

He perhaps had the fearlessness of the young who seldom possess true awareness and understanding of mortality and the preciousness of life, something that maturity and tragedy will temper. And yet, like so many young soldiers in war (First World War, Vietnam, Iraq, etc) he was to taste death before his time:

> *The courage and daring supported him through all the dangers of war. He fell at length by the hand of an assassin. Llawgad Trwm Bargawd or Llawgad Trwn Bargad Eiddyn, whose name is preserved only as the perpetrator of this crime. (Triad 47)*

And thus ends the blood-line of Taliesin – as far as we know. Although presumably Taliesin had a wife on whom he begat Avaon – and she could have bore him other offspring, as well as leaving her own legacy. Alas, the storytellers left her unnamed – and she remains one of the countless anonymous muses who have inspired and supported their poetic partner.

Taliesin's ultimate muse may have been the Goddess herself, Awen incarnate, but his wife must have been flesh and blood to have given him a son.

Yet though it seemed the Penbeirdd's blood-line died out there, his metaphysical lineage continues. Mythopoeically, all those who follow a bardic path are 'Taliesin's sons' (and daughters). Through taking the Way of Awen we become part of that bardic lineage that stretches back to the first storytellers around and the first fires, and will continue until the last tale is told.

Italian Taliesin
13th March 2009

Yesterday received my flight confirmation for the 'Italian job' I am undertaking the end of this month – to run a week's worth of storytelling workshops in an Italian college in Udine to English language students; a gaggle of lively Italian teenagers! I did the same last year in Northern Italy, in the lovely Piedmont region. This year I'm flying into Venice, city of love – my friend Silvana, English teacher and organiser of this trip, is picking me up from the airport, the school is about an hour away. It seems like a tall order, (teaching storytelling in a foreign language) but it seemed to be worthwhile last time – there's a lot more to communicating in another language than just vocabulary, and storytelling is an excellent way of developing these non-verbal methods: body language, tone of voice, expression, gesture, etc. Last year I used a story from the shapechanging epic *Metamorphoses* by Ovid, the Italian Shakespeare – and also from the Bard himself, a sonnet the Swan of Avon wrote about my home city, Bath (I like to show inspiration is always 'under your nose' and it is important to be authentic – to share something distinctive from your own neck of the woods). I wonder if any of my '08 students carried on story-telling? They seemed to enjoy it at the time. Who knows, perhaps one of them will become a great bard, an Italian Taliesin, a 21st Century Boccaccio? Looking at their bright young faces I could see the potential in all of them. They had a spark. Shining brows – on the cusp of venturing out into the world to prove them selves in Maelgwn's court, about to set out on their own 'journey to Deganwy'.

Well, mine has now finished – in terms of the creative process of this book – although, in truth, it never does, if one wants to continue to grow, to hone one's craft. The Bard can become Ollamh – a doctor of verse – if they reach an exceptional level of ability and knowledge (this traditionally took twenty years...), and beyond that, the ultimate accolade of Penbeirdd – but that is a lifetime's achievement to aspire to and is perhaps something only posterity can acknowledge. For now, as Bards, with clarsach on back and a crane-skin bag of tales, it is time to set forth into the world following the path of our calling, the Way of Awen.

The Way of Awen is...

The art of inspiration – leading an inspired life

Tapping into your creativity

Honouring your creative self

Living creatively

Following your dream – making it happen!

Being in the moment, fully present

Being spontaneous

Creative preparedness

Knowing the flow

Living every day fully

Living rightly, living lightly

Not being afraid to think big

Thinking outside of the box

Following your Muse, rather than the crowd

Lucid living

Joy

Living the path of the heart

Creative play

Giving yourself permission to 'fail', to make a mess, and to have fun!

Joining in the dance of creation

A new awe – continually realising the miracle of being alive

From the when of awe, to the now of awe

(A Declaration of Creative Independence, 4th July 2008)

Conclusion:
Living the Way of Awen

When we fail to connect with our creative self (our 'inner bard') we fail to honour the fullness of our soul's potential. Many people postpone their creativity – prioritising work, family, the 'Ten Thousand Things' – anything but what they truly dream of being, leaving it until retirement, an afterthought to their life-story, a hasty addition, an 'errata' slipped into the last pages. And so we lead unfulfilled lives, unless we are lucky enough to be doing what we love.

But how does that happen?

Not by just dreaming about it, but by a conscious act of creativity. William Blake said: '*I must create my own system or be enslaved by another man's. My business is not to reason and compare. It is to create.*' This is the sacred covenant with your self, with your Divine Spark. To be, as Tolkien termed it, a Sub-creator.

We can be creative in many ways – in small, daily ways, in 'reckless acts of living'. We can express ourselves through cookery, gardening, interior design, clothes-making, make-up, hairdressing, dancing, music, conversation, ritual, campaigning, fund-raising…

To make creativity your career you need to go to the next level, one that requires serious commitment rather than 'dabbling'. To become proficient enough to go professional you need to undertake training – your apprenticeship.

It is about making your dreams manifest, and that requires serious commitment and a willingness to learn, to hone your craft, to go beyond the amateur. Book the training course – either evening, part-time or take a year out if possible. But most are happy to bumble along in their hobby, being dilettantes, which still has some merits. Any creative expression is better than none, and it is the process – not the end goal – which is important.

Some let it take over the spare time completely, it becomes a channel for all of their frustrated energies and yearnings – they work to fund their hobby/obsession. The consequence is a schizophrenic existence between a 'work self' and a true creative self. It results in 'sleepwalkers' – those that spend their working day not fully present, not fully engaging. Half-lives don't make happy lives. You see it on the glazed faces of commuters – they have left their dream-self at home. They are empty-shells, forced to be wage slaves. Yet so often we end up working to fund the lifestyle that acts as compensation for having to work: we reward ourselves with luxury goods, cars, clothes, holidays, plastic surgery – things we don't really need. Money gives us the illusion of freedom, of choice – when in fact to earn it we have to relinquish freedom and choice. It is a vicious circle. There's no easy way out, but if you don't start honouring your dreams, then who will? It can start right now – go outside and feel the rain on your skin. Run up the hill and be blown away by the wind. Take a day off and go to the beach – feel the warm sand between your toes. Take off your clothes and plunge into the sea. Cry out at the intense sensation. Wake yourself up. Feel alive.

A final entry in my journal captures this spirit. Spontaneity pays off…

The Hill of Wells
21st March 2009

I am filled with awen having just seen Robin and Bina Williamson perform their Songs for the Rising Year at Malvern Wells village hall – around the corner from where I'm staying (a lovely B&B, the Dell House, sleepily ensconced within its leafy bower as the name suggests). It was a joy to see and hear them both again – a fitting 'end' to my bardic journey (in the context of this book, due in imminently) for Robin is a living embodiment of the Penbeirdd – a worthy inheritor of Taliesin's title for my money. I am a bard, but Robin is on another level entirely, and shows in his consummate skill and stage professionalism how far I have yet to go – not that I imagine matching Robin's huge talent and achievement (he is a living legend, after all). It is rightly humbling to note there is always someone more advanced than you. In truth, we all have our own mountains to climb – and whatever size that, the achievement of reaching its particular summit should not be diminished by the mountains of others.

The fact that I made it here, however humble an immram, is a kind of 'mountain'. This morning I was sluggishly recovering from the previous night – a big night when we launched Jay's book (*Places of Truth: journeys into sacred wilderness* – working on it whetted my appetite for such places) at Waterstones, Bath; an event fellow poet and tutor Mary Palmer asked me to organise (I was to publish a posthumous collection of her work the following year, *Tidal Shift*, after she died of cancer). So I had to co-ordinate the performers, promote it, MC it, and publish Jay's book (being a writer requires more skills than 'just' writing these days – gone are the days of waxing lyrical in ivory towers and perhaps just as well). It was a good night – the awen flowed. All the performers were very professional so helped to carry the weight – it was a collective effort and and credit to all those who took part... And, what a relief, we did it! Despite last minute 'labour pains' we got Jay's book out on schedule (collected from the printers the day before – phew!). It's been an intense couple of weeks – stacks of marking, Jay's book, my book, Waterstones, Bournemouth talk last Monday, Bath Writers' Workshop, my evening classes... I felt I deserved a break. It's essential to replenish the cauldron – and where better than on the hills of wells, where Long Will, as William Langland was known locally, lay down 'tired out from (his) wanderings' and had his visionary dream 'among the Malvern hills' of his divine allegory, *Piers the Plowman*.

Having decided to bunk off 'school' (my marking not quite finished, but the sun was shining and shouting *Carpe Deum*!) I packed my saddlebags and hit the road. It was a lovely sunny road and ride-up along the edge of the Cotswolds and across the Severn plain. When it's like this the bike is a joy to ride. I felt like 'king of the road' again, shaking off the final cobwebs of winter. After I had checked in, I went for an early evening walk – determined to catch the last rays of the day. The golden light had lost its keenness, but in the back of my mind I had my favourite line of English poet (written by Malvern poet, Elizabeth Barrett Browning): '*the sun on the hill forgot to die*'. It was thrilling to think these very hills I ascended might have inspired that line. And true, the light seemed to linger, as I hiked up through the woods like Wandering Angus (a fire in my head fed by the oxygen and kindling around me). The woods worked their magic – it was good to arrive, to connect with the genius loci. To orientate myself. The path zigzagged up through the steep woods. A collapsed retaining wall at Holy Well meant I had to take a more circuitous route to the top, but finally, I cleared the tree-line and made the ridge at sunset – though the sun was obscured behind a low bank of cloud. And yet there was still the dusk to savour. Two guys passed by, but otherwise I was alone. I called for awen on the heights. Satisfied, (planning to return for a proper walk the following day) I descended through the darkening woods.

Now I had to attend to physical needs – sustenance before the concert. The only eating place was a Thai restaurant, not quite what I had in mind. Instead I grabbed a sandwich and a packet of crisps from the garage (served by a cheerful Oriental girl). Not exactly healthy eating but I'd had a good lunch before setting off, and plenty of snacks so I wasn't ravenous. Returning to the B&B I freshened up for the evening's entertainment. It was great to go the nearby gig and enjoy a couple of real ales (which I would not have been able to do if I'd been staying further away – the Dell was a real find). In the break I said hello and Robin remembered me straight away, reminding me to his wife, though I hadn't seen him for a couple of years since booking him for an event in Bath. His lovely wife Bina thanked me for what I said about them in

The Bardic Handbook. I gave Robin a dedicated copy of *An Ecobardic Manifesto* – for he is cited in it as an exemplar. Afterwards we talked further about poets – I mentioned Vernon Watkins, as I'd been on the Gower recently; and Robin talked of Ifor Davies; which brought to mind Phil Tanner, bard of Llangennith. I was flattered when Robin called me 'a pretty good poet' (which, compared to Bob Dylan's comment about Robin – 'not bad' – is positively glowing!) We joked about hanging out on lonely knolls, hoping to bump into the Queen of Elfland. I said I had done this on the Eildon hills, but had no such luck. Robin had been there too – and perhaps faired better!

It was great to sit in the front row – having got the last-but-one ticket earlier that day – and be fed by a master of awen. I am so glad I came – I didn't decide for definite until that afternoon, when I reserved the ticket, found and booked the B&B, packed and blatted up here – it just required faith ... in the Way of Awen.

The next morning, after a peaceful night's sleep and a hearty breakfast, I headed for the hills, making a beeline for British Camp, where Langland was said to have been inspired to write his famous medieval poem. I yomped up the hill in my bike leathers – not ideal for walking in! Breathless, I collapsed on the summit and stared at the blue bowl of sky. Sunlight glittered on the reservoir below and although not quite the original source reminded me of Langland's lines: '*...I lay down to rest under a broad ban by the side of stream, and leaned over gazing into the water, it sounded so pleasant that I fell asleep*'. The hill fort was impressive – its steep flanks would have made a formidable defensive structure – and I wondered whether Tolkien had been inspired by it for his 'the ancient watch-tower of Amon Hen', whilst walking here with Lewis – and by the impressive 'beacons' the beacon fires that Gondor called for aid to Rohan. The local bishops were less friendly, the Earl of Gloucester raising the 13th Century Red Earl's Dyke between their respective bishoprics. Caractacus was said to have made his last stand here, (a small cave, Clutter's

Cave, is said to be the resting place of the British hero who rose to his countrymen's aid) inspiring Elgar, who said in 1934 when suffering from his final illness: *"If ever after I'm dead you hear someone whistling this tune on the Malvern Hills, don't be alarmed. It's only me."* I can see why the composer found such inspiration here. Given long enough it may untap the awen in anyone. Today I only had a brief taste, but it was enough to turn on the taps. Moving onto Black Camp, I parked up, stashed my togs, and followed the undulating ridge north, enjoying its spectacular natural roller-coaster. Turning back along its leeward side, I found a quiet sunny spot overlooking the western vale and penned these lines:

On Malvern Hills
On these lettered hills I find peace.
Thick as cream the Spring sunshine pours
over the wooded wolds, cloistered
from the world. Here song waits, poised,
a bird in the air – waiting
to strike at any fecund second.
The sky is full of poetry, the green Earth
budding with awen.
From these pure springs Masefield, Browning, Auden
drank. Elgar whistled symphonies in the silent folds.
Inklings rambled, forging a landscape of myth and
language, and Langland dreamt his rustic allegory.
From the defiant fastness of British Camp
to Worcestershire Beacon
something positively English
can be gleaned about this charmed island
of six hundred million year old granite,
enduring, quietly conquering
all who reach its sanctuary. From
its many wells it suckles all.

Great Mother Malvern.
Her children take
shelter amongst her skirts,
nourished by selfless springs.
Thank the wild saints, the spirits of place,
for this hallowed spot, this bedrock of Albion.

And so we reach the end of our journey – or at least this stage of it, for in truth, the journey of the bard is a lifetime one, and perhaps even beyond. The story does not end, only where we choose to enter it and leave. It existed before us, and will continue after us. I have chosen to focus on one version of the Taliesin story – and one aspect of that, his formative years. Yet one must remember his story is just one narrative of events, historical or mythopoeic – and that Taliesin's tale continues, indeed, begins in earnest from this point. Taliesin goes forth to fulfil his destiny, as we must – to the best of our ability, as the awen allows.

My point here has been not to provide a definitive analysis of the story, but to show how it can be engaged with experientially. Its wisdom comes alive by how we live it. As Mervyn Peake said in his singular Bildungsroman, *Titus Alone*: '*What a boy had set out to seek a man had found by the act of living.*'

I suggest this is how the story of Taliesin will open up to you – by how you apply it to your own life.

Yet this bardic narrative is not the only one. Another variant of the Taliesin tale talks of how he was kidnapped by Irish pirates:

'Taliesin, Chief of the Bards, the son of Saint Henwg of Caerlleon upon Usk, was invited to the court of Urien Rheged, at Aberllychwr. He, with Elffin, the son of Urien, being once fishing at sea in a skin coracle, an Irish pirate ship seized him and his coracle, and bore him away towards Ireland; but while the pirates were at the height of their drunken mirth, Taliesin pushed his coracle to the sea, and got

*into it himself, with a shield in his hand which he found in the ship,
and with which he rowed the coracle until it verged the land; but,
the waves breaking then in wild foam, he lost his hold on the shield,
so that he had no alternative but to be driven at the mercy of the sea,
in which state he continued for a short time, when the coracle stuck
to the point of a pole in the weir of Gwyddno, Lord of Ceredigion, in
Aberdyvi; and in that position he was found, at the ebb, by
Gwyddno's fishermen, by whom he was interrogated; and when it
was ascertained that he was a bard, and the tutor of Elffin, the son
of Urien Rheged, the son of Cynvarch: — 'I, too, have a son named
Elffin,' said Gwyddno, 'be thou a bard and teacher to him, also, and
I will give thee lands in free tenure.' The terms were accepted, and
for several successive years he spent his time between the courts of
Urien Rheged and Gwyddno, called Gwyddno Garanhir, Lord of the
Lowland Cantred; but after the territory of Gwyddno had become
overwhelmed by the sea, Taliesin was invited by the Emperor
Arthur to his court at Caerlleon upon LIsk, where he became highly
celebrated for poetic genius and useful, meritorious sciences. After
Arthur's death he retired to the estate given to him by Gwyddno,
taking Elffin, the son of that prince, under his protection. It was
from this account that Thomas, the son of Einion Offeiriad,
descended from Gruffvdd Gwyr, formed his romance of Taliesin, the
son of Cariadwen — Elffin, the son of Goddnou — Rhun, the son of
Maelgwn Gwynedd, and the operations of the Cauldron of
Ceridwen.'*
(from Anthony Powel of Llwydarth's MS)

This offers a far more prosaic narrative and although it might be
nearer the historical truth of the real Taliesin it is wide of the
mark of the mythopoeic truth of the more well-known version. It
feels like a rationalisation. But it may yield something to those
willing to plunge into its waters. It is, for instance, salient how
Gwyddno recruits Taliesin as 'bard and teacher' to his son,

Elffin/Elphin. In this version, therefore, Taliesin acts as a mentor figure, a Chiron or Nestor. This strikes a deep truth – that a bard should share his wisdom, teaching either indirectly through tales, or directly through workshops, retreats and so forth. The bard's true gift is to pass on his gift. To light a candle in others. Awen should be for all. We all could do with inspiration to enrich our lives – not to 'wax lyrical', but to live creatively. Not to see the magic as separate from our daily lives, but an intrinsic part of it. To walk with awen by the very 'act of living'. This is the challenge, and there is no greater test than the ability to do this – to delight in all that Fortuna sends us – the vicissitudes of Fate – and dance with it. To sing with joy, to cry with unapologetic pain. To be fully human.

Of the tragic death of Taliesin's son it is said, '*The cheek will not conceal/the anguish of the heart*'. From this it can be assumed Taliesin himself had his fair share of tragedy, and yet he persisted. Of Avaon himself, the Penbeirdd's first-born, it is said he was one of the '*grave-slaughtering ones*'. Art is our weapon in the war against death. With it, with our soul-song ringing out loud and true, we can fully live and we can live on.

I hope this exploration of the journey of a bard has inspired you to pursue your own creative journey with all your heart. Your Taliesin awaits.

See you along the Way

Further Reading:

Bards & Heroes, Carl Lofmark, Llanerch, 1988

Celtic Bards, Celtic Druids, Robin Williamson & RJ Stewart, Blandford 1996

Celtic Heritage, Alwyn & Brinley Rees, Thames & Hudson 1961

Green Fire: magical verse for the wheel of the year, Tallyessin Silverwolf, Awen 2004

Mabon & the Mysteries of Britain, Caitlín Matthews, Arkana 1987

Pagan Celtic Britain, Dr Anne Ross, Cardinal 1974

Places of Truth: journeys into sacred wilderness, Jay Ramsay, Awen 2009

Porius, John Cowper Powys, Overlook Press, 2007

Shamanism: Archaic Techniques of Ecstasy, Mircea Eliade, Arkana 1989

Tales of the Celtic Bards, Claire Hamilton, O Books, 2003

Taliesin – Shamanism and the Bardic Mysteries of Britain & Ireland, John Matthews, Aquarian 1991 (reprinted as *Taliesin – the last Celtic Shaman*, Inner Traditions 2002)

Taliesin Poems, trans. Meirion Pennar, Llanerch, 1988

Taliesin's Travels, Michael Dames, Heart of Albion Press, 2006

The Bardic Handbook: the complete manual for the 21st Century bard, Kevan Manwaring, Gothic Image 2006

The Bardic Source Book, ed. John Matthews, Blandford 1998

The Book of the Bardic Chair, ed. by Kevan Manwaring, RJ Stewart Books, 2008

The Coming of the King, Nikolai Tolstoy, Corgi 1988

The Encyclopaedia of Celtic Wisdom, Caitlín & John Matthews, Element 1994

The Mabinogion, Lady Charlotte Guest, Harper Collins 2000

The Song of Taliesin, John Matthews, Aquarian Press 1991

The White Goddess, Robert Graves, Faber & Faber 1961

Tidal Shift: selected poems, Mary Palmer, Awen 2009

Vernon Watkins, Selected Poems 1930-1960, Faber & Faber, 1967
Wise & Foolish Tongue: Celtic Stories & Poems, Robin Williamson,
    Chronicle 1991

Kevan Manwaring is an author, poet, storyteller and teacher
(MA Teaching & Practice of Creative Writing, Cardiff University).
He has been performing his poetry and stories for over a decade
in venues across England as well as further afield (USA, Italy,
Malta, Egypt) and on BBC TV. In 1998 he was awarded the Bardic
Chair of Caer Badon (Bath) for an epic poem based on a local
legend. With Fire Springs Storytellers he has co-created and
performed in several shows. He has been running creative
writing and performance skills workshops for all ages since
establishing *Tallyessin: awaken the bard within* in 2000. Since then
he has performed professionally at numerous festivals, art
centres, museums, schools, camps, bookshops and private
parties. He teaches creative writing for the Open University and
Skyros Writers' Lab. He lives in Bath, where he has been heavily
involved with the Bardic Chair and the arts scene, hosting the
Bath Storytelling Circle and co-running the Bath Writers'
Workshop. He is often asked to MC and judge bardic events
across the country. He loves walking, visiting ancient sites and
islands, music of all flavours, too many movies and riding his
motorbike. If you see him out and about, a Bard on a Bike, wave.

Selected Works:
The Bardic Handbook, Gothic Image, 2006
Lost Islands, Heart of Albion Press, 2008
The Book of the Bardic Chair (editor) RJ Stewart Books, 2008

For further dispatches on the author's life as a Bard on a Bike,
read his blog: **http://tallyessin.wordpress.com/**

B O O K S

O is a symbol of the world, of oneness and unity. In different cultures it also means the "eye," symbolizing knowledge and insight. We aim to publish books that are accessible, constructive and that challenge accepted opinion, both that of academia and the "moral majority."

Our books are available in all good English language bookstores worldwide. If you don't see the book on the shelves ask the bookstore to order it for you, quoting the ISBN number and title. Alternatively you can order online (all major online retail sites carry our titles) or contact the distributor in the relevant country, listed on the copyright page.

See our website www.o-books.net for a full list of over 500 titles, growing by 100 a year.

And tune in to myspiritradio.com for our book review radio show, hosted by June-Elleni Laine, where you can listen to the authors discussing their books.